Driving Detroit

METROPOLITAN PORTRAITS

Metropolitan Portraits explores the contemporary metropolis in its diverse blend of past and present. Each volume describes a North American urban region in terms of historical experience, spatial configuration, culture, and contemporary issues. Books in the series are intended to promote discussion and understanding of metropolitan North America at the start of the twenty-first century.

Judith A. Martin, Series Editor

Driving Detroit

The Quest for Respect in the Motor City

George Galster

PENN

UNIVERSITY OF PENNSYLVANIA PRESS

PHILADELPHIA

Published by
University of Pennsylvania Press
Philadelphia, Pennsylvania 19104-4112
www.upenn.edu/pennpress

Printed in the United States of America on acid-free paper
10 9 8 7 6 5 4 3 2 1

Library of Congress Cataloging-in-Publication Data
Galster, George 1948–
Driving Detroit : the quest for respect in the Motor City /
George Galster. — 1st ed.
      p. cm. — (Metropolitan portraits)
   Includes bibliographical references and index.
   ISBN 978-0-8122-4429-8 (hardcover : alk. paper)
   1. Detroit Metropolitan Area. (Mich.)—Social
conditions—21st century.   2. Detroit Metropolitan Area.
(Mich.)—Economic conditions—21st century.   3. Detroit
Metropolitan Area. (Mich.)—Race relations—21st
century.   4. Suburban life—Michigan—Detroit
Metropolitan Area. I. Title.   II. Series: Metropolitan
portraits.
F574.D457G35   2012
977.4'34—dc23   011046747

*To my parents, grandparents,
great grandparents, and
great-great grandparents,
Detroiters all. And to my
children and grandchildren,
that they may find a metropolis
of respect to call home.*

Contents

Preface

A great portrait executed in paint has many layers; it builds a depth of character corresponding to the pigment. The best portraits do not merely mimic the surface of their subjects; they also reveal their subjects' characters. The same principles apply to executing in words a portrait of a place, which is the goal of the Metropolitan Portraits book series. In the case of Greater Detroit, many books have portrayed its various surfaces. None, however, have asked, "Why Detroit? What makes it tick?"

Portraits are inherently subjective. They can be flattering, like those of John Singer Sargent, or grotesque, like those of Francis Bacon. My portrait of Detroit combines perspectives that would make both Sargent and Bacon happy, because this place is both beauty and beast. But this portrait is also partly a self-portrait, wherein Detroiters paint their own stories through their lives' brushstrokes. This rich texture of overlaid personal pigments is provided through songs, poems, and oral histories. In the oral history I eschew surnames; the attentive reader will realize identities by the time they have finished the book. At its core, however, the character of place I try to reveal in this portrait will emerge from multiple layers of principles gleaned from economics, sociology, political science, geography, history, and psychology. My goal is to paint a portrait that not only helps us *see* but, more importantly, *understand why* Detroit's social, cultural, institutional, commercial, and built landscape is the way it is.

This goal has shaped my choice of title and subtitle. The title *Driving Detroit* certainly can be interpreted as what Detroit and its primary twentieth-century industry were all about: putting America on wheels (and then updating them every few years, the auto companies hoped). Equally, the title can be interpreted as the act of navigating one's automobile around the environs of Detroit, as indeed I vicariously do with the reader in Chapter 1. But, most importantly, I hope the title is primarily interpreted as a revelation of causal forces that essentially shape this metropolitan area, as in "What *drives* Detroit?" My answer is embodied in the subtitle. Like people everywhere, Greater Detroiters possess basic human drives to attain, retain, and expand basic physical, social and psychological resources, what I summarize in the term "respect." Unfortunately, in this metropolitan area the quest for respect has long been frustrated by three elements. The economy is dominated by the auto industry, which creates distinctive socioeconomic insecurities and psychic damages for its workers: "The Economic Engine of Anxiety." The geography is dominated by a permissive topography and fragmented local political structure spawning a development process that builds excess supplies of housing on the suburban fringe while rendering housing at the core redundant: "The Housing Disassembly Line." The society is dominated by two competitive tensions spawning insecurities: between capital and labor, blacks and whites: "The Dual Dialectic." In concert, these three elements of Greater Detroit make for a place that fundamentally *disrespects* the citizenry. Detroiters have reacted to the perpetual stresses generated by their disrespectful metropolis through a variety of individual coping mechanisms and collective adaptations that give the place its idiosyncratic characteristics: extremes of class and racial segregation, city-suburb disparities, identity politics, violence, intolerance, scapegoating, denial, and myopia. Ironically and perversely, these reactions collectively have frustrated everyone's individual efforts to gain respect by rendering the region incapable of responding effectively to deindustrialization and globalization: "Collective Irrationality." The result is a dysfunctional, unsustainable metropolitan area: "The Auto Mortropolis."

Consistent with the goals of the Metropolitan Portraits book series, the subject of *Driving Detroit* is the entire metropolitan area, what I call Greater Detroit. For most of the region's history, the City of Detroit was essentially the only game in town, so of course the events, industries, and people I describe are often based in the city. Yet it is a huge mistake to focus solely on the City of Detroit, as do virtually all journalists visiting from around the globe. On the contrary, I argue that most of what we see in the city is a result of what transpires in the suburbs and is beyond the power of the city to control. The primary drivers of the region's economy and housing market are geographically concentrated in Detroit's suburbs, though their reckless driving victimizes the city. Similarly, the political and social dynamics of race and class polarization are characterized by a city-suburb dichotomy. It is impossible to understand what drives the City of Detroit by looking only within its jurisdictional boundaries; a metropolitan perspective is required.

Two Daughters of Detroit

Detroit's story is, of course, an amalgam of millions of stories of men, women, and children who have loved, toiled, played, and made lives in this place since 1701 when the city was founded. But the essence of what this city represents, both to itself and to larger social concerns about the role of cities, can be distilled in the lives of two daughters of Detroit: Marguerite (nicknamed Iva) and Helen.

In the summer of 1925, these two preschool girls were about to become neighbors. Marguerite's father, a prosperous physician, had just bought a substantial home in the east side of Detroit at the corner of Garland Street and Charlevoix Avenue for his wife and only child. Only two streets away on Hurlbut lived Helen, cramped among her four brothers and sisters in the modest home that their delicatessen-shopkeeper father had recently purchased. When they got a little older, Marguerite and Helen likely would attend the same Howe Elementary School and later the local Southeastern High School. They would enjoy the same safe, healthy neighborhood, solid schools, and recreational facilities and likely would become friends.

Their fathers, though neighbors, would perhaps have little in common about which to chat, however. After all, Marguerite's father was not only much richer than Helen's but much better educated and traveled, having been awarded bachelor's and medical doctor's degrees and a postdoctoral fellowship in Paris. Helen's father never graduated from high school and had traveled little in the United States, let alone abroad. Marguerite's father had deep American roots stretching back over a century, whereas Helen's grandfathers had immigrated to the United States.

These facts alone might tempt one to predict that Marguerite would have superior opportunities for social and economic success in life than would Helen. But this is Detroit, and the geography of opportunity here is not described by the compass headings north and south, east and west. In Detroit, one's life course is plotted according to the axes of labor and capital, black and white.

Chapter 1

Riding on the Freeway: A Riff on the Place Called Motown

We're goin' riding on the freeway . . . in my pink Cadillac;
We're goin' riding on the freeway . . . and we ain't coming back."
—"Freeway of Love," sung by Aretha Franklin in 1985

The Mother Lode of Symbolism

"Made in Detroit." This seems quaint, now that the label "Made in China" screams at us from virtually every product we pick up, belying the proud industrial heritage that once was America's. This heritage was forged and stamped and pressed and cut and molded in the long-abandoned temples of production that defined Detroit. To understand Detroit, you must understand one thing: in its soul, it is a place that *makes things*—metal things. Ever since it grew to be a metropolis in the late nineteenth century, its dominant businesses were about shaping metal into useful objects. Railway cars, stoves, marine engines, and work boats eventually gave way in the early twentieth century to automobiles, myriad gadgets that kept them running, and accessories that made them more comfortable to drive.

Forty years ago, Detroit also took the lead in making the ultimate auto accessory: driving music. This music was so infectious that it spread like an epidemic from the ghettoized airwaves of "Negro music" into the homes of mainstream white teenagers, becoming "The Sound of Young America." The leading carrier of this epidemic was a home-grown, black-owned and operated record company whose moniker became the region's unofficial nickname: Motown. Detroit's marketing juggernaught used its cars and its music as the flux to weld youth culture to the myth of American freedom and rugged individualism. The result: the still-powerful visage of a muscular motor vehicle rolling along an endless, empty road, its retracted convertible top exposing flowing golden tresses, the wrinkle-free faces in the front seats breaking into satisfied smiles as their favorite Top-40s hit comes on the radio. One cannot imagine an America without the car-music culture Detroit created and so effectively embedded in the nation's psyche. But can one now imagine an America without Detroit?

Detroit did more than just make cars and music to play while driving them; it made both in notably innovative ways. It is well known that Henry Ford designed the world's first moving assembly line for autos in Ford Motor Company's Highland Park plant. This was the largest auto factory in the world—six acres of floor space under one roof—when it came online in 1910. A decade later he could boast of the first vertically integrated auto production facility, at the River Rouge plant in Dearborn. In this wondrous complex, iron ore, coke, limestone, and glass were gulped in at one end and belched out as an automobile a few days later, spawned by the sweat of 102,811 workers at its peak in 1929. It is less well known that Detroit made music in similarly inventive ways. Berry Gordy, Motown Records' founder, developed a record production system that mimicked "Fordism" in its division of labor and its focus on a product attractive for the mass market. Motown Records even designed its music to be appropriate for the first generation of low-fidelity car radios. Long before MTV (or even videotape), it pioneered the pop musical video as a marketing device. The cultural symbiosis among youth, cars, and music was never more powerfully glorified than when Detroit's Martha Reeves and the Vandellas were filmed singing "Dancing in Street" sitting in the back of a Mustang convertible as it rolled down the assembly line at the Rouge in 1965. And it's not surprising, with its alien-like work environments stressing machine-like precision, that Detroit later would become the acknowledged birthplace of Techno music.

Unfortunately, the tragedy of Detroit is that it has never resolved the fierce competition over who was going to make these things and who was going to enjoy the benefits of this production. Thus, Detroit also has innovated in many political ways, both radical and conservative. The Nation of Islam (the "Black Muslims") was founded in Detroit in 1930 by the visionary Wallace D. Fard. The sit-down strike, whereby a well-organized cadre of unionists occupy and then shut down production at a strategic choke point,

was invented in the auto plants in the late 1930s and proved effective in shifting power from the capitalist to the laborer. The Republic of New Africa, a
black nationalist group demanding black control of five U.S. states as repara-
tions, was born in Detroit in 1968. Ironically, the segregationist governor of
Alabama, George Wallace, won the Michigan Democratic presidential primary campaign that same year, based on his electoral strength in Detroit's
prounion but racially and socially conservative white suburbs, the same
places where "Reagan Democrats" would help usher in American neoliberal-
ism in 1980. In response, the Freedom Now Party, the nation's first all-black
political party with an unabashedly radical agenda, bloomed first in Detroit.
Its sibling in the labor union arena, the Dodge Radical Union Movement,
emerged at the same time. And though Detroit did not invent the politically
potent race riot, it perfected it, with new models introduced with ever increasing ferocity in 1833, 1863, 1943, and 1967.

With this history of intense conflicts between labor and capital, black
and white, it is no wonder that Detroit has been at the epicenter of tectonic
shifts in national policy and legal precedents. The United Auto Workers'
early, decisive victories in Detroit spawned reactions as the U.S. Supreme
Court ruled sit-down strikes illegal in 1939 and a conservative Congress
passed the antiunion Taft-Hartley Act in 1947. The urban street disturbances
("riots," "rebellions," what have you) of the mid-1960s reached a crescendo
when the last and biggest exploded in Detroit, prompting President Lyndon
B. Johnson to appoint a blue-ribbon Advisory Commission on Civil Disor-
ders. Emerging in 1968, its famous and prescient report cited Detroit as a
prime example of how northern cites were moving inexorably toward "two
societies, separate and unequal." "White flight," and resultant miserable failure of within-district busing in northern city school districts, was inevitable
when the 1974 U.S. Supreme Court ruled on *Milliken v. Bradley* that suburban Detroit school districts were not culpable in producing segregated
Detroit City schools, and thus remedies could not extend beyond the city
school district.

In 1980, Detroit became the first city to apply powers of eminent domain
to acquiring private property that subsequently was transferred to other private concerns because it was in the "public interest," a brazen legal sleight-
of-hand later vindicated by the Michigan Supreme Court. In the infamous
"Poletown" project, entire neighborhoods were forcibly acquired and demolished to make room for a new Cadillac assembly plant. And, of course, Detroit's auto companies have taken the corporate lead in begging the federal

government for aid in attempts to stave off bankruptcy. Chrysler Corporation successfully sought federal loan guarantees in 1979, setting the national precedent of "too big to fail." It then returned to Washington (in an ill-considered private jet) hat-in-hand in 2008, escorted by a humbled General Motors Corporation. Salvation was not at hand this time, however. Chrysler was forced into bankruptcy in May 2009 and General Motors followed within a month. In both cases, the federal government assumed dominant controlling interests in the companies, transferred substantial financial interests to the United Auto Workers, and circumvented the traditional legal rights of corporate debt holders, thereby setting yet another slew of policy precedents in the uncharted waters of mixed private-state-union capitalism.

Regardless of how the auto companies fare in the future, what has happened in Detroit represents the cutting edge of what will happen across America: an unraveling of the post-World War II social compact originally made in Detroit. This compact had government explicitly and implicitly supporting big businesses that, in turn, would provide welfare-state-like benefits, such as health insurance and generous pensions, to their workers. It was a compact so consensual that Charles Wilson, president of General Motors, could testify before Congress in 1953, without the trace of a smirk or fear of derision, that "what was good for our country was good for General Motors, and vice versa." What far-reaching changes in the American political economy will be associated with the dissolution of this social compact can only be guessed.

But Detroit's most important product is not cars, music, politics, or precedents. It is symbolism. What Detroit inadvertently has always been best at making is a symbol of itself. Americans, and indeed much of the world, have held up Detroit as an icon of either the best or the worst of what a metropolis can be, depending on the era. One hundred years ago, Detroit represented the archetypical "industrial boom town," a place of rampant entrepreneurial and technical ingenuity where the latest, greatest consumer invention was being made affordable to almost everyone through the genius of mass production. By the 1930s, it had come to be seen as the "cradle of industrial unionism," with the UAW rising to preeminence among U.S. industrial unions, a position it held for decades. During World War II, Detroit was known as the "Arsenal of Democracy," a manufacturing behemoth where workers of all races and genders labored tirelessly, side by side, in a gallant effort to defeat the Axis Powers. In the postwar boom, Detroit's product epitomized the ascendancy of American consumerism. It was also, believe it or not, a place widely hailed for its enlightened urban planning and its successful embrace of the "Model Cities" philosophy of the War on Poverty. On the heels of its 1967 upheavals, with its first black mayor elected in 1973 and the first Organization of Petroleum Exporting Countries (OPEC) oil embargo in 1973, Detroit's image morphed yet again into one of postindustrial apocalypse. It came to symbolize the nation's "murder capital," a place of unbridled crime, violence, and racial strife that could be patrolled successfully only by robocops. Detroit became a place dominated by an antiquated industry, glacial in its response to changing international market conditions, instead smugly churning out shoddily built "gas guzzlers." "The Lemon Capital of the World," wags called it. On its better days, contemporary Detroit ought to be represented as resilient people demonstrating amazing perseverance and creativity in the face of enormous obstacles, but it rarely is. With the local "Big Three" automakers shedding so many employees that they more resemble the "Little Three," Detroit is teetering on the brink of another image makeover: ghost town. However represented, the symbolic value of Detroit seems indispensable. If there were no Detroit, America would need to invent one.

As the nature of Detroit's symbolism changed over the last century, so has the nature of those who come to this city seeking enlightenment. It used to be that aspiring industrialists and civil engineers from all over the world visited Detroit's cutting-edge industrial complexes, laboratories, and technical centers. Similarly, progressive international unionists once called reverently at Solidarity House, the UAW headquarters nestled scenically between the Detroit River and Jefferson Avenue. By the 1970s, the curious visitors more often than not were furrowed-browed sociologists asking "What went wrong?" and journalists excavating for the latest outrageous dysfunction that they could sensationalize. Most recently, they come as archeologists to search for clues to the whereabouts of a lost city or as agricultural scientists to explore the feasibility of oxymoronic "urban farming" on its abandoned plains.

Symbols, of course, may be based on some core reality but obscure the deeper reality through simplification and exaggeration. Visit the metropolis called Detroit with me now, and look more deeply: what will *you* find?

Driving the D

Coming to Detroit by air means almost certainly flying Delta Airlines because it accounts for over 80 percent of the flights to the region at one of the nation's busiest airports. But, as in so many realms of this metropolis's life, most passengers here are neither arriving nor departing, merely passing through. As if to compensate for the airport's self-effacing name—Wayne County Metropolitan Airport—the terminal's name reeks with overblown self-importance: the Edward McNamara World Gateway.

Disembarking at the "Big Mac" for the first time is slightly disconcerting for anyone even mildly infected with contemporary Detroit symbolism. This terminal truly is world-class: airy, clean, efficient, safe, multilingual, high-tech, straightforward. You can be excused for allowing the thought to cross your mind, "This *can't* be Detroit; perhaps I got on the wrong flight!" Welcome to "The D," a place that simultaneously manages to confirm and shatter all its stereotypes, a place of stark contrasts juxtaposed in remarkable proximity.

Arriving at luggage claim, immediate reassurance that you got the correct flight appears because Detroit proclaims its identity loud and clear. Ancient visitors to imperial Rome knew they had arrived because of the heroic stone friezes adorning public buildings. The Big Mac's equivalents are four heraldic photomontages adorning the ends of the luggage claim areas. If you are a domestic visitor, you immediately recognize that this place is about sports and politics. On the north wall, there are heavyweight boxing champion Joe Louis, Isiah Thomas of the Pistons, Gordie Howe and Steve Yzerman of the Red Wings, Ty Cobb of the Tigers, Bobby Layne and Barry Sanders of the Lions, and then, as a politically correct nod to the distaff side, Kate Sobrero Markgraf of the U.S. national soccer team and Olympic figure-skating champion Tara Lipinski. And, yes, in case you were wondering, deeply bowing from the waist as you pass these murals is encouraged, so long as you do not trip over someone's luggage in the process.

The second montage in the domestic baggage claim area portrays three home-grown "first" public servants: Coleman Young (Detroit's first black mayor, serving from 1974 to 1993), Ralph Bunche (who in 1950 became the first black to win the Nobel Peace Prize for mediating the Palestine conflict), and Martha Griffiths (Michigan's first female elected to Congress, serving from 1955 to 1974). It includes four union leaders: Walter Reuther and Stephen Yokich, past presidents of the UAW (from 1946 to his death in 1970, and 1994 to 2002, respectively); and James R. Hoffa (past, 1958–1971), and James P. Hoffa, current (since 1999) presidents of the International Brotherhood of Teamsters and native Detroiters. The selection of Jimmy Hoffa, Senior, is curious, given his intimate Mafiosi knowledge and felony convictions and the fact that he was last seen alive (or dead, for that matter) near a restaurant in Bloomfield Township, a northern Detroit suburb. The largest picture of all is reserved for Rosa Parks, the paragon of nonviolent civil rights principles, which also is curious. Although she lived in Detroit most of her adult life and is buried here, Parks acquired her political education and is lionized for her act of civil disobedience in Montgomery, Alabama. I do not know whether her picture adorns the wall of the Montgomery airport and personally have no objections to municipal "double-dipping." Perhaps she appears in Detroit's airport because our two home-grown national civil rights leaders, Elijah Muhammad and Malcolm X, are a bit too radical for the delicate constitutions of white travelers or white local politicians.

By contrast, international visitors see two quite different photomontages, suggesting that this is a place about songs and cars. On the south wall appear the smiling visages of Martha Reeves, Marvin Gaye, Smokey Robinson, The Supremes, The Temptations, The Four Tops, Aretha Franklin, Stevie Wonder, and the founder of Motown Records who brought them fame, Berry Gordy, Jr. It is not uncommon for international visitors to see this mural and spontaneously start humming. Detroit's cultural reach still extends that far: Motown music remains the city's best ambassador.

What international visitors see on the opposite wall are legends of the auto industry, past and present. The mural not surprisingly includes Henry Ford, founder of the Ford Motor Company in 1903 and its president until his death in 1947, William Durant, founder of General Motors in 1908, and Walter Chrysler, founder of the Chrysler Corporation in 1925 and its head until 1936. We also see Henry Ford II, Henry's grandson and Ford's head from 1945 until 1979, and Horace and John (Jack) Dodge, who in 1900 founded the Dodge Brothers Company supplying parts to other nascent auto companies until they rolled out their own eponymous auto in 1917. Two other giants of GM are portrayed: Charles Kettering, head of research from 1920 to 1947, who invented the electric starter; and Alfred Sloan, president from 1923 to 1946, who introduced "planned obsolescence" with annual styling changes and the GM brand price-status hierarchy (Chevrolet, Pontiac, Oldsmobile, Buick, and Cadillac). It is ironic, however, that there are no pictures of the local people after whom the General Motors divisions were named: Louis Chevrolet, Chief Pontiac of the Chippewas and Ottawas, Ransom Olds, David Buick, and Antoine de la Mothe Cadillac. In a poignant (if unintended) testimony to how unstable the industry has become, the mural also portrays the heads of the Big Three when the McNamara Terminal was opened: Robert Eaton (GM), Jürgen Schrempp (Daimler-Chrysler), and William Clay Ford, Jr. Only the last currently retains his position as Executive Chairman.

Got your bags? OK, hop into my SUV. No, we can't take train, subway, or light-rail from the airport because there are no such rail lines. As a matter of fact, there are no fixed-rail passenger lines *anywhere* in metropolitan Detroit, by far the largest metro area in the country with that dubious distinction. The "People Mover," the two-mile monorail system encircling downtown, doesn't count as fixed rail. It indeed moves, but typically with few people: truth-in-advertising would suggest that it be renamed the "No People Mover." Nor does Amtrak count, with its two inconveniently scheduled trains daily sneaking through the city. No one has come to Detroit by train for a long, long time, as a view of the old train station will soon make clear. Come on! This is the Motor City, after all, and that means car motors, not train motors! As for buses, ehhh . . . no. Any metro Detroiters will tell you: buses are for the poor, the elderly, and especially the blacks.

So, driving it is. And don't even *think* of suggesting that I trade in my SUV for one of those sissy, hypotestosterone hybrids; we're riding in a *Detroit* car—and one built by the Big Three, at that: 88 percent of Michigan's auto sales are still held by the Big Three, compared to only 55 percent nationwide.

As you try to navigate metropolitan Detroit for the first time, relax. It's hard to get lost in this place. (Should you somehow manage to get lost, however, act like a native and ask, "Where am I *at*?"). The region's surface street system has a simple design: spokes of strategic radial roads extending from the city center superimposed on a grid. Until this system confronts a river or lake shoreline, each surface road is essentially arrow-straight. If the Detroit region were scaled down to the size of a pancake, its topography would be flatter. The median reference point for this system is located on the central radial thoroughfare, Woodward Avenue, a few blocks up from the Detroit River where the first recorded French explorers landed and later built their stockade. The immediate environs are the only confusing exception to the above scheme, modeled as they were in early nineteenth-century fashion on Pierre Charles L'Enfant's plan for the District of Columbia. This complex, irregular street design was made possible by the "urban renewal" provided by an 1805 fire, which conveniently burned down every building in the town, save one. The pseudo-L'Enfant plan was soon abandoned, however, as the city forsook notions of European urban grandeur to embrace more straightforward American pragmatism. So, all subsequent surface streets were laid out either as radii or on an east-west/north-south grid. The "Big Three" are not only auto

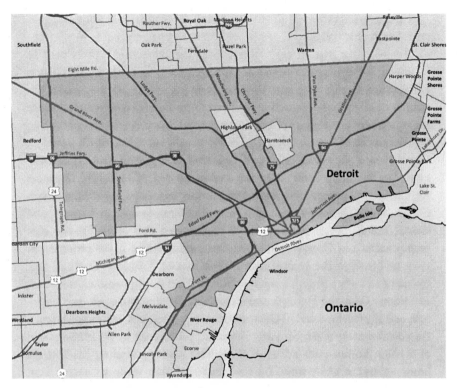

Figure 1. Detroit and its immediate environs.

companies but the main radial avenues that split the compass in roughly equal segments from northwest to northeast. Carrying Michigan state highway numbers to emphasize their primacy—Woodward (M1, heading north), Gratiot (M3, heading northeast), and Grand River (M5, heading northwest)—they are "prime" roads in more ways than one. Several supplemental radial highways also emanate from downtown: Michigan Avenue (U.S.12, heading west), Fort Street (M85 heading southwest), and Jefferson Avenue (heading east). To aid the cartographically challenged, major east-west streets were established at one-mile intervals from the intersection of the three prime highways and then named according to the number of miles distant from it (see Figure 1). Though several of the lower numbered "mile roads" have subsequently been renamed, beginning with Seven Mile Road the system proceeds unbroken through the tricounty metropolitan area. As of fall 2011, development is occurring at 32 Mile Road in northern Macomb County.

No one knows whether the designation "Mile Roads" was done as a low-tech Geographic Positioning System or because Detroiters had so much trouble pronouncing other street names. About the only thing visitors need to remember if they want to pronounce roads correctly in Detroit vernacular is to forget any foreign languages they may have learned. Other tongues are absolutely deadly when deciphering the host of non-English road names that are the region's concrete legacy of a rich immigrant history. It goes without saying that the surfeit of French origin names are usually mangled, which would be expected in a place that calls itself Duh-*troit* or *Dee*-troit, instead of Deh-*twah*. So, St. Aubin Street becomes *aw*-bin instead of Aw-*bahn*, Livernois Avenue becomes *livver*-noiz instead of Lee-vair-*nwah* and, most infamously, Gratiot Avenue becomes *graaa*-shit instead of Grah-tee-*oh*. In fairness, one crucial French-origin place name is pronounced half correctly: the old-money suburb of Grosse Pointe; the first part is never, never pronounced *grow*-see, though the second part is pronounced Point, not Pwahnt. Detroiters don't often practice equal opportunity, but mispronunciation is an exception. Thus, the Dutch-based Groesbeck Road is *gross*-bek, not *hroos*-bek, and the German-based Goethe Street is *go*-thee, not *gair*-tuh. Clarence Darrow famously used this latter linguistic peculiarity in his 1925 defense of a black homeowner accused of murder while defending his Detroit home against a white mob. Darrow suggested that white witnesses were willing to lie under oath because they were such a prejudiced, uncultured lot they did not even know how to pronounce their own parents' language. Perhaps Darrow was being unfair about lack of intelligence. Perhaps metro Detroiters suffer collectively from dyslexia. How else can you explain the common pronunciation of Lahser Road as *lash*-er?

As for freeways, there is no better way for you to understand than by first hand experience. So, as we leave Metro Airport, we zip onto Interstate 94 and set the cruise control at five miles per hour over the posted limit, then stay out of the left lane because that's reserved for folks who *really* want to go fast. I-94, as with so much of prosaic Detroit, has a rich history largely unknown to thousands of daily commuters. Like much modern infrastructure, it roughly follows Native American footpaths. During the nineteenth century it was "improved" to accommodate stagecoaches bumpily plying the Detroit-Chicago route. It assumed its current incarnation as a limited access, divided highway in the early 1940s, as a way to speed commuters to the new Willow Run B-24 Liberator bomber plant, just west of the current Metro Airport. In Detroit I-94 gets personalized with a name, that of Edsel

Ford, Henry's only son, who preceded him in death. One only hopes that this appellation was in memory of Edsel's timeless design of the 1940 Lincoln, not the considerably less elegant 1950s Ford model that posthumously bore his name above its hideous grille shaped like a toilet seat. There are several Detroit freeways named after famous locals: Walter Chrysler (I-75), Walter Reuther (I-696), and two Detroit mayors: Edward Jeffries (I-96), 1940–1948, and John C. Lodge (M10), 1922–1924 and 1927–1929. No one calls these freeways by their full names, though. They are simply the Ford, the Chrysler, the Reuther, the Jeffries, the Lodge. Other freeways are named for their location, such as the Southfield and the Davison. No one seems to shorten these; I have never heard them called "the Field" or "the Dave." Perhaps they are holding these roads in anonymous reserve so the city can sell the naming rights when things get especially tight financially. Whatever the oddities of naming conventions, one thing is certain about metro Detroit freeways: they are plentiful and comparatively uncongested.

> There are days I own
> this speeding,
> sprawled-
> out
> mess,
> drive the freeways
> end to end
> just to feel connected.
>
> Other days it's too much,
> this crazy, cramped culture,
> zipping us down freeways
> vital as veins, spindly things,
> crisscrossing counties,
> linking us in ways
> we never touch. No standing
> on the bus or squeezing
> onto subways here—
>
> Jesus, we rarely even walk
> to the corner—
> just 2.2 million half-ton

capsules cruising highways
as familiar as grandparents,
so integral we name them—
Fisher, Jefferies, Lodge—
memorize each pothole
and speed trap in pathetic attempts
to expedite commutes, reach
wherever we're going
to move on
to the next place
and the next,
always late and never
time to stay, damn
the traffic jam, construction,
anything that slows us down.

"Motor City Trilogy III" by Kristin Palm

Now that we are driving on the freeway, we need only one other thing to complete our local cultural context: Detroit-bred music. This is not a simple matter. Besides the Motown superstars we met at international baggage claim in the Big Mac, we could choose from among a dizzying array of artists who defined the sound of many genres. In the R&B/Soul category, Detroit contributed John Lee Hooker, Jackie Wilson, and Parliament/Funkadelic. Jazz greats are numerous: Dorothy Ashby, Marcus Belgrave, Kenny Burrell, James Carter, Regina Carter, Betty Carter, Kenny Garret, Charlie Haden, Milt Jackson, Earl Klugh, and Yusef Lateef. The multiple Winans family acts have dominated gospel singing. Pop female songbirds include Anita Baker, Gladys Knight, Madonna, and the Marvelettes. Home-grown rock options abound, with Insane Clown Posse, Mitch Ryder and the Detroit Wheels, Motor City (MC) 5, Ted Nugent, Iggy Pop, and Bob Seger and the Silver Bullet Band among the alternatives. If we wanted to sample the diverse modern Detroit music scene, we could check out Blanche, Detroit Cobras, Eminem, Kid Rock, Soledad Brothers, White Stripes, or Von Bondies. Techno may be your thing, so we could try the acknowledged inventors of the genre, The Belleville Three (Juan Atkins, Derrick May, and Kevin Saunderson), or other stars like Carl Craig, Richie Hawtin, and Underground Resistance. If you prefer classical, we could dip into the vast discography of the superstar maestros who have taken the Detroit Symphony Orchestra to the pinnacle of international success, such as

Ossip Gabrilowitsch, Paul Paray, Neeme Järvi, and now Leonard Slatkin. Perhaps you are drawn to underappreciated, invisible geniuses; if so, Detroit can offer up the Funk Brothers, the nonpareil Motown studio band that played on more #1 hits than the Beatles, Rolling Stones, Beach Boys, and Elvis combined. I could also surprise you with hundreds of unknown CDs because Detroit's musical talent pool is so deep that world-class artists who have never broken out grace the stages of local venues every weekend. To spare you choice angst and inevitable second-guessing, let me make it simple. I'll play Aretha Franklin's "Freeway of Love." Sorry, my pink Cadillac is in the shop, so the requisite street-cred SUV, tricked out with chrome spinners, will have to do.

Their voices seemed so large
That I studied them in regret
And wasted evenings after school
When the city seemed to sweat rain like tears
And I drug it on home.

With the radio on, I applied
My makeup, and then washed it off,
Only to reapply it—so satisfied
With my new shell and skirt
While doing a few hip steps.

As I combed, then put the rollers
In my hair, all the lyrics—
Each subtle nuance of voice I knew by heart
From the very pace of the city
Until I could not tell their voices from my own.
    —"My Sister Chicken Recalls How She Listened to the Supremes
        on the Radio as a Young Girl" by Charles A. Gervin

As we reach the intersection with the Southfield Freeway, we could head north a mile into Dearborn and visit Greenfield Village, a collection of historical buildings gathered from across the nation and assembled into a faux nineteenth-century village, complete with role-playing actor "citizens." Notable buildings include Thomas Edison's New Jersey laboratories, Orville and Wilbur Wright's Ohio aeroplane shop, and Henry Ford's Dearborn boyhood farm home. Henry Ford wanted to celebrate American ingenuity and industriousness in Greenfield Village. But perhaps its more powerful effect on the region's psyche comes through its subliminal nostalgic message, which unwittingly embodies the dominant, ultimately destructive "metanostalgia" of Detroit: "Boy, how *good* it used to be."

But I have decided to skip Greenfield Village and instead go a couple of miles over to I-75 because it offers a much more dramatic entrance into Detroit. I-75 climbs a huge bridge as is zooms over the Rouge River, named by the early French settlers for the hue of its muddy water. The Rouge River now squeezes through the region's most dense concentration of heavy industry, ingesting a century's worth of accumulated pollutants and thereby displaying the continuing accuracy of its name. As we approach the crest of the I-75 bridge, the magnitude of this fire-breathing, steam-spewing industrial landscape becomes clear. The Zug Island steel plant is on our right, the Marathon Oil refinery on our immediate left. And farther left is the sprawling Ford Rouge complex. Then, as we crest the bridge, it is hard to keep from catching our breath. Here spread before us is what seems nothing less than a magical city. A fine suite of distinctive skyscrapers, dominated by the five towers of the Renaissance Center, demarcates the downtown nestled hard by the Detroit River. The majestic Ambassador Bridge spreads its suspension cabled arms across the river to the far Canadian shore in Windsor, as if offering a welcoming embrace (see Figure 2). Under it glide pleasure boats and an improbably long, narrow freighter carrying iron ore. Ahead we can make out the silhouette of Belle Isle Park in the middle of the sparkling river, the blue expanse of Lake St. Clair beckoning beyond with endless possibilities.

This view must have buoyed the spirits of hundreds of thousands of southern black migrants over the years, arriving by bus to search for a better life in the Motor City. They must have been awed by the dramatic juxtaposition of gritty industrial sinews, shiny commercial citadels, light-bejeweled bridges, and glistening water vistas. To capture this spirit of thrilled optimism, I pop into the CD player the upbeat jazz composition of guitarist Wes Montgomery, "Goin' on to Detroit." But I don't let this song play to the finish because that would leave the wrong message. Far too many black opportunity seekers would soon change their tune when they saw Detroit up close. The stark contrasts and incongruous juxtapositions first beheld from the crest of the I-75 bridge over the Rouge River were real enough, but the promises of opportunity often were broken, cruelly and systematically.

Driving farther on I-75, our eyes cannot help but be drawn to a solitary, fifteen-story building sitting apart from the downtown skyline. Approach-

Figure 2. Renaissance Center and Detroit central business district; Windsor, Ontario, is to the right (south) across the Ambassador Bridge.

ing, it becomes clear that the building is abandoned and hollow (see Figure 3). Shards of glass protrude from the frames of over 900 windows. Here and there, black smoke stains from uncounted fires compete with bravely applied graffiti to coat the extravagantly detailed limestone façade. A magnificent entrance hall protrudes from the front of the tower, its three multistory archways flanked by sixteen fluted columns adorned by Corinthian capitals. This neoclassical marvel, produced by the architects of New York's Grand Central Station, is the fossil of the Michigan Central Rail Station. Opened on December 26, 1913, its last passenger train arrived in 1988. In its heyday, this was the terminal where thousands arrived daily to join the industrial boomtown. Yet, like so much of Detroit, its exterior beauty concealed a grimmer reality. Trains heading for the Deep South from the Michigan Central before World War I had racially segregated coaches to generate less hassle when they crossed the Mason-Dixon Line. Today no one rides the train in Detroit, whether segregated or not. So the Michigan Central stands like a forlorn headstone marking the remains of a buried civilization.

Figure 3. Ruins of Michigan Central Rail Station.

We soon merge onto the Lodge and confront yet another tall building drawing attention to itself: The MotorCity Casino (see Figure 4). Retrofitted from an old bread factory, currently the site focuses on a different sort of "dough." This and its two sibling casinos, Greektown and MGM Grand, represent the latest, desperate gambit to revitalize Detroit's core. The Motor-City Casino's hotel is capped with a roof treatment reminiscent of the tail fins that emerged from Detroit's 1950s car factories. Its flanks are draped in LED panels that nightly provide garish (though free) lightshows for the neighbors; they are worth every penny. The MotorCity Casino sits amid acres of open fields in the heart of Detroit. Its only neighbors are elderly residents of a high-rise public housing development across the street.

Now the Lodge ducks under the vast concrete complex comprising the Cobo Convention Center, Cobo Arena, and Joe Louis Arena (home of the Red Wings). It is strange (and perhaps revealing) that the region's major visitors' complex is named after Al Cobo, the Detroit mayor (1950–1957) who made race-baiting a political art form. That this complex sits a block from the current municipal building, named after the city's first black mayor, seems bizarre. But

Figure 4. MotorCity Casino.

it is the Joe Louis Arena ("the Joe," of course) where the fears that cleave the region are made concrete, figuratively and literally. Designed in the late 1970s when crime was at its most virulent and the memory of race riots was still fresh, the Joe is a veritable fortress. It is a giant cement pill box accessed only by steep stairs that could (if needed) be easily defended from a mob at street level below. Located on prime riverfront land where one might expect spectacular views across to Windsor, the Joe boasts not a single window. The vast, multi-level parking garage is connected to the Joe with hermetically sealed metal walkways—so white suburban hockey fans can make the fearsome transition from car to game securely. And it *is* a racial thing. Former Detroit Pistons star Grant Hill was once interviewed after watching a Red Wings game at the Joe. He remarked that, while he enjoyed the game well enough, he couldn't help but notice that the only other black in attendance was the puck. The antiurban fortress design of the Joe suggests two things: suburbs and city interact based on fear, and hockey fans are not as tough as they think they are.

The Lodge swoops up to street level after passing under Cobo and ends abruptly, as if taken aback by the arresting view. Jefferson Avenue, a wide landscaped boulevard that leads to the tony Grosse Pointe suburbs, opens before us. A wall of skyscrapers, including the block-long Coleman A. Young Municipal Building, dominates the field of vision on the left. On the right, the expansive Hart Plaza fronts the Detroit River, bracketed by the Ford United Auto Workers Training Center and the imposing Renaissance Center world headquarters of General Motors (the "Ren Cen"). In case you needed reminding, Detroit displays its contending pillars of power conspicuously in the opening scene it presents to visitors. Auto companies, unions, and local government, all are rendered concrete (and stone and glass) in juxtaposed architectural icons.

Swing around the riverside plaza and palm-filled shopping court that General Motors added to the Ren Cen in 2003, its beautifully redesigned corporate headquarters purchased in 1996. Swing through the always hopping Bricktown and Greektown entertainment districts. Turn up Woodward Avenue, the spine of the metropolis, and gawk at the shiny new office buildings: the recently renovated and reopened Book Cadillac Hotel, abandoned since 1981, and the newly built Campus Martius roundabout park. For two blocks up Woodward, the century-old and long-vacant retail stores now sprout upscale condominiums. A few blocks farther north, Comerica Park and Ford Field, homes of the Tigers and Lions, anchor the sports and entertainment district, boasting major theaters and dozens of trendy bars and restaurants. The Fox, Fillmore, Music Hall, Opera House, Fisher, and Gem theaters collectively comprise the largest collection of stage theater seats west of New York City.

Icons of twentieth-century commercial architecture abound wherever you turn downtown. The fantastic interior of the 36-story, 1929 Guardian Building looks like a Mayan temple on amphetamines. The 1928 Penobscot Building, the city's tallest at 47 stories until surpassed by the Ren Cen, inspired the Empire State Building. The 1963 Michigan Consolidated Gas Building served as a prototype for then-little-known local architect Minoru Yamasaki when he designed New York's World Trade Center two years later. Love it or hate it, John Portman's 1977 Ren Cen, a rosette consisting of a 73-story hotel and four surrounding 39-story office buildings, is an archetype of concrete brute gigantism style. In stark contrast, the 2003 opening of Compuware's World Headquarters showcased how airy and light-filled office buildings could be. Confronted with all this, an objective observer is forced to reconsider some stereotypes. Downtown Detroit is *not* abandoned; it actually seems an interesting, vital place.

Yes, this is *one* reality. But like so many aspects of Greater Detroit, two contrary realities exist side by side. Despite its stirrings of life, this downtown is more down than town. Woodward Avenue and its immediate environs are largely devoid of pedestrian traffic, except for special celebrations and major sporting events. Stretching invitingly for miles along the Detroit River from the Joe and Hart Plaza to the Belle Isle Bridge, the beautifully landscaped Riverwalk would attract thousands of pedestrians, joggers, and cyclists in most cities. But on a perfect May 2011 Sunday, most people using it were security guards. Retail stores are woefully absent. There has not been a department store in downtown Detroit since Hudson's closed its million-square-feet flagship in 1983. Two office skyscrapers, the 19-story 1919 David Whitney Building and the 34-story 1927 David Broderick Building, forlornly flank the northern entrance to Woodward Avenue at Grand Circus Park. They are hollow shells, despite optimistic signs perpetually affixed to their plywood windows announcing imminent redevelopment. Like dozens of other 1920s-era buildings rotting away in the downtown, they exude an unmistakable aura of sadness. Unwanted ruins, crumbling symbols of glory days long past: Detroit's Acropolis.

Come nightfall, the downtown takes on a more eerie quality. A few venues hum with life and light and laughter, but on the next block buildings sit vacant or abandoned, their dark, haunting shapes passed by a few furtive pedestrians. Life amid the ruins. This disconcerting aspect of downtown Detroit at night is well known to city planners. Indeed, as the city was preparing to host Super Bowl XL in 2006, it arranged to have lights installed behind selected windows of many vacant towers to give naïve visitors a different impression: Detroit as Potemkin Village, Detroit as façade-omy.

The Torn Urban Palimpsest

In contrast to the straightforward, self-congratulatory symbolism at the Big Mac airport terminal, reading Greater Detroit's built environment is considerably more challenging. The metropolis is a palimpsest, a tablet on which multiple generations, ethnicities, races, and classes have written their stories. These accreted tales each have an internal logic and meaning, but superimposed on each other they create a deeply conflicting set of Detroit visions. Perhaps nowhere is this conflict stronger than at the metropolis's

Figure 5. *The Fist* (Joe Louis Memorial) with *The Spirit of Detroit* behind.

historical center at the intersection of Woodward and Jefferson Avenues, Hart Plaza, where the messages of five sculptural monuments powerfully clash (see Figure 5).

At metropolitan Detroit's symbolic heart sits a small traffic island. Here a huge, amputated, bronze forearm bearing a clenched fist is horizontally suspended from two triangular frames, aiming a knockout punch at an ambiguous target. Ostensibly a monument to Detroit's own heavyweight champion boxer Joe Louis, it represents much more. Perhaps it represents a gesture of defiance from a city that is home to 68 percent of the region's black population, aimed at the suburbs starting eight miles north that hold 96 percent of the white population. Perhaps its target is only a few hundred yards north on Woodward at Campus Martius Square. There a heraldic pylon proclaims "Celebrating Relentless Advancement in Commerce," with more than a touch of pathetic irony. Perhaps the fist offers a counter to an even larger bronze statue just north across Woodward in front of the Coleman A. Young Municipal Building, *The Spirit of Detroit*, depicting a white family being gently supported in the palm of a giant, toga-clad, seated white demigod. Life is to be confronted with a closed black fist instead of an open white hand. Or perhaps the Joe Louis fist is punching out the optimism embodied in the two monuments placed just to the south in Hart Plaza. The first, *Transcending*, celebrates the union movement and its successes in improving common people's quality of life. It is a three-story high polished silver ring set on edge, with a gap at the top—does it mean that the union's job is not completed or that the circle has been broken for people of color? The second, *Gateway to Freedom*, farther down the plaza, celebrates the Detroit terminus of the Underground Railroad safe passage for escaped slaves. An antebellum black family in bronze points hopefully across the river to Canada and impending freedom and prosperity. Having just viewed the Michigan Central station, questions arise for us. Was the 1860 Underground Railroad to Detroit a better vehicle for enhancing blacks' opportunities than the overground railroad in 1910? Or 1960? Are we sure that *Gateway to Freedom* portrays a historical black family, not a contemporary one? Have they turned their backs on Detroit, figuratively and literally, because they can no longer achieve freedom and prosperity here? Are they rejecting the violence of the punching black fist a few hundred yards behind them, or are they grateful for its begrudging rear-guard action that covers their escape?

Greater Detroit has never successfully resolved the conflicting messages of these vexing, inscrutable monuments at its core. This fact foreshadows a more fundamental problem. Greater Detroit is a region devoid of consensual symbols, communal messages, unifying visions. It is overlaid with contradictory spaces, rendered more dramatic by their startling spatial juxtaposition. It is almost as if random layers of Detroit's palimpsest of place have been half torn away, one story abruptly ending and another emerging in stark relief. These stunning disparities in the built environment reflect deep inequalities among the groups that live in this complex metropolis.

Prismatic Place Icons

At this point in our introductory sojourn, it matters little which direction from downtown we drive because iconic places are everywhere. Greater Detroit's icons come in three flavors: industrial, religious, and recreational, all distinguished by their internally contradictory symbolism; these icons are both famous and infamous.

Earlier on our drive, we already skirted the industrial behemoth that is the Ford Rouge complex (see Figure 6). It is no exaggeration to say that at its opening it was the internationally acclaimed pinnacle of massively scaled, vertically integrated industrial efficiency. Nazis and communists alike would

Figure 6. Ford Motor Company River Rouge Complex and the overpass over Miller Road.

try to copy its secrets. Not as well known is that it continues to be a leader in motor vehicle manufacturing technology. The new F-150 pickup truck plant here is cutting edge for its use of robotics inside and its ecofriendly processes outside. Yet for all its ongoing productive prowess and positive innovations, the Rouge cannot be divorced from its other identity as ground hallowed by blood spilled in battle for labor rights. In 1932, outside the Rouge's Gate 3, five unemployed demonstrators were slain and fifty wounded in a hail of bullets fired by Dearborn City police and Ford's thuggish security corps, euphemistically known as the "Service Department." On the Miller Road overpass from the employee parking lot into the Rouge, a young Walter Reuther and his fellow United Auto Worker organizers were beaten senseless by the same "service" in 1937. The Rouge was the last auto factory to succumb to unionization, in 1941, after years of martial-law conditions, internal espionage, and desperate, violent, race-baiting picket line confrontations along that same Miller Road.

As if one icon of productive might combined with heady conflict were not enough, Detroit has yet another. It is the Dodge Main plant, located in central Detroit adjacent to Hamtramck. Started by the Dodge brothers, with capital supplied by Henry Ford's purchase of their Ford Motor Company shares, this behemoth was a more prosaic facility than the Rouge but proved no less significant in the region's history. During the 1939 UAW union strike, the Chrysler Corporation used Dodge Main as a proving ground for "strikebreaking through race riot," as they cynically pitted black strike-breakers against white picketers surrounding the plant. In 1941 the Dodge Main management set the industry-wide precedent for racially discriminatory transfers of workers into new lines of defense work, thereby violating the union seniority rules and further intensifying workplace racial tensions. These tensions remained unresolved for over a quarter century, as Dodge Main bred a path-breaking, black-led labor organization, the Dodge Radical Union Movement (DRUM), aimed at countering perceived UAW conservatism. Protest of workplace racism and UAW indifference at Dodge Main came to a head in 1968 with the DRUM-led wildcat strikes, immortalized by black strikers literally "dancing in the street" as African-style drummers pounded out rhythms on the picket line. Ironically, this Dodge Main monument to racist management and iconoclastic, black labor activism no longer exists. It is buried under its larger and equally famous 1980 successor, the General Motors Cadillac Hamtramck Assembly Plant. As we will see, the City of Detroit's eventual acquisition of the Dodge Main site and its still-occupied Poletown neighborhood environs, and subsequent transfer to General Motors, still stands as one of the nation's most controversial urban economic development strategies.

There is no shortage of candidates for Detroit religious institutional icons. Second Baptist Church, terminus of the Underground Railroad; St. Albertus Catholic Church, spiritual heart of the first Polish immigrant enclave; the Shrine of the Little Flower, parish of Father Charles Coughlin, the world's first media preacher; or The Perfecting Church, the epitome of the fundamentalist megachurch headed by a superstar clan (in this case, Grammy Award-winning, Gospel-singing Winans) would all seem obvious finalists. However, New Bethel Baptist Church gets my nod because it was the epicenter of major events in the turbulent 1960s civil rights era (see Figure 7). And like other Detroit icons, it symbolizes both the best and the worst. The era's New Bethel pastor, the Reverend Charles L. Franklin, had an oversized local reputation enhanced by his close association with Dr. Martin Luther King, Jr. It was at New Bethel where King and Franklin planned, prayed, and prepared for the unprecedented, daring civil rights march held in Detroit in June 1963.

Figure 7. New Bethel Baptist Church.

In September 1963, New Bethel hosted the first meeting of the Detroit Council on Human Rights, a multiracial group dedicated to nonviolent change. As the civil rights movement turned more radical after Dr. King's 1968 slaying, New Bethel remained in the vanguard, hosting a meeting of the newly founded Republic of New Africa in 1969. The bloody gunfight and subsequent mass incarceration of meeting-goers when the Detroit police tried to intervene in this meeting proved a bellwether in the growing storm over racially biased and brutal police behavior.

New Bethel Baptist Church also is iconic for its intersection with another domain of Detroit dreams with a darker side: pop music. It was here that Rev. Franklin's daughter Aretha sprang from singing in the church's choir to international fame. As she serenaded Dr. King at her home church before the 1963 march, no one could have imagined this as merely an overture to the main act: Ms. Franklin singing "Precious Lord" at King's funeral five short years later. New Bethel Baptist Church also held the funeral in February 1976 for Florence Ballard, "The Lost Supreme," scandalously pushed out of the group in 1967. The play and film *Dreamgirls* told this thinly

Figure 8. Belle Isle and the MacArthur Bridge, with downtown Detroit in distance.

disguised story, as Jennifer Hudson won an Academy Award for portraying Ballard in the 2007 film version. This funeral drew 5,000 fans dressed in everything from work clothes to evening gowns, who booed Diana Ross as she exited her limousine. Perhaps they were protesting Ross's culpability in the death of one dreamgirl, or was it Motown Records's flight from Detroit and the resultant death of a dream for many? With the Four Tops serving as pallbearers, the organist played the recessional over and over: the Supremes' hit "Someday We'll Be Together." New Bethel Baptist Church still serves a city whose implicit motto might well be that subtext-laden recessional.

Greater Detroit's recreational icon is Belle Isle Park, the thousand-acre island playground in the Detroit River midway between Canada and the United States, about two miles upriver from downtown (see Figure 8). Frederick Law Olmsted, famed landscape architect of New York City's Central Park, transformed the swampy island after its purchase in 1879 for $200,000. For countless Detroiters, Belle Isle has served as a sweet spot of memories: picnicking, boating, biking, fishing, cruising, dancing, canoeing, skating, deer-feeding, concert-going, ball playing, walking, and just lying in the sun watching the giant lake freighters steam by, almost within reach. Many more private memories undoubtedly were made on summer weekend nights, when Belle Isle's décor was transformed by "wall-to-wall car-petting."

Belle Isle has often hosted events that captured the public's imagination. Bicycle races held at the dawn of the twentieth century were often won by local hero Barney Oldfield, who later made himself and his sponsor nationally famous racing automobiles made by the upstart Ford Motor Company. Crowds in the Roaring Twenties breathlessly watched Harry Houdini, manacled hands and feet and nailed into a weighted shipping crate, being tossed from the Belle Isle Bridge into the frigid Detroit River. Failing to recognize the river's powerful three-mile-per-hour current, Houdini unexpectedly emerged from the water 100 yards downstream and far from his rescue boat. He escaped death in Detroit this time but not on his next visit. Suffering from acute appendicitis, Houdini still insisted on performing his act in Detroit's Garrick Theater. He collapsed on stage and died from peritonitis in Grace Hospital five days later, Halloween 1926. Gar Wood, the Detroit Yacht Club commodore on Belle Isle, skippered his "Miss America" series of speedboats to dominating victories over his English rival in the semiannual Harmsworth Trophy races between 1921 and 1933 on a course next to his club. Such fan-pleasing events continue, as Belle Isle still hosts the auto-racing Detroit Grand Prix and the American Power Boat Association Gold Cup for hydroplane boat racing.

Belle Isle today boasts an impressive palm house, perennial gardens, fountains, maritime museum, waterslide park, beach, fishing piers, tennis courts, ball fields, golf course, nature preserve, and the nation's largest yacht club building. On any summer weekend, it overflows with families bathing in the joyous mix of music, laughter, and barbecue smoke, as it has for generations. What Belle Isle does best, though, is provide a vantage point for Detroiters to stand back and take a look at their city. Seen from Belle Isle's shores, Detroit's buildings and natural setting are impressive indeed, the city's potential palpable. The vista as the summer sun sets behind downtown's glistening towers, its waning rays turning the river and the sails of harbor-bound boats to gold, is nothing short of wondrous.

Yet, like so much of iconic Detroit, Belle Isle serves as another palimpsest of revealing stories, many without happy endings. Barely ten years after being acquired, Belle Isle's development was threatened by an early manifestation of the ugly capital versus labor politics that would haunt the region for the next century. Republican aldermen representing wealthier wards on the city's fringes, with support from real estate development interests, opposed park improvement bonds, preferring instead that the city raise funds to complete Grand Boulevard, a proposed ring road to be built about three miles from downtown. They argued that their (well-heeled) constituents did not need Belle Isle Park. The *Detroit Evening News* took the lead in attacking this "Speculators' Boulevard" position. In one scathing 1889 editorial, it played up the class divisions the Belle Isle issue brought to the surface.

> The rich do not need it. Their own dooryards are in many cases beautiful parks. In summer they go to the seaside, and if they wish an airing without going away, their fine horses and carriages can whirl them off to their villas at Grosse Pointe. They will probably take little comfort in the island park even when it is completed, for the poor will be there in their homely garments, and with their homely ways, to offend the eyes and ears of my lord and my lady. But the [city] council will make a mistake to accept this indifference of the rich towards the park as an index of popular opinion. The masses of people want it. It is seaside, villa, air, water—everything in the way of rest and comfort—to which they can escape from the squalid and often unwholesome surroundings of their homes.

Another example is the Scott Memorial Fountain, designed by Cass Gilbert, architect of the U.S. Supreme Court and the Woolworth Building in Manhattan. It is a magnificent marble mélange of spouting sea beasts that spills its foaming waters down long steps into a huge reflecting pool at Belle Isle's strategic downriver apex overlooking downtown. Casual visitors cannot imagine the fountain's deeper representation of another fundamental Detroit feature: pragmatism trumping moralizing. By the time he died in 1910, James Scott had a public reputation both large and infamous. It proved a great moral quandary for upstanding Detroiters when Mr. Scott's will designated that the then-fantastic sum of $300,000 be used to construct a fountain on Belle Isle, but the gift required that a life-sized statue of James Scott be part of the fountain. "Memorialize in perpetuity on a prime site a drinker, gambler, and all-around libertine? Never!" fumed the City Council and collective preacher-hood in righteous indignation. The furor abated dramatically after the Council's public hearing at which U.S. Senator Thomas Palmer, recent donor of land for Detroit's other great public park, archly noted, "I've known in my time many a good church worker . . . enjoy quietly the very things James Scott enjoyed publicly." A fountain construction contract signing eventually replaced hypocritical posturing, but not until fifteen years had passed.

Next to the graceful MacArthur Bridge connecting Belle Isle to the mainland sits a huge vacant parcel. Its seemingly prime riverfront location belies the fact that it is a toxic brownfield, resulting from generations of stove manufacturing, tire production, and metal smelting. It is an inescapable reminder of the redevelopment challenges posed by Detroit's industrial legacy, as poignant as it is visible. Looking in the other direction, however, reminds Detroiters of another reality. There, close across the Detroit River, basks Windsor, Ontario. Saddled with the same economic base, Windsor's shoreline of immaculate parks flanking upscale, high-rise apartments stands in stark contrast to Detroit's planning failures. Those with good memories also realize that the island's infrastructure is but an atrophied version of its glory days. Over the years, the island's horse stables, canoe livery, zoo, and aquarium have successively closed, victims of the city's perpetual financial exigencies. The second, once-great yacht club located on the island, the Detroit Boat Club, sits abandoned and crumbling amid the rotting remnants of its docks. In the 1960s the city nearly evicted the Detroit Yacht Club from the island over its racially exclusive membership policies.

But Belle Isle's dark side is best symbolized by the events that happened there on June 20, 1943. As the city strained to accommodate hundreds of thousands of new black and white workers in the war materiel factories, interracial tensions in neighborhoods, public places, and workplaces inexorably accumulated, like so much kindling awaiting a spark. The interracial brawls breaking out on Belle Isle that Sunday provided the spark, lighting flames of violence that, spread by rumors and police brutality, eventually set the entire city ablaze with one of the deadliest race riots in U.S. history. Belle Isle, like Greater Detroit itself, contains accreted layers of beauty and bestiality, harmony and hysteria, fabled pasts and faded possibilities.

> It had not seemed so long since we last gazed from Sunset Point
> The river's ice floes reflecting downtown's gilded towers
> Fading Mardi Gras masks for a city whose party was definitely over
> Perpetual lent with no resurrection in sight.

Much was the same yet much had changed.

Still kids ran after seagulls oblivious to stepping in goose poop
Their unquenchable optimism no match for their savvy wings
    slicing
Smoke from a hundred charcoal fires tickling the nose with their
    potpourri
Ribs, chicken, dogs slow cooked fallin'-off-the-bone delicious
    come-an-get-it y'all
Dinner-gong river waves drumming their polyrhythms against the
    debris-girdled banks
Reverberating from the cigarette boat destined for uncharted Port
    Machismo
Mocking baby-boomer boys' toy hydroplanes whining around the
    model yacht basin
Under a sky so blue screaming June in Michigan at last!

Yet now windows-down pulsating cars cruise to rap, Motown being
    long passé
Indian players clad in royal blue and chartreuse festoon the oddly
    circular pitch
The thwak! of ball against bat no baseball game but cricket
No tennis, no basketball, no soccer, no football games either
Padlocked golf course fairways indistinguishable from rough
All casualties of the city's serial fiscal murderer
Half-filled rusted freighters with perhaps their last load of iron ore
    slink past
Despondent fishermen looking for all the world indifferent to
    potential role reversal
Bait for giant fish splashing ashore to swallow them out of their
    misery
Frustrated fathers toss their blissfully innocent children into the
    uncertain air hoping
They will land more gently in the twenty-first century than they.
          —"Father's Day on Belle Isle" by George Galster

Greater Detroit's icons, whether industrial, religious, or recreational, share
something else beyond their rich, contradictory symbolism. The meaning and
sentiment attached to them depend on whether one is a capitalist or a unionist,

black or white. Capitalists, for example, view the Ford Rouge complex as a paragon of vertical integration and efficiencies of large scale, while unionists see it as a paragon of labor victory, despite years of capitalist repression and violence. Blacks see the Rouge as a place where they proved their loyalty to one of the few employers who would give them industrial jobs, while whites see it as a place where blacks acted as strikebreaking scabs and auxiliary security guards, slugging it out with picketing white strikers. These icons are *prismatic*: what one sees in them will be colored by class and racial point of view. Greater Detroit is loaded with prismatic icons. Its failure to create icons with a *common, universal* symbolism represents one of the region's defining characteristics and most damaging legacies for its future.

Edgy Eight Mile

Now I can make two suggestions about where we should drive next. Nothing better shows the bittersweet icons and jarring contrasts of Greater Detroit than driving along the region's two most storied byways: Eight Mile Road and Woodward Avenue. If we were hungry before we started, there's no shortage of longtime classic restaurants that still dish out treats reflecting their ethnic heritage: the Parthenon (Greek), Dakota Inn Rathskeller (German), Cadieux Café (Belgian), Roma Café (Italian), or Polonia (Polish). But we can also fortify ourselves with two of Detroit's home-grown basic food groups—a "coney" (a hotdog smothered in meat sauce topped with raw onions) and a Vernor's (a tangy-sweet, bright yellow ginger ale)—and hit the road again.

Eight Mile Road is laid out like so many of Greater Detroit's major surface arterials: eight lanes of traffic separated by a wide, landscaped median. At major intersections left turns are prohibited. To turn left from Eight Mile, drivers must pass the intended street, bear left into a special lane carved into the median, and await a separate traffic light controlling their eventual U-turn back toward the desired street, whereupon they execute a right turn. To do this from a cross-street, drivers first turn right onto Eight Mile (in the wrong direction), then execute the same U-turn at the next break in the median. Reputedly created to speed traffic flows and avoid "T-bone" collisions at intersections, the gyrations needed for the idiosyncratic "Michigan left turn" prove endlessly frustrating to first-time visitors.

Despite its design, Eight Mile Road is not a beautiful boulevard. Like most regional thoroughfares, it is flanked by a bewildering profusion of small retailers, gas stations, entertainment venues, motels, car dealers, strip malls, commercial offices, manufacturing companies of various scales, and residential enclaves of differing qualities, all seeming to appear and disappear randomly. The cacophony of signage is visually exhausting and often ambiguous. What, for example, is "Christian Ho Down, Friday Nights" advertising? On the working man's Rodeo Drive, one can never be too sure—parking-lot prostitution at a particular Eight Mile big-box building supply company is so energetic that the spot has been dubbed "The 'Ho Depot." Eight Mile Road's distinctive ugliness is crowned by aluminum totem poles that carry high-tension electric wires down much of its length; these are not the only totems along its twenty-seven-mile length.

Superficially, the two sides of Eight Mile seem identical. A closer inspection reveals crucial distinctions that emphasize its role as the most powerful symbolic and substantive edge in Greater Detroit. For one thing, seventeen miles of Eight Mile Road forms the dividing line between Wayne County on the south and Oakland and Macomb Counties on the north. This also means it is the boundary between the City of Detroit on the south and the cities of Southfield, Ferndale, Hazel Park, Warren, and Eastpointe on the north. These jurisdictional distinctions are important in several ways.

One trivial but endearingly bizarre way is that "gentlemen's clubs" (aka strip joints) are only permitted on the Detroit side of Eight Mile. If nothing else, this ensures plausible deniability for husbands who claim they're stepping out for a quick "run for the border," even though not visiting a Taco Bell as implied. These clubs carry fascinating names that encode Greater (male) Detroiters' fantasies, with allusions to big money ("Tycoons," "Trumps," "Players"), exotic locales ("Luxor," "Coliseum," "Penthouse Club"), and exceptional women ("All Stars," "Hot Tamales," "Booby Trap"). Detroit's City Council has sagely declared that such venues be separated by a minimum distance. It is not clear whether this requirement means to keep the clubs' nuisance factor at a tolerable level for their Detroit neighbors or to make these diversions equally accessible to randy suburban customers along the length of Eight Mile. This does, however, promote incongruous land use juxtapositions. The Coliseum strip joint proffers a faux swanky exterior, its entrance drive graced by a phalanx of two-story, internally lit obelisks. Next door to the Coliseum entrance, however, is a junkyard selling auto parts, which has propped a yellow pickup truck high in the air to draw attention. In a classic example of inadvertent advertising, the signs on the truck proclaim "Parts Galore" and "U Pull 'Em and Save Big $$" (see Figure 9).

Figure 9. Parts Galore and the Coliseum, collaborative advertising on Eight Mile Road.

A more substantive distinction is commercial. The region's (and one of the nation's) first two enclosed shopping malls, Northland (1954) and East-land (1955), were built on Eight Mile. Northland was located next to the Lodge Freeway in Southfield, Eastland near I-94 in Harper Woods. Neither contributes to the tax base of the City of Detroit; they suck retail dollars and affiliated jobs out of it. Both malls were anchored by a Hudson's Department Store, whose president, Oscar Webber, pledged in 1950 not to build stores outside the city. These retail centers, like the new housing and industrial complexes sprouting in green fields nearby, represented the cutting edge of postwar sub-urbanization that would eventually slice the City of Detroit's jugular.

Eight Mile's final fundamental distinction is racial. For generations, Eight Mile has been an informal but powerful boundary between black city and white suburb, enforced through countless illegal actions of individuals, police forces, and city governments. U.S. census data underscore the con-tinuing effectiveness of this bounding, especially in the suburban munici-palities bordering Eight Mile east of Woodward—Ferndale, Hazel Park, Warren, and Eastpointe. Only 5 percent of the population in neighborhoods in these four municipalities adjacent to the north side of Eight Mile Road is black, while 87 percent is white. By contrast, the population in the Detroit neighborhoods they face across Eight Mile is 79 percent black and 15 percent white.

Given these facts, it is not surprising that "crossing Eight Mile" carries a host of potent social, political, economic, and psychological connotations for Greater Detroiters, whether for blacks looking north or whites looking south. Some of these were perceptively explored by Eminem in his 2002 film *8 Mile* and his song of the same name. Down the middle of Eight Mile Road indeed stretch lines of high tension, in terms of both electricity and racial symbolism.

> It's different, it's a certain significance, a certificate
> of authenticity you'd never even see;
> But it's everything to me; it's my credibility
> —"8 Mile," sung by Eminem

The Avenue of Greater Detroit

Woodward Avenue is named after Augustus Woodward, judge, city planner, and first governor of the Michigan Territory, who in 1807 both devised downtown's radial street scheme and rendered Detroit's most egregious legal decision regarding slavery. It proceeds in a north-northwesterly direction, perpendicular to the Detroit River—arrow-straight for twenty-five miles—connecting downtown Detroit with Pontiac, a once-distinct municipality now engulfed by suburban sprawl. It is officially designated an American Heritage Highway and for good reason. No street is more redolent with poignant history, shocking contrasts, and heady symbolism.

Heading north on Woodward out of downtown, it is difficult to comprehend how Silas Farmer in his 1890 *History of Detroit and Michigan* could have written that it "has no superior on the continent." Only four mansions remain from that era. One is now a restaurant, another is law offices, and two are Wayne State University offices. Instead of grandeur, the dominant impression is of abandoned retail stores and immense tracts of empty land occupying what in most cities would constitute prime locations. These glimpses of nothingness from Woodward are but the tip of the abandonment iceberg.

When we reach the Mid-Town corridor, however, the picture changes dramatically to new construction and renovation amid meticulously preserved architectural treasures. The 1919 Orchestra Hall, the Detroit Symphony Orchestra's acoustically superb home, was renovated and significantly expanded in 2006 by the Max Fisher Music Center. New buildings of the Wayne State University campus and its expansive Medical Center mushroom around its restored Old Main Building. The Italianate splendor of the 1921 Detroit Public Library, another Cass Gilbert design, glistens as the centerpiece of the Cultural Center. Directly across from it gleams another white marble-clad classic: the 1927 Beaux Arts-style Detroit Institute of Arts, handsomely expanded with a Michael Graves design in 2007. Nearby, the refurbished nineteenth-century mansions on Ferry Street now comprise a classy boutique hotel complex. A few blocks north, the New Center district is anchored by the neoclassical-style, Albert Kahn-designed former General Motors building. GM Corporate headquarters from 1923 to 1996, it was the world's second-largest office building when it opened. Now retitled Cadillac Place, after conversion into state offices in one of the largest historic renovation projects ever attempted, it elegantly holds 1.4 million square feet of floor space. Across from it sits the incomparable Fisher Building, a 30-story office-retail-theater complex financed by the Fisher Brothers from selling their car body fabricating business to GM. Also designed by Albert Kahn Associates, this art deco gem boasts a three-story, barrel-vaulted lobby festooned with forty varieties of marble; it deservedly won the New York Architectural League's "Most Beautiful Commercial Structure Award" in 1928. This Cultural Center-New Center precinct, with its suite of four National Historical Landmark-designated buildings clustered within a mile, is nothing short of stunning.

But there is one more jewel here that cannot be seen from Woodward Avenue. So, let's hop out of the SUV for a moment and enter the main interior court of the Detroit Institute of Arts. There we can marvel at *Detroit Industry*, the 27-panel fresco masterpiece of Mexican artist Diego Rivera, painted in 1932 and 1933 and commissioned by Edsel Ford. The main panels on the north and south walls dramatically portray auto manufacturing at Ford's Rouge factory. Workers strain mightily with tasks as challenging as they are dangerous, encircled by monstrous machines threatening to mangle them at every turn, all carried out under the scowling visages of foremen and Henry himself. Overarching these scenes are mysterious allegories on creation, nature, and the comparative roles of religion and science in human progress. Rivera's powerful images of life-shaping experiences and fundamental questions raised by the industrial metropolis were created with pigments mixed with plaster, so they are embedded in the museum's walls. No less powerfully, they are also embedded in the souls of Detroiters.

Now let's resume our drive. You likely will have noticed by now that Mid-Town's streets are periodically punctured by huge geysers of steam spewing from manhole covers. Produced by the most prosaic of processes—burning garbage at the municipal incinerator to produce energy for commercial buildings across Mid-Town—this escaping excess steam lends a ghostly, fairy-tale-like quality to the environs. It is as if, as one imaginative child exclaimed during her first visit, "there were dragons living under the street!" And, like dragons and other fairy tales, the visage of Mid-Town is ephemeral.

All the public and private grandeur we have just experienced evaporates within a half mile north of New Center. We're now left to contemplate weedy lots, boarded-up convalescent centers, and burned-out storefronts, interspersed among the neon-clad party stores and grandly crumbling churches with their vestigial congregations. Then, miraculously, yet another discordant vision emerges when we reach the Boston-Edison historic district, with its magnificent mansions reflecting turn-of-the-twentieth-century opulence. There on Woodward also sits the glorious Cathedral of the Most Blessed Sacrament, seat of the archbishop of Roman Catholic Detroit. This sudden morphing from dream to nightmare and back again, in endless, random repetition, is the dominant visual experience of driving the D.

Beyond the four parallel streets comprising Boston-Edison, the world we see from Woodward again jarringly collapses into ruins and debris-strewn lots. This condition only intensifies as we cross into Highland Park, a tiny municipality completely surrounded by Detroit, that, throughout the twentieth century, stubbornly maintained its independence to hoard its then-robust industrial tax base. The symbol of this since-vanished tax base is the shuttered 1910 Ford Highland Park plant, legendary home of the first moving auto assembly line, the Model T, the $5 a day wage of 1914, and Walter Reuther's first place of employment with Ford in 1927. With no production there since 1976, the decomposing corpse of this eight-story dinosaur sprawls over 200 acres behind the down-market strip shopping center, Model T Plaza. The shopping center was built where the executive offices and the power plant of the factory once belched edicts and effluents. The City of Highland Park is now bankrupt, running on the artificial life support of state receivership, making ends meet by a lone cop strictly enforcing speed limits on Woodward.

We soon spy an omnipresent illustration of Greater Detroit's core commercial architectural evolution: the best retail buildings are not demolished but are adapted to the down-market trade. The most popular uses seem to be party stores, pawn shops, play spots, and places of worship with no known institutional affiliations. Here at Woodward and McNichols (Six Mile) Road, there once stood an imposing, 1920s-era bank, regal in its neoclassical garb of fluted stone columns. The bank departed along with the community's disposable income, the empty building converted first into an adult movie venue and, most recently, a strip club called (accurately, if ironically) "Deja Vu," a commercial evolution from tellers to "no-tellers," if you will.

As we leave Highland Park and reenter Detroit across McNichols Road, things noticeably improve again, at least on the west side of Woodward. There basks the expansive Palmer Park complex of trails, woods, golf course, pool, tennis and basketball courts, and ball fields. This vast tract was bequeathed to Detroit in 1897 by Senator Thomas Palmer, future defender of James Scott, whose family owned a farm there. The remainder of the Palmer farm was platted in the 1910s for considerably less altruistic motives: an upscale residential subdivision. We glimpse the result after passing Seven Mile Road. It is the Palmer Woods historic district, a collection of Tudor Revival homes, the epitome of *faux*, old-money, gentry architecture built for the aspiring *nouveaux riche* Detroiters of 1920s. Turn your head the other way and you are forced into another Woodward double-take, for now the Michigan State Fairgrounds appears. For over a century, the proud purveyors of Michigan's best cattle, sheep, chickens, and horses gathered every August in an inconvenient corner of the state, in its least agricultural county, in its biggest city, to show their wares and gorge on the combination of fried food, carnival rides, and washed-up, old-timer musical acts gasping for breath in the humid Michigan air. Like much of the land bordering Woodward, the State Fairgrounds has soaked up both glory and gore over the years. In 1936 it was the site of "every man's horse" Seabiscuit's first major stakes racing victory; in 1967 it was the marshaling point for federal paratroopers dispatched by President Lyndon Johnson to quell the civil disturbances in Detroit. The State Fairgrounds is now closed, awaiting a fate unknown.

Now we have reached a place we have already explored: Eight Mile Road. But this is no ordinary surface intersection. This is the only place in its entire length where Woodward rises on an overpass, its apex marking the point where we have officially entered a different municipality and county. The fact that Woodward requires a bridge over Eight Mile reinforces the dual world symbolism of city and suburb. Here, in this suburban world along Woodward, the racial composition of the neighborhoods is suddenly overwhelmingly white. Housing deterioration, abandoned buildings, and vacant land are rare. Retail storefronts are occupied; indeed, they are omnipresent along

Woodward from Eight Mile to Fifteen Mile Road. Yet even in this very different suburban world, the bizarre parade of bittersweet icons continues.

Two municipalities bisected by Woodward, Royal Oak at Eleven Mile
Road and Birmingham at Fifteen Mile (Maple) Road, epitomize contemporary American notions of good town planning. They are most un-Detroit-
like in this regard, for the region is notable for its dearth of governmental
controls on land uses or concerns about environmental sustainability. The
only planning of note has been aimed at making traffic flow more smoothly.
So it is more than a little bizarre that these two towns, as if to bite the automotive hand that feeds their prosperous residents, have consciously developed
pedestrian-friendly, higher-density, mixed-use environments. They seem to
be popular, but if they were generalized across the country, the demand for
cars would plummet (even further!), taking Royal Oak, Birmingham, and the
rest of the region down together.

At Twelve Mile Road in Royal Oak, we reach the Roman Catholic Church
of the Little Flower, founded by the nationally (in)famous 1930s radio personality Father Charles Coughlin. The current church, completed in 1936,
features an octagonal sanctuary seating 3,000 and the eight-story Charity
Crucifixion Tower, all financed by listeners to Father Coughlin's radioed en-
treaties. The imposing tower looming over Woodward prominently features
both a 28-foot statue of Jesus and a somewhat smaller one of Bishop Michael
Gallagher, Coughlin's protector and mentor. This prototypical "radio priest"
used his technologically cutting-edge pulpit of the airwaves to bash the nascent United Auto Workers Union, promote reactionary anti-Semitism, and
rationalize the atrocities of Nazi Germany. Nevertheless, the U.S. Council
of Catholic Bishops in 1998 designated the church one of only five national
shrines in the country.

The stream of irony runs still deeper through this spot on Woodward
Avenue. In 1947 Royal Oak took the lead among suburbs in thwarting developers' attempts to rezone single-family residential areas for apartment complexes. Although both the first site proposed on Webster Road and the second
two years later off Vinsetta Boulevard bordered a busy railroad line, a coalition of homeowners associations successfully lobbied city officials to maintain the zoning. Their arguments represented the prototype of privileged
whites' superficially unprejudiced framing of exclusionary intents, couching
their opposition in terms of promoting the "public health, safety and welfare" of the city, by restricting residence to "homeowner citizens" and so
maintaining their property values. Their position was ultimately upheld by

Michigan's Supreme Court in 1949. Where did these homeowner associations meet to sharpen their segregationist strategies? The Church of the Little Flower's own Shrine School on Woodward.

But the fundamental symbolic importance of Woodward Avenue for Detroiters is defined more by what has occurred *on* it, not what sits next to it. For two centuries, Woodward has been the place for innovation, celebration, and aspiration. Yet, like every Detroit icon, it carries a tainted legacy.

Woodward has been the site of several important innovations, not surprisingly all related to the car culture. Concerned about the increasingly unruly traffic downtown during the First World War, Detroit police officer William Potts adapted railroad semaphores' red-yellow-green format to create the nation's first automated, tricolor traffic light. It was installed at the corner of Woodward and Michigan Avenues in 1920. A few miles north in Highland Park, Woodward passes over the Davison Freeway, the first below-grade, limited access, divided urban highway in the U.S. when it opened in 1942. The stretch of Woodward from Six Mile (McNichols) Road to Seven Mile Road represents America's first mile of concrete highway, paved in 1909.

Since its inception, Woodward has been the gathering place to celebrate major civic events. Down Woodward have marched successive waves of successful troops returning from conflicts as far back as the War of 1812. For a score of years beginning in 1948, every Democratic presidential candidate launched his campaign with a Labor Day rally at Cadillac Square, hosted by UAW President Walter Reuther as the acknowledged general of the nation's most successful and highly organized industrial-political army. Today Woodward Avenue annually hosts the Thanksgiving Day Parade, Labor Day Parade, and Labor Day jazz festival. Along it parade Detroit's latest incarnation of professional sports champions. The Tigers, Pistons, Red Wings, and Shock have all made this trip during the last decade; the Lions are another story.

For the last decade, Woodward has been the venue for celebrating something even more basic: the region's raison d'être. The Dream Cruise is a loosely organized, August weekend-long parade of tens of thousands of hot cars, old and new, along suburban Woodward. The archetypical driver is a baby-boomer steering a vehicle that he or she could only fantasize about owning when a teenager. The route is festooned with massive billboards glorifying the automobile and scoffing at chic cultural icons of the country's more glamorous parts. One billboard shows a closeup of a rakishly angled tail fin with the caption "Some towns do art fairs." Another features the enclosed spare tire case prominently mounted on the gleaming rear bumper of a 1957 Chevy, boasting, "Some 50 year-olds look good with a spare tire." Automaniacs line endless miles of Woodward with their beach chairs and coolers, making a weekend of exaggerating recollected teen exploits and exclaiming admiringly over the revving chrome. You only hear engines though, not tires squealing. The event has become so congested with classic (and not-so-classic) cars that the Dream Cruise is more accurately a Dream Crawl. Still, over a million attend annually, easily exceeding combined attendance of all the other events I have listed. What an implicit affidavit of Detroiters' priorities and fantasies! It is also another manifestation of Detroiters wallowing in metanostalgia: life was good here when I was a teen and cruising.

Woodward has also harbored other sorts of dreams—and nightmares. In 1861, it was the point of mass recruiting rallies for the U.S. Army, seeking cannon fodder for the Civil War carnage to come. The bittersweet march of the gaunt survivors took place there four years later. In a century-lagged echo of unfinished business, on June 23, 1963, between 150,000 and 200,000 civil rights advocates marched twenty blocks down Woodward to the convention center. Leading the march arm in arm were Rev. Martin Luther King, Jr., Rev. Charles L. Franklin, UAW President Walter Reuther, Detroit Mayor Jerome Cavanagh, and Michigan Governor George Romney. Those assembled in Cobo Hall heard a new King speech, distinguished by its effective repetition of a single line, rising in volume and power with each repetition. It was the draft of what two months later would become the internationally acclaimed "I Have a Dream" speech, thundering across Washington, D.C., from the Lincoln Memorial. There was no little symbolism involved in King's taking the prototype "I Have a Dream" for a test drive on Woodward that hot June day. Twenty years earlier, on April 11, 1943, a group less than a tenth in size had marched down the same stretch of Woodward, to protest discrimination in the war plants and racially stained police brutality; Reuther then was the primary speaker. Within two months, on June 21, 1943, this same Woodward pavement would be covered in blood as white mobs pulled black passersby from cars, buses, and trolleys and beat them mercilessly. Who would have guessed then that only five years after the Great Civil Rights March, on April 4, 1968, Woodward would quake with anger and grief as the outraged gathered to decry King's assassination in Memphis. So, of course, it had to be Woodward where thousands of Detroiters spontaneously gathered, abandoned their traffic-jammed vehicles in the middle of the street, and began hugging strangers on the night of November 4, 2009, to celebrate the election of President Barack Obama.

Woodward: the avenue where dreams were born, dreams were driven, dreams went bad, and a few dreams came true—the avenue that *is* Detroit.

> A city like Detroit only exists in a prose poem. No stanza or line break could contain it. But paragraphs—big blocks of words—that's what Detroit is. Run-on sentences border its streets, parking lots: heavy miles of guard rails and fences. Cars live here: carburetors, catalytic converters, automatic transmissions, power brakes, power steering, white sidewalls, fuel injection, radiators, front suspension, mufflers, bucket seats, leather, chrome, head room, leg room, ride like million, can we build one for you, highways of your mind, luxury ride, down 8 mile, 7 mile, 6 mile, 5 mile, down till they don't count no more, down to the Renaissance Center, and the mass transit that nobody gives a shit about, down to the very guts which is not blood or heart or even steel but riding fast smooth down the leg of Woodward Ave., windows open, radio blasting. Keeping alive.
>
> —"Detroit" by Linda Nemec Foster

Detroiters

The main problem with driving around Detroit is that it precludes conversations with the denizens of the D. These are invariably informative and revealing, if not always comfortable.

It is perilous to stereotype the people in a metropolis of over four million. But I venture to guess that it won't take a visitor much time outside the car chatting with the locals to observe several common things. Four are paramount. First, Detroiters publicly exhibit a host of contradictory traits. They are proud and insecure, friendly and intolerant, generous and suspicious, religious and profane, warm and violent, often virtually simultaneously. Second, Detroiters are unpretentious. Self-importance is hard to preserve when they so often hear other Americans' reaction, "You live *where*?" followed by a knowing, frowning silence, as if to say, "Oh, I'm *so* sorry . . ." Third, Detroiters are active agents. They have often expressed this in highly violent and counterproductive ways, but they are not typically passive victims. Finally, Detroiters are deeply antiurban. As soon as the Friday workday ends (often before), Detroit families decamp for their "weekend places up north," significantly shifting the population center of gravity of Michigan's lower peninsula. Though primarily a "white thing," black families also have traditionally escaped the metropolis to their own haven of Idlewild, to hunt, fish, swim, boat, and otherwise recreate in the absence of anything urban.

As we explore the history of this place, we will confront many internationally famous Detroiters, names such as those in the baggage claim areas at the Big Mac. Yet equally important in understanding this place are the contributions of many unknown to most Detroiters, names like Thornton and Ruth Blackburn, Charles Bowles, Lewis Cass, George Edwards, William Faulkner, Charles Freer, James Weldon Johnson, Sheila Kelly, Hazen Pingree, Gladys and Ossian Sweet, and Joseph Workman. But even more fundamentally, Detroit's story is a compendium of millions of stories of the historically anonymous, those who have quietly toiled, struggled, and sometimes succeeded in building a life and, thereby, a city. In this book, we will explore the way the city has been experienced by five generations of one of these no-name families. The story of this family is neither unique nor representative, yet it is pure Detroit.

> How we shop for groceries only on Saturdays (at Eastern Market)
> How we never leave returnables in our cars
> How we drive to the suburbs for *The New York Times*
> How we treat stoplights as optional
> How we open galleries and theaters in auto supply shops and
>   Bohemian halls
> How we look out for one another
> How we say we are going to leave.
>   "The Straits" by Kristin Palm

Stunning

Driving Greater Detroit teaches several lessons. It is a place that is about making music and metal things and then viciously fighting about the spoils. It possesses an unusually rich trove of iconic cultural artifacts, buildings, and places, populated by equally iconic historical figures directing, or being directed by, epic events. The symbolic meanings these icons convey are immensely powerful. There are vast racial, economic, and physical disparities in Greater Detroit, and they are clearly etched on the character of spaces and faces, easily observed while driving its thoroughfares. These disparities shift not along gentle geographic gradients but tumble over steep cliffs.

Greater Detroit is stunning. It is stunning in its legacy of industrial, labor organizing, and artistic achievements juxtaposed against its legacy of race and class warfare. It is stunning in its contrasts between poverty and plenty, decay and splendor, ugliness and beauty, hate and love, despair and resilience, all implausibly proximate on the urban landscape. It is stunning in that it has represented to the world both the best and worst of what cities can be, all within the span of half a century. It is stunning in that it represents *to itself* a palette of internally inconsistent, prismatic symbols whose meanings depend on the class and race of the viewer.

But curiosity demands the obvious follow-up question: why? Why *is* Detroit—the place, the people, and their interrelationships—like this? *What drives Detroit?* In this book I will offer some answers, beginning with a broad hint.

> *RESPECT*
> —the only message on a large billboard on Woodward Avenue seen while crossing Eight Mile Road entering the city, June 2010

Chapter 2

Sculpting Detroit: Polity and Economy Trump Geology

Its borders are so many vast prairies, and the freshness of the beautiful waters always keeps the banks green. The prairies are bordered by long and broad rows of fruit trees which have never felt the careful hand of the vigilant gardener. . . . Under these broad walks one sees assembled by the hundreds the timid deer and fawn, also the squirrel bounding in his eagerness to collect the apples and plums with which the earth is covered. . . . Golden pheasants, the quail, the partridge, woodcocks and numerous doves swarm in the woods and over the country, which is dotted and broken with thickets and high forests of full-grown trees, forming a charming perspective, which sweeten the sad loneliness of the solitude. The hand of the pitiless reaper has never mown the luxurious grass upon which fatten wooly buffaloes, of magnificent size and proportion. . . . There are ten species of forest trees. . . . The fish are here nourished and bathed by living water of crystal clearness, and their great abundance renders them none the less delicious. . . . In a word, the climate is temperate, and the air purified through the day and night by a gentle breeze. The skies are always serene and spread sweet and fresh influences which makes one enjoy a tranquil sleep.

    . . . If the situation is agreeable, it is none the less important because it opens and closes the door of passage to the most distant nations which are situated upon the borders of the vast seas of

sweet water. None but the enemies of truth could be enemies to the
establishment so necessary to the increase of the glory of the *king*.
—Cadillac's account of Detroit in 1701, as reported
by historian Silas Farmer, 1890

If you cut away the hyperbole and cut him some slack for exaggerating (OK,
lying) to make a political point to his boss, you must admit that the founder
of the City of Detroit got to the heart of its rationale. Detroit started because
of its living natural amenities and strategic location. It was set here for
the beasts, trees, dirt, and the width of a river. Once established, however,
the morphology of Greater Detroit would be sculpted more by politics
and the economics of industry than by geology.

Geopolitics and Geology

Detroit's founding was rooted in the geopolitical shenanigans of late
seventeenth-century North America. The fortified trading posts of New
France, scattered across what now is Ontario, Minnesota, Wisconsin, Illinois, Indiana, and Michigan were in economic, political, and military trouble as the century drew to a close. As the Natives swamped these outposts
with so many beaver pelts that their barter price fell dramatically, the French
found that they could secure highly favorable terms of trade by offering "fire
water" in the swap. The Natives' rapidly rising preference for fermented spirits over ancestral spirits caused consternation among their chiefs and the
French Jesuit priests alike. Coupled with growing threats from the pesky
English to the south, the rising tide of wilderness unhappiness led the Court
of King Louis XIV to consolidate its garrisons, abandoning all but two outposts.

Caught up in this geopolitical maelstrom was French soldier-merchant-
explorer Antoine Laumet, who, following a socially astute marriage, became
known as Antoine de la Mothe, Sieur de Cadillac. This name change proved
fortuitous in a later era of Detroit's economic history. After all, who could
imagine naming a luxury automobile a "Laumet"?

Cadillac was the commander of one of the recently abandoned posts,
Fort De Buade. Frustrated by the loss of both his military command and the
associated lucrative personal gains, Cadillac set off for France in 1698 to con-

vince the Court to build a new fortified trading post as a strategic replacement for military and economic reasons. He knew the perfect spot.

After over two years of haggling, Cadillac finally convinced the minister of marine, and King Louis approved a payment of approximately $300 to build the new fortification. In early July 1701, Cadillac left Montreal with 25 canoes, 50 soldiers, and 50 assorted farmers and artisans. His band took a series of rivers eventually leading to Lake Huron, thence south to Lake St. Clair, avoiding the threatening Iroquois along the direct route through the southern Great Lakes. On July 24, 1701, Cadillac's party landed at the narrowest part of a river connecting Lake St. Clair and Lake Erie. Striding manfully ashore (according to subsequent paintings), he ascended the modest bluff and founded Fort Pontchartrain du Détroit. This name was a diplomatically astute and cartographically clever choice, representing a dual commendation of Cadillac's benefactor (King Louis' minister of marine, Count Pontchartrain) and the defining geography of the place (*détroit* in French means "straits" or "narrows"). In 300-year hindsight, Cadillac botched the name, because Detroit has rarely since been on the straight and narrow.

And here is where the story changes from geopolitics to geology. The way many cities develop physically, economically, and socially is deeply determined by their natural geological attributes. Geology in most metropolitan areas sculpts their socioeconomic destinies. It constrains where and how city building can occur and at what cost. It draws topographical boundaries of home turfs for competing groups. It often supplies abundant subterranean minerals. It sometimes provides an element of risk, threatening periodic cataclysms, such as earthquakes and floods. Not so for Detroit.

Instead of being directive, geology has been benignly permissive in southeast Michigan: no deposits of gold, iron, or coal to exploit as the core driver of urban expansion. Detroit's only sizable mineral deposit was not even discovered until the city was already well into its industrial expansion and was merely an economic afterthought: salt. Ironically, from today's perspective it seems as if nature played a cruel joke, rubbing that salt deposit into an open wound of deindustrialization.

Detroit's geological gifts were twofold: an extensive, navigable, freshwater lake and river system to the east, and a temperate, moist, fertile, featureless plain spreading seemingly endlessly to the north and west. Glaciers were very kind to Detroit. Glaciers were the region's first "site developers," bulldozing the topography into "ready-to-build" sites and scooping out a passel of lovely little depressions that would become lakes as the glaciers retreated. Water thus was plentiful for thirsty people, industries, and lawns alike. Cleared of the valuable (and irreplaceable) hardwood forest cover by the mid-nineteenth century, southeast Michigan proved easy to farm, especially for Easterners more accustomed to thin, rocky soils. Wood, brick, and limestone were plentiful, and the topography permitted building practically everywhere. Construction was thus cheap and geographically ubiquitous. Detroit builders never confronted swamps, deserts, hills, or valleys of consequence. Apart from the rare tornado, Detroiters never needed to worry about natural disasters. Never in recorded history has the region suffered a damaging earthquake, nor has the Detroit River ever flooded. The river's current was, however, swift enough to carry untreated effluents from the burgeoning city downstream into Lake Erie. An added benefit to this from Detroiters' perspective was that some of their pollution might contaminate Ohio's water supply, potentially weakening the hated Ohio State University football team.

So, geopolitical considerations motivated where Detroit was sited, and the local geology provided the benign environment for the new settlement's sustainability. But what opportunities would this permissive geological stage really provide for the region's development?

Manufacturing Dispersal

The first answer is manufacturing dispersal. By the time industries arose in Detroit in the mid-nineteenth century, geopolitical considerations had given way to economic ones. Detroit's nascent industrial base—shipbuilding, iron smelting, chemicals—clustered along the riverfront. Although this riverfront-dominant land use pattern continued through the nineteenth century, the advent of the railroad eliminated the need to locate near water for most manufacturing firms. Early portents were already visible by the 1870s: the Michigan Car Company, a builder of railway carriages, relocated to the western fringe Springwells neighborhood, at the intersection of the Michigan Central and Grand Trunk rail lines. By 1900, dozens of substantial industries with 400 or more employees had sprouted up along Detroit's hinterland-opening railways, including American Car and Foundry, American Radiator, Detroit Steel and Spring, Detroit Bridge and Iron Works, and Daniel Scotten and Company (producers of tobacco products).

But the auto companies were the real shock troops of Detroit's manufacturing dispersal. Within the next twenty years as this industry mushroomed, earlier patterns were reinforced and replicated further out from the core, following the newly built circumferential railroads. The industrial landscape of Detroit by 1920 assumed a distinct pattern of two concentric crescents, each with an open side toward the river, each with a nexus of railroads at its core. The inner crescent roughly paralleled Grand Boulevard. On its eastern side ran the Michigan Central Railroad, where Packard Motor Car Company, Dodge Brothers Automobiles, Hupp Motor Company, and Briggs Manufacturing Company were located. Just to the west along the Grand Trunk Railroad were Studebaker Automobile Works, Cadillac Motor Company, Hayes Manufacturing Company, and Northway Motor and Manufacturing Company. Farther west and southwest on the inner crescent lay the Lincoln Motor Company, Kelsey Wheel Company, Motor Truck Body Company, and Paige-Detroit Motor Car Company. Roughly two miles farther from Detroit's downtown was the outer manufacturing crescent, following the Detroit Terminal Railroad. It was anchored on the east (near Connors and Jefferson Streets) by Hudson Motor Car Company, Chalmers Motor Car Company, and Continental Motors Company. At its northwest apex near Woodward and Six Mile Road was Ford Motor Company's Highland Park factory; just south was Maxwell Motor Company. In the southwest, the outer crescent boasted another Paige-Detroit Motor Car plant, Savon Motor Company, and Springfield Body Company and terminated at Ford Motor Company's River Rouge factory complex in Dearborn.

Unlike nineteenth-century Detroit, with its homogeneous, unbroken industrial district extending for miles along the riverfront, this rise of the dual manufacturing crescents meant that factories inevitably rubbed shoulders with homes. This dominant and distinctive mixed manufacturing/residential landscape within the same neighborhood was as remarkable then as it is now. The Detroit City Directory of 1920/21 observed:

> A peculiar situation has developed in Detroit . . . with regard to the location of industries. There are no well-defined factory districts, such as are found in most cities. Instead the plants are to be found in every section. The rapid increase in population . . . has caused the city to spread out, so the many large plants, which only a few years ago were located far outside the city limits, now are found in the center of some otherwise pleasant residence district.

But the manufacturing dispersal evident by the 1920s was only a tepid foreshadowing of what would occur after World War II. Again the auto industry, now consolidated and mightier than ever, would lead Greater Detroit's process of industrial suburbanization. In the 1950s, Detroit's auto companies built 25 new plants in southeast Michigan; none were in City of Detroit. From 1950 to 1956, 124 other manufacturing firms located in the suburbs; 55 moved out of Detroit to do so. Even greater dispersion followed, as firms increasingly switched to trucks as their dominant distribution mode, freed as they were from inner-city congestion by the region's burgeoning network of limited access, high-speed roadways.

Transportation infrastructure alone did not drive manufacturing dispersal, however. Land-extensive production processes were also a prime driver. Within the first decade of mass auto production, industrial engineers discovered that assembly line processes could be much more efficient if raw materials, parts, and semifinished products were all on the same floor. Moving from multi- to single-story auto plants meant that a given amount of factory floor area would require more land: a shift from intensive to extensive use of land. This technological innovation is dramatically illustrated by the shifting designs of Detroit's premier industrial architect, Albert Kahn. Early in the twentieth century, he designed the two iconic factories of the era: the six-story Ford Highland Park plant and the five-story Packard plant on Grand Boulevard in the heart of Detroit. But a decade later, he radically altered his design. The land-extensive watershed was Kahn's Building B at Ford's Dearborn Rouge complex, a half-mile-long steel and glass structure on one story, opened in 1917 to build Eagle boats for World War I.

Unfortunately, by the end of the auto industry's 1920s heyday, few factories had been built in this new, land-extensive style. Then came the Great Depression, with little motivation to build new facilities. Then came World War II, with no opportunity to build new auto plants. Not surprisingly, the pent-up postwar boom in land-extensive auto factory construction occurred at the fringes of metropolitan Detroit, where large tracts of land could be inexpensively assembled. The new suburban factories consumed three times as much land per worker as the older, land-intensive plants. Indeed, to accommodate the City of Detroit's existing manufacturing employees at the density of the newer, land-extensive factories would have absorbed almost half the city's land area. This new suburban construction put older Detroit plants at a competitive disadvantage. During the 1950s alone, 840 manufacturing plants in the city closed, headlined by the Packard and Hudson auto companies' massive facilities. This deindustrialization of the city has continued unabated since, producing fiscal, environmental, and psychological catastrophes.

The magnitude of this dispersal of employment from Detroit to its suburbs is nothing short of staggering. In every twenty-year period since the end of World War II, Detroit lost roughly half its remaining manufacturing jobs. This meant that, of the 333,000 manufacturing jobs located in the city in 1947, less than 10 percent—only 23,000—remained by 2007. By contrast, the suburbs of Greater Detroit had 189,000 manufacturing jobs in 2007. Of course, we have witnessed substantial reductions in the region's manufacturing employment in both city and suburban areas in recent years. But this should not obscure the overarching point that a dramatic intraregional shift in the location of *all* economic activity—manufacturing and nonmanufacturing alike—occurred in the last half century.

Between 1970 and 2000 alone, the number of jobs in Detroit's three-county suburban ring grew 2 percent per year, on average, while jobs in the city declined by 2 percent annually on average. This means that today over *three-fourths* of all the region's jobs in retail and wholesale trade, construction, finance, insurance and real estate, business and repair services, personal services, and professional services—as well as manufacturing—are beyond the city limits. Even in the transportation, communication, public utilities, and public administration sectors, most employment is now located outside the city.

If job counts don't paint a sufficiently vivid portrait of city decline and suburban growth, try establishments. The suburbs have over 400 first-run movie screens; Detroit has 10. The suburbs have 110 bowling alleys; Detroit has two. The suburbs have dozens and dozens of Starbucks; Detroit has two. The suburbs have 130 7-Elevens; Detroit has none. The suburbs have 21 major indoor shopping malls; Detroit has none. Nowhere else in America is a city so thoroughly overshadowed economically by its suburbs.

But why is most economic activity outside the City of Detroit? What prevented it from continually expanding its boundaries, as it had done earlier? After all, from 1880 to 1900 Detroit ballooned 76 percent from 13 to 23 square miles; by 1926 it would expand another 504 percent to its current 139 square miles. The answer lies in geopolitics of identity played on a featureless plain.

Searching for Boundaries

The geology of southeastern Michigan did not only affect how industrial patterns developed, of course. It also shaped the region's demographic and, ultimately, political contours. Groups of households who distinguished themselves by race, ethnicity, religion, or class could not use topographic features as intergroup boundaries. There are no rivers, ravines, or hills to subdivide turf naturally. The only clear geological barriers, the Detroit River and Lake St. Clair, form an international boundary at the region's eastern edge. All boundaries on the Michigan side, less visible and impermeable, had to be constructed by humans. Lacking geographic markers, the socially constructed boundaries between Greater Detroit's adjacent groups proved more contingent, subject to alteration and contention. And violently contest them Detroiters did.

One attractive option for those seeking economic and personal security, identity, and advantage within clear boundaries is to have a distinct jurisdiction where their group is politically dominant. In this regard, Michigan's state politics proved as permissive as the geology. Formed out of the old Northwest Territory, Michigan swore fealty to the Jeffersonian principles of government "close to the people." Thomas Jefferson's grand idea behind the young nation's Land Ordinance of 1785 was that the Northwest Territory's lands and jurisdictions would be structured rationally. All land would be surveyed and divided into mile square sections. Each square would contain 640 acres that could be easily subdivided into, for example, sixteen forty-acre farms. Local political jurisdictions called townships would be created by joining 36 of these one-mile squares into a larger square, six miles on a side. These, in turn, would be joined to create counties. This scheme is still patently obvious in the jurisdictional geography of Greater Detroit, three centuries later. As illustrations, Oakland County is a 900-square-mile square, five townships (thirty miles) wide and five high; Macomb County is three townships wide and five high.

Michigan's fascination with Jeffersonian democracy compounded the fragmentation of political power across this multitude of local governments twice. The first instance was the state's 1837 constitution, which granted extensive "home rule" powers to townships and municipalities, rather than reserving them for the state. One of these powers related to how land would be used and the nature of any land development. This constitutional diffusion of land use planning responsibility ultimately hamstrung the region's ability to shape growth in a sustainable fashion, coordinate economic development, or share resources.

Another "home rule" constitutional power granted to townships was the ease with which they could incorporate. After lying dormant for almost a century, this provision began to be resurrected in southeast Michigan early in the twentieth century. Some suburban townships realized that municipal incorporation could be used as a defense against any perceived land grab by the City of Detroit. Incorporation often was undertaken not for high-minded Jeffersonian principles but to protect valuable industrial tax base assets. Greenfield and Hamtramck Townships provide prime—and ironic—examples. In both cases, the dominant employer in the township—Ford in the former and Dodge in the latter—vigorously opposed annexation, fearing higher Detroit taxation. They led the successful political efforts to incorporate the townships into the cities of Highland Park and Hamtramck. To this day, Detroit completely surrounds these municipalities, odd little territories that make a novice Detroit map reader think the color-coding has been botched. Incorporation decisions would come back to haunt these tiny enclaves a half century later. Both Ford and Dodge closed their massive factories, leaving these vestigial cities virtually bereft of industrial tax base. At this writing Highland Park is being operated under state receivership.

But Greenfield and Hamtramck Townships were the exception. Around 1900, most suburban townships eagerly voted for annexation by Detroit, anticipating the extension of city infrastructure to a predominantly rural, undeveloped area. Indeed, between 1900 and 1925, Detroit quintupled its area through annexation. This came to a screeching halt in 1926, with Michigan's second major act of fealty to Jefferson's ideal of "small box" government. The state legislature passed a law making annexation much more difficult; Detroit never tried this again. This was not likely troubling at the time since plenty of vacant land remained within the 1926 city limits. But by the early 1950s, land-locked Detroit, surrounded by other incorporated municipalities, found itself shut out from the big suburban party of industrial and residential development.

After a respite during the Depression, suburban incorporation reignited. From 1940 to 1965, 31 new home rule governments were incorporated and ten villages reincorporated as cities, collectively encompassing an area almost twice the size of Detroit itself. Yet most of these new incorporated jurisdictions were smaller than ever before (the exceptions being Livonia, St. Clair Shores, Southfield, and Warren); 12 were home to fewer than 3,000 people in 1960.

Today, the urbanized area of Greater Detroit has spread over a seven-county region containing 27 villages, 89 municipalities, and 115 townships. While this proliferation of home rule territories may have given residents some sense of control over clearly demarcated turf, as eighteenth-century proponents had envisioned, the resulting political fragmentation has proven desperately dysfunctional in the competitive contemporary world of international capitalism. First, it produced a prosprawl development bias. Developers have the upper hand where the metropolis is expanding. Rural townships and tiny incorporated places typically lack skilled public managers or professional planning staffs, and their part-time elected officials are easy to seduce, bully, or bribe. This has produced a grotesquely sprawled region, both environmentally and economically unsustainable. It fueled a perverse housing disassembly line that has destroyed the city core. Second, this intense parochialism, enshrined in these tiny political entities, eroded a sense of common community, encouraged cut-throat interjurisdictional competition, abetted stereotyping, and reinforced inequalities along class and race lines.

Divided Suburbs

Greater Detroit's suburban landscape is not only politically fragmented: Detroit's suburbs look different on the ground. They manifest distinct physical, economic, and sociological characteristics, as if the force of political jurisdiction fragmentation had split geography into-component parts. The suburbs of Greater Detroit come in four basic varieties: "engulfed," "boxed," "wanna-bes," and "watered."

"Engulfed" suburbs were once distinct, stand-alone villages and towns that served as local commercial and retail centers in the rural hinterland. Long after their inception, the ever-expanding edge of Detroit's urban conurbation swept over them, ending their rural character but not their economic function. Today, they maintain commercially vibrant cores built on the small-town template established a century earlier. Ironically, their "old-fashioned" architecture and urban design, with storefronts adjacent to sidewalks and residential spaces above, has become *chic* in the vernacular of "New Urbanism" planning. Examples include Utica in Macomb County, Ferndale and Rochester Hills in Oakland County, and Northville in Wayne County. Two have created the region's hottest residential high-rise and upscale loft markets by aggressively building on legacies of compact, walkable, mixed-used cores: Birmingham and Royal Oak in the Woodward Avenue corridor in Oakland County.

"Boxed" suburbs are so named because two types of boxes of radically different sizes dominate them: huge manufacturing complexes and tiny bungalows built for the people who labored in them. The first generation of these industrial suburbs includes the "downriver" Wayne County towns of River Rouge, Ecorse, Wyandotte, and Trenton, all with substantial industrial operations along their Detroit River fronts by the late 1800s. The second generation was driven by the auto industry's early development. Besides Highland Park and Hamtramck, a passel of auto factories also appeared by the 1920s in Pontiac, twenty-five miles up Woodward from the river. But Dearborn is the quintessential example of this second generation of boxed suburbs. It was incorporated out of Springwells Township, southwest of Detroit, as an explicit company town under Ford Motor Company's rule. Not only did the 1,200-acre River Rouge megacomplex dominate Dearborn's visual and economic landscape, but Henry Ford also built his Fairlane residential estate, the Ford Airport, The Henry Ford Museum, and Greenfield Village there. At one point the company owned fully one-fourth of Dearborn's land, and over the years it donated 1,000 acres for municipal purposes. So dominant was this patriarchy that Dearborn residents still speak of going to work at *Ford's*, not Ford. After World War II, this corporate dominance was reinforced further by Ford Motor Company's development of Fairlane Center in the heart of Dearborn, still the nation's biggest contiguous, privately owned piece of urban real estate, containing numerous hotels, offices, and restaurants, a shopping mall, and a corporate campus with Ford's world headquarters. The third generation of boxed suburbs sprang up during and immediately after World War II. West of Detroit in Washtenaw County, Ypsilanti mushroomed adjacent to the Willow Run B-24 bomber plant opened by Ford in 1942. North of Detroit in Macomb County, Warren similarly boomed from the wartime construction of a major Chrysler tank factory. It was soon boosted further by the 1956 opening of the General Motors Tech Center, the first comprehensive corporate campus of offices, labs, and training facilities in the U.S., hailed by *Life Magazine* as the "Versailles of Industry."

The two "wanna-be" suburbs of Greater Detroit are Southfield and Troy, both in southern Oakland County. They both want to be downtowns. Like a downtown, each has a well-defined core of office and hotel skyscrapers surrounded by high-density residential clusters and significant retail capacity. Unlike a traditional Midwestern downtown, however, in these two "edge cities," high-rises rise up behind expansive lawns set next to wide, landscaped boulevards that connect to multiple expressway intersections nearby. Southfield's retail base is anchored by one of the nation's first enclosed malls, Northland. Troy's retail is anchored by the latest-generation citadel of consumerism, the Somerset Collection (note: it is not a mall, it is *a collection*). Southfield and Troy perhaps should not be labeled "wanna-bes" because they have won the battle with Detroit's historic Central Business District. Indeed, each now contains considerably more office space than downtown Detroit and immeasurably more retail activity.

Finally, the "watered" suburbs are predominantly middle- and upper-income residential districts close to recreational lakes and rivers. Many, like Orchard Lake, Waterford, and Walled Lake in northwestern Oakland County, have used their wealth of glacier-carved lakes as centerpieces of real estate development built on a "recreational/resort" lifestyle. The same strategy propelled other suburbs on nonindustrialized stretches of Detroit's wet eastern boundary, such as Grosse Ile in Wayne County (located in the lower Detroit River) and St. Clair Shores in Macomb County (located on, as one might guess, the shore of Lake St. Clair). But the prototypical watered suburb is the set of five villages known collectively as Grosse Pointe, nestled at the far northeastern tip of Wayne County between Detroit and Lake St. Clair. Wealthy Detroiters were already building luxurious "summer cottages" along this lovely, unpolluted shore during the late nineteenth century. By 1920, Grosse Pointe's uniquely exclusive character was so firmly entrenched that even Detroit's own directory grudgingly gave it credit for boosting property values in adjacent areas of the city, noting blandly (but with prescience, as it turns out) that the Pointes "are of the highest class with high restrictions." Grosse Pointe's lofty reputation was further elevated later that decade when Edsel Ford moved his family into an elaborate lakeside mansion there; the community has been home to various Ford family members ever since. Regardless of the fates of the Fords and their motor company, Grosse Pointe will always have its water. One of America's most idyllic urban drives is along its Lakeshore Drive: mansions on one side, the pristine expanse of Lake St. Clair stretching to the horizon on the other, the vista interrupted only by the occasional yacht club, two majestic miles of human-made and natural opulence (see Figure 10).

Just once more,
I'd like to take a ride in my father's car,
The way we did when we were small.

Figure 10. Grosse Pointe Yacht Club and Lake St. Clair, as seen from Lakeshore Drive.

"Lets go for a drive," he'd say,
never liking movies or TV.
We went "adventuring"
On the East side, the mysterious Orient
of small tool & die factories,
remote auto-maker's mansions,
the blue-gray expanse of St. Clair,
and the Pointes,
their perfect greenery, noiseless streets,
and quaint, inviolate shops
like replicas of shops—too nice
for customers.

                         "Motoring" by Mitzi Alvin

As one might surmise, distinctive populations also distinguish the split suburbs of Greater Detroit. From the earliest periods when substantial real estate development took place beyond the city limits, suburbs were designed for a particular sort of person, sorted by ethnicity, race and class.

At one extreme of this sorting, Grosse Pointe in 1920 was exclusively upper-class white: 40 percent native-born Americans and virtually all the rest of Anglo-Saxon immigrant extraction. Despite many household servants living on the premises of the mansions, Chinese, Poles, Hungarians, Greeks, and Italians were virtually absent; even Germans were scarce.

Another 1920 extreme was Brightmoor, a rural area of Wayne County, west of the city limits. It was developed by Burt E. Taylor as "affordable housing" (meaning unpaved roads and outhouses) for white, working-class households recruited from Appalachia to work at Ford's. Unsurprisingly, it was to prove a hotbed of Ku Klux Klan activity.

At yet a different extreme was a large tract north of Detroit at Eight Mile and Wyoming Roads. Developed in the mid-1920s for former southern black sharecroppers who could build their own homes here, the spacious plots of land permitted subsistence farming to offset the insecurity of their industrial jobs. Local legend has it that the Eight Mile-Wyoming enclave was targeted for black occupancy by a white developer who wanted revenge on an adjacent land developer. As postwar subdivisions eventually engulfed it, the Eight Mile-Wyoming community became a lightning rod for white stereotypes, particularly for its Eight Mile Road border where employers could drive up and hire a black day-laborer. Sneering white commuters dubbed it "the slave market" as they sped by.

The final example of racially divisive suburban development involved Henry Ford. For varied political and economic reasons, he found black workers useful in his Rouge factory, but not so useful that he wished either his white workers or himself to live with them within "his" city of Dearborn. Conveniently, an informal, black-only settlement abutting Dearborn on the west had been developing where these new Ford workers could live. Either by appalling insensitivity or stunning illiteracy, when this all-black area incorporated in 1926, it adopted the surname of the Scotsman who had operated an 1860s sawmill in the area: Inkster.

These perhaps extreme cases are not atypical of the fine-grained demographic splintering abetted by Detroit's earliest suburbs. Both Hamtramck and Highland Park in the 1920s had roughly 60 percent of their households employed in auto manufacturing, and both were virtually all white. But in Hamtramck, 60 percent of household heads were Polish immigrants, and 85 percent were blue-collar factory workers. In contrast, most of adjacent Highland Park was native-born, Anglo-Saxon stock, with a sizeable share of white-collar and managerial employees. Yet another pattern existed just outside southwest Detroit in Springwells Township, where 70 percent of the population was non-Anglo-Saxon, working-class households, with an unusually diverse mixture of immigrant Czechs, Yugoslavians, Hungarians, Russians, Rumanians, Armenians, and Austrians.

> It's a neighborhood
> you're glad you don't live in
> tired bars
> hang-around types
> with chronically thin wallets
> girl-women who parade their emptiness
> on a faded street
> peddling the only product they own
> and those who crowd the files
> of caseworkers . . .
>
> —"Four Decades Ago" by Irvine Barat

United Suburbs

The close of World War II saw a miraculous psychological transformation uniting both the older Detroit suburbs and the deluge of new ones about to spring up. Despite considerable ethnic variation, their residents began to see themselves as "white," not as a hyphenated American of a particular ethnic background. This symbolic suburban unification was based on owning a single-family, detached home.

From its earliest days, Detroit's residential landscape was dominated by single-family, detached homes. The comparative household affluence, combined with inexpensive land and building materials bequeathed by nature, made this situation possible. By the mid-nineteenth century, it was further encouraged by enclaves of skilled carpenters who set up home-building businesses within each ethnic community. Foreshadowing Habitat for Humanity's construction principles, households often worked alongside these skilled workers to build their own homes after their regular work shifts. By 1880, Detroit had the lowest number of persons per dwelling of any of the top-twenty U.S. cities. A turn-of-the-century housing survey of the twenty-five largest cities stated unequivocally that Detroit had "no block buildings or tenements." Indeed, in 1900, over 70 percent of native whites, blacks, Canadians,

British, Irish, and German households lived in single-family dwellings; Poles were the only major group where a majority did not live in single-family homes. By 1960, single-family units made up 75 percent of all dwellings in Greater Detroit, a remarkable figure for a major urban area. Single-family dwelling units reached a 76 percent regional share in 2009, compared to only 67 percent for the nation as a whole.

Home ownership walked hand-in-hand with this type of low-density housing construction. Already by 1900, over a third of Detroit's citizens owned their own homes; by 1960, this statistic had skyrocketed to 71 percent, a full nine percentage points above the national average. In 2009, the home-ownership rate in Greater Detroit remained at 71 percent, compared to only 66 percent on average for the U.S. Of course, home ownership by 1960 was especially common in Detroit's suburbs and virtually exclusively reserved for white households. This was not accidental but resulted from concerted efforts by local, state, and federal levels of government and private institutions. So suburban Detroiters could sublimate their ethnic differences under one crucial commonality: the need to maintain property values and defend turf on economic grounds. As *white* property owners, they were entitled to certain "inalienable rights," such as freedom to avoid undesirable neighbors whose mere presence would devalue their homes and erode their quality of life. "Whiteness," thus, came to be defined in oppositional terms: *not them*. It was as if the postwar Detroit suburbs used the solvent of home ownership to create a "selective melting pot," dissolving European ethnics into a gruel called *white*, while leaving other groups out of the pot altogether—primarily blacks but to some extent Latinos, Asians, and Middle Easterners—to remain distinct in all their supposed inferiority. This white homeowner-voter mentality would prove a political boon to the likes of George Wallace, Richard Nixon, and Ronald Reagan, as Richard Sauerzopf has documented. The phrase "Give a man a porch, and he becomes conservative" was practically invented in the Detroit suburbs.

The Topography of Inequality

Inevitably dispersed manufacturing, suburban jurisdictional fragmentation, and the selective geography of home ownership would spawn staggering socioeconomic disparities across the landscape of Greater Detroit. Indeed, the jagged topography of inequality is one of the region's defining characteristics. Socioeconomic contours here change not along gentle gradients: they drop off steep precipices. This spatial inequality can be seen at both the neighborhood and regional scales.

At the smaller scale, neighborhood-by-neighborhood variations in household economic status are dramatic. Paul Jargowsky found that Greater Detroit had the greatest economic segregation among the country's largest metropolitan areas. And this dubious distinction held for whites, blacks, and Latinos alike. Regardless of race or ethnicity, Detroiters cluster with their own class. Of course, they also cluster by race and ethnicity. Statistics computed by John Iceland and Daniel Weinberg show that Greater Detroit has the highest levels of black-white neighborhood segregation in the nation by most measures, though segregation of whites from the region's small Latino and Asian populations is comparatively less virulent.

At the larger scale, city-suburb differentials have grown stark in both economic and racial dimensions. In 1950, the median family income in the City of Detroit was $28,140 measured in inflation-adjusted 2002 dollars, while the figure for the suburbs was $28,890—only 3 percent higher. By 2000, these figures had changed to $36,810 and $71,350; the suburbs' median income is now 94 percent higher. In 1950, the city had an 18 percent poverty rate, the suburbs 19 percent. By the end of the prosperous 1960s, the city's poverty rate had dropped to 15 percent but had fallen even more in the suburbs, to only 5 percent. Both suffered in the 1970s and 1980s, but even after the late 1990s boomlet reduced the city's poverty rate to 26 percent, the suburban rate was in the 7 percent range. Now, in the grip of a recession that has seen unemployment rise for ten straight years, the city's poverty rate has surpassed 36 percent (the nation's highest), while the suburbs' poverty rate has barely pushed into double digits at 11 percent in 2009.

As for racial patterns, in 1950, 58 percent of all whites in the region still lived in Detroit, as did 84 percent of the region's blacks. By 2009, 68 percent of the region's black population continued to live within the city, but only 4 percent of the region's white population lived there.

To see the stark gaps across the lines separating spaces in Greater Detroit, we return to our familiar byways, Woodward Avenue and Eight Mile Road. Imagine that, if we now were to drive along Woodward, we could observe for each block-group a sign showing its median household income. If we graph these figures, we paint the portrait of geographic inequality portrayed in Figure 11. The horizontal line represents Woodward Avenue. The left-hand side of the line depicts its south end ending at the Detroit River in the Central

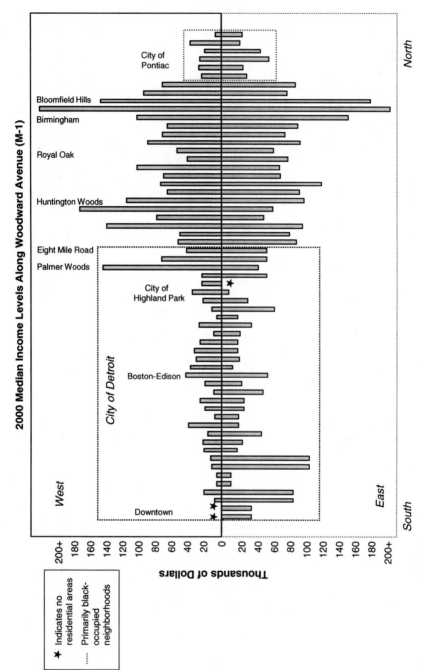

Figure 11. Median family income for block groups abutting Woodward Avenue, 2000.

Business District. The right-hand side shows its farthest northern reach as it ends in Pontiac. Eight Mile Road separates the City from suburban Oakland County. Above this horizontal line representing Woodward are shown each of the block-group neighborhoods adjacent to Woodward on the west; below the line are shown neighborhoods adjacent to it on the east. The length of the line for each neighborhood represents its median income in thousands of dollars. Rectangles formed by dashed lines designate neighborhoods that are predominantly occupied by black households.

What is immediately apparent is how abrupt the changes in median income are from one neighborhood to the next, whether you stay on one side of Woodward or cross it. The Palmer Woods neighborhood in Detroit and the posh suburbs of Huntington Woods, Birmingham, and Bloomfield Hills clearly stick out, graphically and literally, in terms of their relative affluence compared to their immediate environs. Closer examination reveals that the predominantly black-occupied neighborhoods of Detroit and Pontiac have considerably lower median incomes than the predominantly white-occupied ones north of Eight Mile Road in the suburbs. However, vast economic disparities exist among black- or white-occupied neighborhoods. In Greater Detroit, the topography of inequality has distinctive racial and economic precipices, as the jagged contours along Woodward Avenue show.

Planning Palsied

How did local government planning shape Greater Detroit? With few exceptions, such planning concentrated on building and improving transportation infrastructure and neglected other aspects. Efforts to create a more beautiful, healthier, inspiring, sustainable place were palsied.

Obvious remnants of the first public effort to impose form on Detroit can be seen in the parallel streets running perpendicular to the river just east of the downtown. Their names are Beaubien, St. Aubin, St. Antoine, Chene, and Dequindre, all reflecting the first French settlers granted titles to farm this land in 1707. To provide each farm with vital river access, Cadillac instituted a system of "ribbon farms," plots as narrow as 200 feet but extending up to three miles inland. Eponymous streets coincided with the boundaries of these ribbon farms.

We also can see the legacy of the square-mile units that served as building blocks of Jefferson's 1785 Land Ordinance for organizing the Northwest

Territory. The east-west base line from which this surveying scheme is measured across Michigan is the western extension of Eight Mile Road in Detroit. Many of the roads in southern Oakland County and the northern sectors of the City of Detroit are products of this square-mile system, congruent with one or more of its borders. Running north-south are Livernois, Wyoming, Schaefer, Greenfield, and Southfield; running east-west are Fullerton, Fenkell, McNichols, Seven Mile, Eight Mile.

Probably the best-known vestige of Detroit's early city planning came about following the July 11, 1805, fire, which destroyed almost the entire city. Judge Augustus Woodward, with fresh degree in hand from Columbia University, arrived later that year and convinced new Michigan Territory Governor William Hull to postpone rebuilding the ruined city until Woodward could concoct a plan. What chutzpah! Of course, Woodward's plan was worth the wait. Its grand and ambitious design took full advantage of this unique opportunity to envision a definitive Detroit. Sadly, like so many long-term city visions forwarded subsequently, the Woodward Plan was abandoned in December 1817, after only a few dozen square blocks were realized. Perhaps Woodward's vision was too far ahead of its time. After all, the major public policy issue in Detroit circa 1817 was whether domestic hogs should be allowed to roam freely. On the plus side of this fierce porcine debate was a free garbage removal system; on the minus side, the disruption of carriage traffic, inconveniently sited swine effluent, and rooting up of unwilling host families' gardens. The issue was resolved by requiring all hogs to have their noses ringed before being turned loose on the citizenry. Ever pragmatic, early Detroiters also cast an implicit referendum vote on Woodward's plan by using the nascent Grand Circus Park as a dumping ground for dead cats. Nevertheless, the Woodward Plan still defines the core of downtown Detroit, giving it a quirky "necklace" design that is unique among American cities, save the District of Columbia.

Over the next two centuries, Detroit would execute precious few grand civic plans for urban transformation. Unlike Chicago, Cleveland, or Philadelphia, Detroit never undertook a Daniel Burnham-inspired City Beautiful plan. Its biggest park, Belle Isle, was more a fortuitous topographical accident than conscious city planning. It's not that leadership was lacking. Mayor Hazen Pingree argued in his 1891 annual message to City Council that Detroit should develop a major park downtown:

> A large park, in the center of the city, would boom Detroit more than
> the establishment of half a dozen Union Depots or of 18 or 20 facto-

ries. The Grand Circus Park was wisely designed . . . after the fire as a hub of a park system, consisting of broad avenues radiating from it as a common center. The only mistake which they made was in not making this Central Park large enough for the subsequent growth of the city. . . . A glance at the map of the city will show that the spaces, southeasterly and southwesterly from the Grand Circus . . . could be obtained by the city either by purchase or condemnation for a reasonable amount. The space . . . if made into a common or central park would be of untold advantage to every other part of the city . . . such a magnificent space of 82 acres . . . would be a lasting monument to the wisdom of the city fathers who procured it, and would justly entitle all who aided in the cause to the gratitude, not only of this generation, but of generations yet unborn.

Mayor Pingree was correct (though unintentionally) that this park would be "a lasting monument to the wisdom of the city fathers"; they never built it. The mayor did not relent, arguing with laser-like prescience in 1897 for filling in the riverfront downtown to create a convention center based on its economic development benefits:

Already Detroit has become a favorite resort for visitors from the Southern States during the summer months, and an attractive city for the conventions of the various State and inter-State organizations for the promotion of private enterprises. But . . . there is a lack of facilities for the accommodation of conventions of the first class, such, for example, as the national conventions of the political parties.

Again, the plan was unrealized but the vision persisted. Famed Finnish architect Eliel Saarinen, a visiting professor at the University of Michigan at the time, drew up a dramatic plan for Detroit's riverfront civic center in 1924. Once again, despite the wealth of the city during this period, a shortage of political capital doomed it. Not until Cobo Hall Convention Center and Arena opened in 1960 and Joe Louis Arena and Hart Plaza were finished in 1979 was Mayor Pingree's dream finally realized. The 1980 Republican National Convention was the first for the city. It was also the last.

By contrast, planning involving transportation infrastructure seemed to gallop unscathed through the minefield of Detroit politics. The first railroads to come to town were granted easy waterfront access from both directions, converging at the foot of Woodward Avenue. This "inner belt" of rail lines was soon overcrowded, so in the early twentieth century, the city built the "outer belt" Detroit Terminal Railway, from east of Waterworks Park to cross Woodward about six miles from the river before circling west to join Michigan Central Rail lines.

But railroad construction paled compared to highway construction in shaping twentieth-century Detroit. Many limited access highways were begun during World War II to meet defense production needs. Their construction accelerated after the war, brutality slicing through many neighborhoods. Unlike many cities, Detroit's freeways encircled the downtown and penetrated into it. Neighborhood opposition never stopped a major highway plan in Greater Detroit. This *was* the Motor City, after all.

Thus, Detroit's palsied planning efforts abetted sprawl. Its failure to create a high-quality residential and civic environment reduced the core's attractiveness. At the same time, first railroad and then highway construction encouraged manufacturing and household dispersal. To be fair, a few visionaries tried to resist sprawl. In 1894, Mayor Pingree vetoed the Board of Education's plan to build a massive high school at the city's fringe in a sparsely inhabited area, then about 2.5 miles from the river. His veto letter stated, "The majority of the citizens . . . are opposed to a location so far north. The selection of a site within the mile circle [centered at Woodward and Jefferson Avenues] would be more satisfactory." The Board eventually prevailed, building its new school on the "so far north" block bounded by Warren, Hancock, Cass, and Second Avenues. This building is now known as Old Main, the heart of the Wayne State University campus, in the region's core.

The Sprawl Recipe

Greater Detroit created a distinctive recipe for sprawl. Start with a featureless, temperate, well-watered plain. Fold generous amounts of government investments in railroads and express highways into a base of land-extensive manufacturing concerns. Add equal measures of relative worker affluence and cheap building materials to produce a crust of owner-occupied, single-family homes. Sprinkle over all an allspice of fine-grained, local political jurisdictions produced by a "home rule" state constitution, yielding a distinctly pro-development, laissez faire flavor.

This recipe has been passed on and refined for generations. Consider the following assessment made a century ago:

> Congestion [in Detroit] has been retarded, notwithstanding the rapid growth of the population, in a number of ways. The land is without hills or valleys to raise natural obstacles to normal expansion.... Other obstacles to congestion were the diffusion of population in special industrial districts along the river front, with its twelve miles of factories, the Parkway (Grand Boulevard) and its factory districts, and their routes by which the railroads have entered and completely encircled the city.... To these hindrances to congestion must be added the possibility of almost unlimited expansion, with easy access to places of labor. It is significant that practically all of the automobile factories, which have been built in the last five years, are located in the outskirts, where before there were great tracts of vacant land.
> —Myron Adams, "Detroit—A City Awake," 1911

Today Greater Detroit continues to cook up sprawl, gorging itself on land as if it were an all-you-can-eat buffet. According to the Census Bureau's 2009 American Community Survey, the Detroit urbanized area was home to the eleventh-largest population in the U.S. but ranked only eighty-fifth in people per square mile of land area. It has roughly a third of the population density of the San Francisco, the most dense U.S. urbanized area. But this low density belies its idiosyncratic hollowed-out center. Among the largest metropolitan areas, Greater Detroit ranks first in dispersion of jobs away from the historical core and clustering them in distant subcenters.

The Accidental Metropolis

The original French settlement was named Detroit for the one natural attribute that held an important military advantage: a strait that could potentially become a strategic choke point against the hated English. The area's other amenable natural attributes allowed the settlement to flourish and encouraged hinterland trapping, agriculture, and forestry exploitation. This, in turn, gave Detroit some mercantile raison d'être. Still, there was nothing special about this location that made an *industrial* metropolis inevitable. Many other Great Lakes locations had navigable water and even better access to industrial raw materials like coal, iron ore, and limestone and to consumer markets where industrial products would be delivered. No, there was nothing inevitable about industrial Detroit.

Detroit at the dawn of the twentieth century had the happy accident of having attracted an unlikely agglomeration of innovative, entrepreneurial engineers interested in developing a new product, one that ultimately would prove as ubiquitous as it was revolutionizing in American life. Given that economic spark, the city grew dramatically, but its physical form was also largely accidental. Weak and fragmented local governments neither guided nor constrained Greater Detroit's morphology, while concerted efforts by planners to build a city that was beautiful, humane, or rational simply withered. Instead, local government was the great enabler, bowing to developers and building transportation infrastructure willy-nilly. Fundamental land use decisions were idiosyncratically driven by major corporate interests—manufacturing industries and residential developers alike. Because the region's topography was so permissive, this atomistic development regime consumed huge amounts of land. For their part, households sorted themselves across this sprawling space by ethnic, racial, and economic hierarchies, abetted by the narrowly self-serving land use policies promulgated by a crazy quilt of local political jurisdictions. The result was a galaxy of distinctive social worlds that began by orbiting around the city but increasingly spun off on their own centripetal trajectories. The human price and unsustainability of this sprawl recipe will become apparent.

When you get right down to it, Detroit was an accidental metropolis. There was no compelling reason why this benign spot in southeast Michigan should have become a city, let alone the Motor City, the dominant industrial metropolis of its day. And now that its future as the Motor City seems in jeopardy, one must confront the next question: why should *any* metropolis exist here in the future? Will this piece of geography witness another happy accident that provides a new rationale for urbanization, or is that asking for lightning to strike twice in the same place?

Chapter 3

From Fort to Ford to . . . ?

Drive your Chevrolet in the USA,
America's the Greatest Land of All
— General Motors advertising jingle sung by Dinah Shore
in the 1950s

Though popular consciousness permanently welds the auto industry onto the economic frame of Detroit, for two-thirds of its history the city did something else for a living. The region has had three distinct economic bases. From its inception until the close of the War of 1812, Detroit served an important geopolitical function. While supporting a substantial military garrison proved a vital economic engine, it was clear from the outset that Detroit was more about making money than protecting royal empires or, later, a fragile new nation's frontier. By single-mindedly pursuing profit, Detroit evolved from a trading post and exploiter of natural resources into a diversified manufacturing economy, supplying a dizzying array of products for businesses and households, and, finally, into the epitome of oligopolistic auto production. The potent legacies of this last evolutionary stage portend poorly for how Greater Detroit's future economy may evolve.

Fortifying Excess

Although the forts that the French and the Americans built over the years in this place called Detroit served a larger military purpose, they also offered a modicum of security that allowed markets to develop. These markets were worth protecting because, from the very beginning, it was obvious to European settlers that money—lots of money—was to be made here. Very early on, Detroiters began worshiping a mercantile principle that would guide them for three centuries: *No Success without Excess.*

The city's founder unwittingly established this principle; he epitomized greedy excess before his canoes and buckskin had a chance to dry out. Within four years of the outpost's establishment, the local Jesuit priests were grumbling and writing accusatory letters about Cadillac's misdeeds in managing the lucrative fur industry. We can only surmise that this "management" involved a healthy "consulting fee" for the Monsieur and an inadequate cut for the local parish. Though Cadillac would be arrested, tried, and acquitted of these crimes in 1705, he hardly seemed chastened. On the contrary, Cadillac set a standard for a Detroit demi-deity leadership hubris that continued unbroken until the reign of Mayor Kwame Kilpatrick three centuries later. Cadillac next honed a new act of excess: neofeudal landlord. In exchange for the land title to new farms in and around Fort Pontchartrain, Cadillac demanded annually a cash rent, a share of the produce, and a designated amount of labor to be performed on Cadillac's own farm. Apparently these terms were so onerous and generated so much uproar that Count Pontchartrain, Cadillac's French patron, complained to him in writing in 1709 that he showed "too much greed." Cadillac ignored this warning, sequestering himself in his lavish home safe inside the fort's walls. But by 1710, less than a decade since founding Detroit, Cadillac was disgraced and gone, forced to leave his fiefdom by the French government and posted to ... of all god-forsaken backwaters ... Louisiana.

Never fear. Cadillac may have left, but his administrative descendants' excesses never flagged, regardless of the flag they flew. Through the early eighteenth century, the British pressured French territories across North America, encroaching on their profitable trade with the natives. By 1752 the Governor of New France, Marquis Duquesne, had had enough: French greed must be protected against British greed! Duquesne organized a war party in Detroit with 250 French and Ottawa soldiers, who defeated the combined British-Miami forces at Piqua, Ohio, in June. This demonstration of French resolve apparently was impressive, as several native groups returned to trading with Detroit. Over the next few years, Detroit prospered further, growing to 2,000 inhabitants, as it became a major staging point in the French and Indian War. But its very success made it a key British target. Fort

Pontchartrain surrendered to the British on November 29, 1760, ending forever French rule (and, sadly, French pronunciation) in Detroit. Reportedly the French settlers regarded this administrative change with indifference; being pragmatists, they expected the mercantile status quo to be preserved. Their *savoir faire* proved justified because exploitation of the natives transcended the particulars of European nationality. Indeed, British trading methods were even more excessively greedy than those of the French. Terms of trade became so outrageous that the Ottawa, led by Chief Pontiac, laid siege to Fort Pontchartrain on May 10, 1763. During this 153-day siege, Pontiac's exploits emboldened native groups throughout the region, who then captured many British garrisons. Nevertheless, Detroit never fell to Pontiac, evincing a stubbornness (and perhaps devotion to excess) that characterize it to this day.

Of course, Detroit eventually did fall under American control in 1796, was retaken by the British in 1812, and then taken back once and for all in 1813. This political seesaw could not obscure the reality that the economic base that sustained Detroit for its first century was about to change abruptly. By the early decades of the eighteenth century, Michigan's native people were pushed off their lands through a series of swindles called "treaties." Moreover, due to excessive hunting, the once-lucrative fur trade began to decline by 1821. This meant that no longer was much to be gained by trading primitive goods with natives. The second great economic base of Greater Detroit was at hand.

From Market to Manufactory

Fortunately, the future had recently puffed up and docked at the foot of Woodward Avenue at the end of its inaugural voyage from Buffalo. The *Walk-in-the-Water*, named after a Wyandotte chief, made the first steam passage across the Great Lakes on August 27, 1818. Then the Erie Canal opened in 1825. Detroiters' entrepreneurial longing became logging because their state's wood could now be economically shipped long distances east and west. As fast as the forests receded before the axe, the lumber barons' mansions arose along Woodward Avenue (the David Whitney mansion is the most prominent remnant). By 1853, a Hart map of Detroit shows no fewer than a dozen saw mills operating on the waterfront.

If steam-powered watercraft were not enough to save Detroit's economy, yet another new steam-powered device soon appeared: the railroad. By mid-century, the railroad had connected Detroit with Ohio and Pennsylvania's coal and with the Upper Peninsula of Michigan's iron ore and copper, efficiently lacing the state with log-transporting capacity. The railroads also linked Detroit with markets to the East and to Chicago.

This joint emergence of steamboat and railroad shipping options arrived in the nick of time, boosting Detroit's prospects just as the fur-trading economy was dying. New settlers poured into Michigan through Detroit, buying locally all sorts of frontier-styled household goods and services. But early Detroiters were no longer content to exploit the land and forest bounty and serve as merchant outfitters. Transportation innovations were about to spawn something entirely new: an industrial economy.

Detroiters must have figured, "If we depend so much on steamboats and railroad cars, why don't we build them *here*?" So they did. The year 1827 saw the first steamboat built in Detroit: the *Argo*. This wooden-propeller boat was launched from the forerunner of the Detroit Dry Dock Company. A shipbuilding hub grew on the waterfront just east of downtown, soon surrounded by component manufacturers supplying boilers, steam engines, and iron fittings. Railroad car production—primarily but not exclusively for freight—boomed a bit later. The Detroit Car and Manufacturing Company, established in 1853, produced the first rolling stock west of Albany. The burgeoning local demand for malleable metals, combined with the new-found ease in transporting raw materials, led to the Eureka Iron and Steel Works being formed downriver in Ecorse Township in 1854, soon followed by the Wyandotte Rolling Mills nearby. These two firms became the area's largest industrial employers of the 1850s. The Detroit and Lake Superior Copper Company built the world's largest smelter during this same period.

Civil War procurements were a boon to Detroit's nascent industrial base, foreshadowing how the city would be molded by the demands of many hot and cold wars to come. Significant new firms arose: the Detroit Bridge and Iron Company, the Michigan (rail) Car Company, the Detroit Stove Works. Wood products, ships and their steam engines, rail cars, metal products of various kinds, paints and pharmaceutical chemicals—all poured out of the city's burgeoning factories to meet the Union's needs.

Greater Detroit's early industrial base rapidly diversified after the Civil War, like a gangling adolescent trying on various identities. By 1880, according to Census Bureau data tabulated by Olivier Zunz, clothing, hats, and shoes were being made by 121 establishments, food processing by 113, lumber and furniture by 104, transportation equipment (carriages, ships, rail cars) by 82, tobacco (mainly chewing and cigars) by 63, foundries and machines by 24, and iron and steel by seven. The number of establishments roughly corresponded to employment levels in these sectors: clothing, lumber, tobacco, and food sectors clearly dominated, employing 6,210 workers, while transportation equipment, foundries and machinery, and iron and steel sectors employed 3,271. This sprouting industrial economy was noteworthy not only for its variety but also for the small scale of its enterprises: of the 919 manufacturers listed in the 1880 Detroit census, only 4.5 percent had 100 employees or more. The three biggest operations were the Pullman Palace Car Company (736 employees building passenger rail cars), Detroit Stove Works (625 employees), and D.M. Ferry Company (596 employees making seeds).

Detroit's new economy came none too soon because excess once again destroyed a pillar of the old economy as logging became unsustainable. Now "self-made men" needed to find paths to wealth other than through the forest. Having been an apprentice in Detroit's first tobacco factory, formed in 1840 by George Miller, Daniel Scotten bought his own tobacco store in 1856. His brands proved so popular that, by 1875, he was cranking out over two million pounds of tobacco annually from his own (and the city's largest) tobacco factory, a three-story behemoth on West Fort Street. A druggist named Frederick Stearns also began producing small batches of pharmaceuticals in 1856 in the back of his shop, with the help of one assistant. A quarter century later, Stearns employed over 400 in one of the nation's largest pharmaceutical factories. In 1866, future mayor Hazen Pingree left his job at Baldwin's boot and shoe factory to set up his own footwear workshop. Within twenty years, he had developed a semiautomated shoe-making process, employing hundreds in another giant factory.

Over the next score of years, the adolescent industrial economy matured and muscled up. Detroit's industrial landscape of 1900 looked considerably different, with foundries and machine shops rising to become the largest sector, with 6,544 workers. Pharmaceuticals, too insignificant to be listed as a separate category in 1880, now employed 2,155. Though George Pullman pulled out of Detroit in 1897 to consolidate operations at his ill-fated social experiment in his eponymous Illinois company town, the void was amply filled by American Car and Foundry, the region's largest employer, with its 2,200 workers. The brawn of the 1890 Detroit economy is obvious from its "tale of the tape": largest producer of stoves in the U.S.; second-largest producer of pharmaceuticals (Parke-Davis being Detroit's largest); second-largest producer of tobacco products (mainly 5-cent cigars); and producer of three-fourths of all ships on the Great Lakes. This first was memorialized in typical, excessive fashion by the Michigan Stove Company, by making the "biggest Stove in the world," large enough to sleep an entire family, as a gimmick to display at Chicago's 1893 Columbian Exposition. Then for half a century it sat outside the firm's Detroit stove works, on Jefferson Avenue at the entrance ramp to the MacArthur Bridge to Belle Isle. It now forlornly rests rusting in the shuttered State Fairgrounds, near the corner of Woodward Avenue and State Fair Drive, distracting curious but uncomprehending motorists.

*   *   *

George Jacob aimed to be the next great Detroit "self-made man," following in the path of Scotten, Stearns, and Pingree. That they were Anglos and he was a first-generation German immigrant did not dampen his aspirations. He had rejected the agrarian roots of his German-born father, Johann Georg, but not his ethic of advancement through skill and its diligent application. Now, just before the dawn of a new century, despite belching Detroit smokestacks that often obscured the sunrise, George Jacob clearly foresaw his means to success, illuminated by the eerie glow of the smelting hearth.

It was 1898. A new automotive industrial epoch was about to start, but George Jacob did not realize it. He had finished scraping up enough investors within the large, prosperous German-American community on Detroit's east side to construct a small iron foundry and machine shop. For his part, father Johann Georg had donated a section of the family farm on Canfield and Moran, two blocks west of Mt. Elliott Avenue, for the factory site. George Jacob was in the mood to celebrate. He had just turned forty, and his entrepreneurial dreams had come true. What better way than to take Amelia, his wife of twenty-four years, to some newfangled fad called a "moving picture show." So they hopped a streetcar downtown to the Wonderland Theater and saw the first movie ever shown in Detroit, *Empire State Express*. It proved a sensational evening. The film's climactic scene showed a locomotive coming straight at the audience, making shrieking women faint and startled men jump into the aisles. Little could the audience suspect the all-too-real train wreck their city would become within a century.

Acme Wire and Iron Works opened for business in 1899. Always the pragmatist, George Jacob hedged his bets. The artisan part of the business would make decorative wrought iron objects for the home, such as fireplace tools, settees, railings, candlesticks, and cigar ashtrays. The prosaic part would weave wires together to make tool cages, parts baskets, machine guards, and window protectors for factories. Acme was an immediate success in both production lines. George Jacob was probably too busy to note the low-key opening that same year of the Olds Motor Works on Jefferson Avenue, Detroit's first automobile factory.

Soon, however, George Jacob would confront head-on the leading edge of Detroit's looming third economic epoch. He may have paid little attention to the new auto industry in town, but it paid attention to him and his new wealth. In 1903 he was approached by a young engineer seeking to raise capital for a factory to build a basic, affordable motor car. George Jacob thought the notion harebrained. Besides, the engineer's two previous auto companies had failed in short order. But the final straw was probably that the guy was an Anglo. So, George Jacob declined the opportunity to get in on the ground floor of the Ford Motor Company. His four sons, George, Arthur, Emil, and Fred, would one day inherit the tiny Acme Wire and Iron Works but not a fortune.

Henry Ford had offered George Jacob an alternative—a riskier but potentially much more lucrative—path to success, but he was too conservative and myopic to see it. At least George Jacob was ahead of his time in one respect: his conservative myopia would come to be the industrial and cultural norm—and debilitating disease—for Greater Detroit.

Enter the Motor City

Like any industry that springs up to produce a brand new invention, the early years of auto and auto parts production were littered with hundreds of small-scale corporate startups and almost as many failures. According to Steven Klepper, each year 11.5 new firms entered the U.S. auto industry, on average, from its inception in 1895 to 1900, rising to 36.8 from 1900 to 1905 and peaking at an astounding 82 new firms in 1907 alone. Though new entrants annually averaged 15 from 1911 to 1922, tellingly there were only 15 more entrants thereafter as the national auto industry matured and consolidated. The total number of automobile and associated firms in the U.S. peaked in 1909 at 272; by 1941 it had plunged to only nine.

Detroit followed the same pattern of growth then shakeout. Starting with its first firm in 1899, by 1914 no fewer than 43 different auto companies were manufacturing cars in Greater Detroit. These included such unfamiliar names as Aerocar, Detroit Electric, Dort, Durant, King, Huber, Herreshoff, Leland, Maxwell, Peerless, Sommer, and Welch. But by the late 1920s, there were only eight left, with the outlines of the Big Three—General Motors, Ford, and Chrysler—firmly in place. Within only thirty years, the base of Detroit's economy had evolved into a textbook case of oligopoly: a clutch of large-scale producers practicing restrained competition and erecting high practical barriers for new firms to enter the industry. Long gone were the small shops of craftsmen who could built a motor car essentially by hand, financed by a modest amount of capital. Henry Ford could get his start in 1903 with only $28,000. Fifteen years later, the minimum production scale had ballooned so rapidly that the new Lincoln Company required over $6 million in startup costs for plant and equipment.

Coincident with consolidating this industry into a few large firms was an even more rapid spatial consolidation. The U.S. auto industry was widely scattered at first. Eight states had significant numbers of new auto companies spring up early on. Ironically, Michigan was a latecomer to this party; none of the first 69 auto firms began here. But what a grand entrance Michigan, and Detroit in particular, would eventually make, with 135 auto startups during the twentieth century! The first was Ransom Olds in 1899, who built a three-story auto plant on Jefferson Avenue near where the Belle Isle Bridge would eventually be. Other future industry giants soon followed, with 1903 as a remarkable watershed. James Packard opened his Albert Kahn-designed factory on Grand Boulevard, after moving his successful luxury car manufacturing operation from Ohio. David Buick switched from making bathtubs to producing gasoline internal combustion engines on Jefferson Avenue, near the current location of the Renaissance Center. Cadillac rolled out its first vehicles. Ford Motor Company was incorporated and started building a pre-Model T model on Mack Avenue; its success necessitated a move to a larger, 1.4-acre factory on Piquette Avenue a year later and then to the much-larger Highland Park facility by the end of the decade. By 1905 approximately 15 percent of all U.S. auto producers were located in Greater Detroit, and by 1941 this had grown to over half. Market shares show even more Detroit geographic dominance. Already in 1910, seven of the top ten national auto producers were Detroit-based, generating roughly two-thirds of all sales. Detroit's market share would grow to a whopping 85 percent by 1925, firmly validating being called "Motor City."

The Accidental Metropolis, Again

Just as the location of Detroit was an accident of the French-British contest for North America in the early eighteenth century, so the early twentieth-century Detroit auto industry concentration was fundamentally accidental. Two categories of chance elevated Detroit to the status of Motor City: innovation and personality.

Certainly around 1900 Detroit possessed various prerequisites to produce automobiles. First, there was a large cadre of skilled metal workers, the legacy of the railroad car, ship, and stove industries. They knew how to cast, forge, refine, grind, cut, and bend metal into usable objects. Second, the Great Lakes and the railroads allowed cheap transportation of raw materials and final products. Third, there was venture capital, accumulated by the earlier exploitation of Upper Peninsula copper deposits and logging the forests that once covered the state, which bankrolled the Olds, Buick, and Cadillac car companies. Though important, none of these preconditions were unique to Detroit; indeed, they were quite common across the Midwest. Cleveland, Pittsburgh, and Chicago also had all these assets, as well as their own clutch of turn of the century auto-manufacturing firms. What these auto-production pretenders lacked was the dual good fortune of seminal innovations and irrepressible entrepreneurial personalities.

Detroit innovations came in many varieties: product, process, management, and marketing. Henry Ford introduced the prototype "economy car," the Model T, in 1908. The six Fisher brothers invented the fully enclosed auto body in 1908, the same year they incorporated their Fisher Body Company. John and Horace Dodge introduced all-steel car body construction and a twelve-volt electrical system in 1914. David Packard was a noted technological leader in the automotive field, developing novel products like accelerator pedals, H-gate gear-shift patterns, and steering wheels.

But the most famous and important production innovation occurred when Henry Ford adapted the moving assembly line to auto production, installing it in his Highland Park plant from 1910 to 1913, following the principles of the management guru *de jour* Frederick Taylor. According to

Steve Babson, this reduced average production times for engines by more than half and for chassis by 88 percent. Prior to this innovation, as Ford himself described it in 1922, "We simply started to put a car together on the spot on the floor and workmen brought to it parts as were needed, in exactly the same way that one builds a house." In contrast, Ford's process switched the stationary and mobile elements: the particular auto component being manufactured (engine, body, chassis) moved slowly along a track amid a set of fixed worker stations, each assigned one small, repetitive task, for which requisite parts were within easy reach. This not only saved worker time but also divided the production process into simpler tasks, permitting less-skilled labor to be employed. Moreover, it reduced the flexibility that each worker had in completing an assigned job, giving more power to management. The second significant local auto industry process invention was vertical integration, again pioneered by Ford. The Ford Rouge facility began with raw materials, produced intermediate goods from them like paint, steel, and glass, formed them into auto components, and then assembled them into the final product, all on the same site. This achieved significant transportation savings and avoided markups charged by independent suppliers, creating huge value-added for one corporation. The benefits of these process innovations to consumers can be seen in the Ford Model T prices. When introduced in 1908, the car sold for $850; by 1923, its price had fallen to $265.

Early auto industry management innovations were numerous, but General Motors was a clear leader. Pioneered by GM Vice President Donaldson Brown in the 1920s, the "standard volume" accounting system specified the average costs of producing a car, standardized across all the divisions, allowing the central office a codified way to assess rates of return for each model in each division. Significantly, this standard volume scheme spread the fixed costs of research, development, plant, and machinery over the ups and downs of a business cycle; it allowed managers to focus on achieving their long-term goals of 20 percent annual rates of return and on maintaining a 40 percent market share for the corporation.

Henry Ford's process innovation—installing the first moving auto assembly line—required a management innovation because work on the line proved so distasteful that costly labor unrest and turnover skyrocketed. In 1913 Ford needed to hire 52,000 workers to maintain an average workforce of 14,000. Although new to Detroit in 1912, the Industrial Workers of the World (IWW) union quickly capitalized on worker discontent and organized its first strike at another manufacturing firm in 1913. Ford was deemed by some a madman when he unilaterally raised his workers' pay from $2.25 to $5 a day in 1914; then it became clear that the "madman's" labor absenteeism and turnover rates plummeted, and the IWW never gained a foothold in a Ford plant. By 1920, most other auto manufacturers had installed moving assembly lines, along with significantly higher wages, implicit testimony to the "madness" of Ford's managerial inventiveness.

Marketing was yet another area of innovation. Ransom Olds was the first automaker to advertise in a women's publication, a 1903 *Ladies Home Journal*. In a wonderfully prescient (if sexist) anticipation of the "car as shopping machine" and the mall culture, it portrayed a stylishly dressed woman, proudly sporting her new hat, entering her Oldsmobile outside a millinery shop. The accompanying ad text read, "The ideal vehicle for shopping and calling—equally suitable for a pleasant afternoon drive or an extended tour . . . operated entirely from the seat by a single lever—always under instant control. . . . The mechanism is simple—no complicated machinery." Under the leadership of Alfred Sloan, who became president in 1923, General Motors won the marketing Triple Crown. The first was annual model changes and "planned obsolescence." The second was a new hierarchy within the GM stable of autos: the young family of modest means would buy a Chevrolet and steadily move up the ranks as "purse and preference dictated"—from Pontiac to Oldsmobile to Buick to Cadillac—all within the GM "ladder of success." Last but not least, if you could not afford to buy a car outright, the manufacturer itself would lend you the money to do so. The General Motors Acceptance Corporation (GMAC), founded in 1919, pioneered this radical marketing idea.

But beyond the multiple dimensions of innovation, there was something else special about the cluster of idiosyncratic engineers in Detroit from 1900 to 1920. Henry Ford thought it was "an idea in the air." I would call it "entrepreneurial spirit," a desire to try to make good on your new automotive idea under the umbrella of a firm that you control. Ford's desire to call all the shots himself is well documented; at the founding of the Ford Motor Company in 1903 he owned 25 percent of the shares; by 1919 he had gained 100 percent control. Upset with the new management at Olds Motor Works, Ransom E. Olds broke away to form his own company producing cars whose nameplate, REO, left no doubt who was in charge. Similarly, Horace and John Dodge created their own car in 1913, after tiring of only supplying auto components and feeling "carried around in Henry Ford's vest pocket," according to John. William C. Durant founded, bought, sold, and merged numerous auto companies in these decades. These were only a few of many entrepreneurs who epitomized a vital industrial incubation process that helped Detroit dominate the early auto industry: spinoff firms founded by those who previously had worked for another firm in the same industry. Detroit's proclivity for spinoffs was distinctive. Klepper has shown that 48 percent of the entrants into Detroit's auto industry were spinoffs from parent companies already located in the area, compared to only 15 percent of the industry located elsewhere in the U.S. The Greater Detroit auto cluster literally built upon itself through innovative, profitable parent companies that spawned entrepreneurs founding similarly performing offspring: success through incest.

Stamping Instability

An automobile's mystique is comprised of many elements—power, speed, reliability, creature comforts. But perhaps none is more central than the lines of its body. These lines are formed in the stamping plants, where giant hydraulic presses noisily crush sheet metal against molded dies. So, too, was Detroit's twentieth-century economic base stamped by the dominant auto industry with an indelible shape: cyclical instability. As a relatively expensive durable good, automobiles are far more vulnerable than most goods and services to the vagaries of credit markets and of consumer confidence. When the national economy is optimistic and credit is cheap, people buy new vehicles. When unemployment and interest rates rise and uncertainty grows, people drive their old cars a little longer and forego new vehicles.

This crucial aspect of the auto industry can be seen in Figure 12. It shows on comparable visual scales American consumers' year-to-year variability in all spending and their purchases of domestically produced autos during the half century after World War II. The recessions of 1959, 1974, and 1981, for example, show up as modest slippages in consumer spending, but dramatic declines in car sales.

History reveals the booms and busts that were forcibly stamped on Greater Detroit, pounding deep imprints on the region's psyche. From 1900 to 1929, Detroit's economy witnessed an unprecedented boom as the young auto industry gobbled up an ever-increasing share of the nation's rapidly expanding auto market. Klepper documented that auto production in Greater Detroit rose at a mind-boggling pace: from 13,000 in 1905, to 800,000 in 1915, to 3.8 million in 1929. Although most automakers also engaged in military production during World War I, auto production then neither ceased

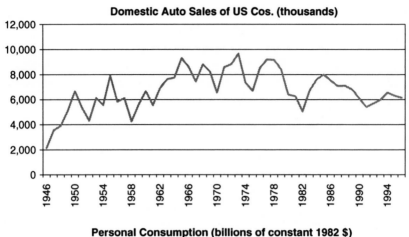

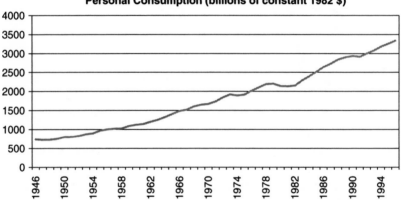

Figure 12. Comparative cyclical instability of U.S. personal consumption and auto sales, 1946–1996.

nor seriously slowed. These were heady times indeed, when Detroit's international reputation for productivity and wealth were at its peak. A 1927 *New York Times* article encapsulated the conventional wisdom by exclaiming, "Detroit is growth. . . . Detroiters are the most prosperous slice of average humanity that now exists or that has ever existed."

Yet even before this boom busted in October 1929, Detroit labor tasted its first bitter appetizer of auto industry instability. By the mid-1920s General Motors had introduced yearly model changes, a bevy of price points across its stable of nameplates, major advertising campaigns, and GMAC auto financing, all but crushing Ford's antique Model T, which remained essentially unchanged for two decades. Ford was forced to close its plants in 1926 for a lengthy retooling that would ultimately yield the cutting-edge, eight-cylinder Model A, and restore Ford's competitiveness. One of the tool and die makers hired in 1927 at the Highland Park Plant to facilitate this massive changeover was Walter Reuther. He was one of the few lucky workers, however. Ford employment fell from 120,275 in January 1926 to 99,739 in June 1926 to 82,890 in June 1927, according to Paul Kellogg.

As tough as it was for labor to swallow this, Ford's changeover was a meek foreshadowing of the desperate times to come. Between 1929 and the Great Depression's first major trough in 1932, auto production fell by two-thirds and employment by more than half. Employment at Ford dropped to 37,000, only 30 percent of what it had been in the prior peak. Michigan's jobless rate reached 40 percent by the winter of 1932. One-third of Detroit's families were without any financial support whatsoever. It was during this desperate time that the durable urban legend arose about the "roast that went around the block." A group of seven neighboring families in Detroit's Brightmoor neighborhood devised this scheme: a designated family would buy a roast and have it for Sunday dinner, pass leftovers to the family next door for Monday supper, who would continue the process until, by Saturday, the seventh neighbor family would cook a thin beef stock with the remaining bones. The next week the seventh family bought the roast and ate first.

But, cycles being cycles, a rebound came, as documented by Reynolds Farley, Sheldon Danziger, and Harry Holzer. Between 1932 and 1937, auto production tripled. After a mild slump in 1938, output by 1940 was again booming ahead of the 1937 rate. Things were so profitable by this point that the automakers were very reluctant to become what later would be hailed as the "arsenal of democracy." Responding to President Franklin D. Roosevelt's 1940 call to shift from consumer to military production, UAW president Walter Reuther argued that up to 50 percent of the auto industry's tools and machines were suitable for war production and that substantial unused capacity could be coordinated across auto firms to mass produce 500 airplanes a day. Reuther's initiative was actively opposed by the Big Three, which did not want their now-profitable auto plants converted. Instead, they held out for the government to grant them fat, "cost-plus" military contracts, permitting them to build new defense factories, such as those eventually constructed for tanks in Warren and bombers in Willow Run. Henry Ford refused to sign a contract to build Merlin aircraft engines in his existing plants. In the first half of 1941, GM devoted less than 10 percent of its total output to the defense effort. It would take a declaration of war in December 1941 and the subsequent centralized control of industry by the national war planners for the auto industry to get beyond narrow self-interest and cease producing automobiles.

But eventually Greater Detroit's factories did churn out war materiel exclusively, and in impressive fashion. During World War II, the region's productivity doubled; by the end of the war, it had manufactured 20 percent of the country's military output. Chrysler built tanks; GM produced guns, artillery, and bombs; Ford contributed vehicles and B-24 heavy bombers.

After a brief respite at the end of the war while the industry switched back to predominantly civilian auto production, the boom resumed. From 1946 to 1950, auto sales tripled. As of 1950, employment in the region had grown 39 percent in the prior decade, from 857,000 to 1,120,000. Greater Detroit's industrial economy had expanded to such an extent that, by 1951, historian Milo Quaife could declare without fear of contradiction that Detroit was "the center of the most advanced industrial development on earth."

This 1940s boom ended abruptly as the U.S. headed into the 1952 recession. As usual, the national effects were magnified in auto-dominated Detroit (see Figure 12). The industrial shake out left two prime local casualties: Packard went bankrupt in 1954, and Hudson closed its Detroit operations after merging with American Motors in 1956. These twin blows closed two massive factory complexes on Detroit's east side, with seventy thousand jobs and millions of tax revenue dollars. It also triggered racial scapegoating that plagues the region to this day.

After peaking again in 1956, auto sales plummeted in 1958. But this merely set the stage for the longest postwar period of domestic automobile sales expansion through the mid-1960s. Times were particularly flush for the industry in 1963: remarkably, all the Big Three made over a 20 percent return. The largest and most profitable of the trio, GM, had $2.5 billion in cash reserves that year, a sum so large that the *Wall Street Journal* quipped, "It's rumored in Wall Street that the General Motors Corporation is saving up to buy the United States Government." Only an idiot would have imagined then that forty-six years later the roles would be reversed.

Domestic auto sales were especially volatile in the 1970s, pummeled by the new Organization of Petroleum Exporting Countries (OPEC) oil embargos, a stagnant economy, and political instability from the Vietnam War and Watergate scandal. Noticeably stronger import competition also marked this decade, as the Big Three's 1980 U.S. market share slipped to 74 percent from 82 percent in 1970. Spawned by record interest rates and gasoline prices, the period 1979 to 1982 is locally known as the Second Great Depression. At five million vehicles, domestic auto production in 1979 had not been so low since 1958. That same year, Chrysler Corporation was so weakened that it sought (and received) loan guarantees from the federal government and wage and benefit concessions from the UAW, to stave off bankruptcy.

During the late 1980s, domestic auto sales again rebounded without reaching the prior decade's peaks, before falling once more as the economy sputtered entering the 1990s. But Detroit carmakers introduced two new products—the minivan and the sport-utility vehicle—which proved so popular that the Big Three catapulted into a decade-long parabola of profitability, despite a market share that eroded to 65 percent by 2000. GM made a profit each year from 1993 to 2004, a whopping cumulative figure of $48.4 billion. Ford also scored well, with a North American operations profit every year but one from 1999 through 2004, a cumulative $20.9 billion. Prosperity for the region's auto workers peaked earlier. Detroit-area auto manufacturing, parts manufacturing, and transportation equipment employees held steady at 417,000 through the mid-1990s, then grew steadily to a peak of 516,000 by 2000.

This 1990s miniboom now seems like ancient history as the region foundered after 2000 in its Third Great Depression. Employment in Greater Detroit's auto manufacturing, parts manufacturing and transportation equipment sector fell precipitously by over 100,000 from its 2000 peak. The miniboom bypassed local the machine tool industry: from 1995 to 2005, employment shrank 38 percent, from 555,000 to 344,000. Delphi Corporation, a Detroit area-based auto components manufacturing conglomerate spun off from GM in 1999, foretold an even more ominous employment outlook when it declared bankruptcy in October 2005. At that point, it was ranked 63rd on the Fortune 500 list in sales, with 185,000 employees nationwide.

In 2007, as the national economy plummeted into the worst recession since the 1930s, the pain was magnified in Greater Detroit. Falling new car sales forced Chrysler into bankruptcy in May 2009 and, unthinkably to Detroiters, General Motors followed suit within a month. Although these corporations received substantial cash infusions from the federal government and later emerged from bankruptcy, they were hollow apparitions of their robust former selves, having shed tens of thousands of white- and blue-collar jobs locally and jettisoned millions of dollars in pension liabilities that formerly propped up tens of thousands of local retirees. By the end of 2009, the Big Three's market share had fallen to 44 percent. Though the Big Three's bottom line has improved in mid-2011, the bottom of the Third Great Depression for Greater Detroiters is not yet in sight—restored profitability came at the expense of lost jobs, wages, pensions, and health care benefits.

In 2009 *Time* and its sibling news organizations assigned a handful of journalists to live in Detroit and report during the ensuing year on the disaster that had befallen its economy. The magazine bought a large house in Detroit for the journalists to stay in, paying less than $100,000. The collaborative's first major exposé was the October 5, 2009, *Time* cover story, emblazoned with the headline "The Tragedy of Detroit," superimposed on a photo of the derelict Packard factory. This was the same magazine that had once featured on its cover the iconic likenesses of Henry Ford (1926), Alfred Sloan (1926), and Walter Chrysler (1925 and 1929) during the city's glory days, providing mute testimony to the instability that the industry indelibly stamped on Greater Detroit.

> I do not believe we should make such awful profits on our cars. . . . A reasonable profit is right, but not too much.
> —Henry Ford, 1919

> If you can find a better car, buy it!
> —Lee Iacocca, chairman of Chrysler Corporation, in a 1980 TV advertising campaign to restore consumer confidence in his company after the federal bailout

> If you don't like it, turn our car back in within 60 days!
> —Fritz Henderson, chairman of General Motors Corporation, in a 2009 TV advertising campaign to restore consumer confidence in his company after the federal bailout

The High-Octane Hangover

The century-long dominance of the automobile industry stamped an indelible imprint on Greater Detroit's economy. But past is also prologue, and the region staggers into the future as if suffering from a high-octane hangover. This excessive imbibing on all things automotive left four powerful legacies related to the nature of capital, labor, technology, and race relations.

The first legacy is the nature of capital organized as a gigantic oligopoly. Detroit's auto industry had very limited domestic competition for many years, was sheltered (by political, military, technological, and financial factors) from intense competition from abroad, and had only self-restrained competition from within. So it did not need to optimize production or managerial efficiency, aggressively invest in world-class research and development, or pay rapt attention to either its customers' emerging wants or to new market forces. Neither did it need to resist stubbornly 1950s and 1960s union demands for concessions that would not only raise current wage and benefit costs but also indefinitely saddle it with huge pension and insurance legacy costs for retirees. Because the corporate structures were both huge and vertically organized, many functions that otherwise might have been provided by independently owned and operated firms located nearby, and many business services such as financing, marketing, design, and accounting, were instead internalized. The few business services that were contracted out essentially rendered these firms lackeys of the Big Three, wholly dependent on the practices of their behemoth benefactors. Because the auto companies were so large that they had to operate bureaucratically, there emerged an institutionalized reluctance to take risks and think "outside the box." It also created a complacency associated with a "too-big-to-fail" mindset.

The net results of these features of the region's dominant form of capital were that an independent, multi-faceted and creative financial and business service sector, innovative entrepreneurial spirit, and aggressive venture capital sources were steadily underdeveloped as the twentieth century wore on. *Crain's Detroit Business* estimated in 2004 that Michigan should be getting 3.4 percent of the nation's venture capital dollars, based on its population and gross domestic product, but that the state had not gotten even 1 percent since 1994. In 2006, Detroit Renaissance (a business-led economic development organization) and *Crain's Detroit Business* surveyed more than 350 executives, entrepreneurs, venture capitalists, real estate developers, and institutional board members in the region. The pollsters concluded that the region's large-company culture discourages entrepreneurship. Their poll revealed that 46 percent felt that "businesspeople were not interested in supporting and investing in startup ventures" and that 48 percent believed that "the business culture does not accept failure as a part of learning and innovation." It thus appears that the long-term consumption of a high-octane oligopoly has given Greater Detroit's business community a collective case of amnesia: they have forgotten that Henry Ford tried three times before his company eventually succeeded.

The second legacy of an economy with a high-octane hangover is the progressive deskilling, disempowering, and redundancy of the blue-collar workforce. The transition to an auto-dominated economy in the early twentieth century brought a profound change in the nature and organization of work. Generally, small factories, with workers doing a variety of skilled, craftsman-like tasks completed at their own pace, were steadily replaced by huge factories where more and more workers did repetitive, robotic tasks on an assembly line whose speed was set by management. The resulting demands for skilled workers were predictable, as the Highland Park plant demonstrates. In 1910, one-third of Ford employees were classified as skilled workers; by 1917, this had been reduced to only one-fifth.

It is a cruel irony that, while the auto industry depended on skilled metal craftspeople for its very birth, much of the industry's subsequent efforts aimed to render these craftspeople obsolete through the assembly line's inherent division of labor. Not only were assembly line laborers cheaper to train and easier to control, but they were easier to replace, either with robots or with equally unskilled but even less expensive labor abroad. Was it cynical, then, for the Johnson administration's Office of Economic Opportunity to promote auto jobs for minority youth by sponsoring the 1965 video of Martha and the Vandellas singing their new hit "Nowhere to Run" from a Mustang convertible on Ford's Rouge assembly line? Truth in advertising would have required that subtitles be shown as the song was sung, since redundancy through automation and outsourcing were the inescapable destiny of the Detroit autoworker—indeed, "Nowhere to Run."

The third legacy of the high-octane hangover is the postwar shift in auto production that required single-story, large-scale production facilities that consumed large tracts of land. This land-extensive technology meant an ever-outward expansion of Greater Detroit's economic engine—the driver of unsustainable land use patterns and the bankruptcy of the central city jurisdiction. By contrast, metropolitan economies dominated by finance, insurance, real estate, business services, higher education, research and development, retail, wholesale, government, or arts and culture sectors grow by agglomerating at high densities at the core, as in Boston, New York, Chicago, and San Francisco. Even metropolitan economies dominated by heavy industries like steel production (such as Pittsburgh) were constrained to cluster on navigable waterways to accommodate the magnitude of raw materials used as inputs. Not so for auto manufacturing, whose inputs and final products can easily be shipped via railroads and trucks. Greater Detroit's twentieth-century economic engine was a powerful driver of sprawl compared to other regional economies. It is, thus, no accident that among the largest U.S. metropolitan regions Greater Detroit has the least spatially concentrated job pattern and the smallest relative share of central business district jobs compared to suburban centers.

Huge auto production facilities also leave another legacy at the end of their lifespan: massive brownfield sites that are incredibly expensive to reuse. As in the archetypical cases of the Ford Highland Park and Packard Motor Company plants, it is likely that these gigantic industrial remnants will continue to haunt the landscape a century after their original construction, polluting their environs, discouraging development, and serving as omnipresent reminders of past glories. They are the region's crumbling billboards of meta-nostalgia.

The last legacy of the high-octane hangover involves race relations. The auto industry shaped race relations in Greater Detroit in two main ways. Directly, it actively fomented racial divisions as a means to fight union organizing efforts in the pre-World War II era. Indirectly, it generated high wages for its primarily white work force at precisely the historical period when new homes were sold only to whites, owing to systematic discriminatory practices of the housing development, real estate brokerage, and mortgage industries, abetted by racist policies promulgated by local, state, and federal governments. This meant that the white working class would be hypersegregated (often in jurisdictions outside the City of Detroit) and incentivized to fight integration as a threat to the value of their homes.

Heavy Metal Forever?

Like drunks who can't get started on a twelve-step program because they can't admit they have a problem, Greater Detroit has never seriously tried to wean itself from its addiction to the high-octane oligopoly or to manufacturing in general. True, the share of regional employees working in the broad manufacturing industrial sector has dropped over the last three decades from roughly one-third to one-sixth. But this is in line with America's general deindustrialization. It was not intentional policy. Yet, the relative importance of manufacturing—especially the auto subsector—to Greater Detroit's economy compared to the rest of the U.S. remains stunningly high. David Crary, George Erickcek and Allen Goodman documented that the share of local employees working in Greater Detroit's manufacturing sector is 49 percent higher than the national average. Yet in certain manufacturing subsectors, the current overrepresentation of the metal fabricating economy that emerged over a century ago is even clearer. In the industrial machinery subsector it is 75 percent higher than the national average. In the fabricated metal products subsector it is 149 percent higher. In the motor vehicles and related equipment subsector it is 1,082 percent higher!

This industrial addiction is not only reflected in the workforce composition, but in the minds of Greater Detroiters. A 2009 *Washington Post*-Kaiser Family Foundation poll asked a representative sample of 1,205 Detroit area residents the question "What's the first word that comes to mind when thinking about the Detroit area today?" The three most frequent responses were "depressed," "unemployment," and, close behind, "auto industry"; 70 percent believe that "the auto industry must recover in order for the Detroit area economy to improve."

The reasons for this addiction are many and difficult to prioritize. Some I presented above as legacies of Big Three dominance: vertical integration, entrepreneurial spirit squashed by gigantism and bureaucratization, and lack of venture capital. Another is that the historically high union wages in the auto sector set high compensation standards for nonunionized sectors, discouraging new startup firms and entrepreneurial efforts. As Timothy Bates emphasized in 1997, the generally low educational levels of the population also made it less likely that new startups would succeed, let alone prosper enough to change the character of the region's economic base. Finally, the element of accident enters the Greater Detroit saga yet again. Two fateful events occurred early in the eighteenth century that would forever limit the potential diversity of Detroit's economic base. In 1837, a land company donated forty acres to the state to create a new campus for the then Detroit-based University of Michigan; the acreage was located in the faraway village of Ann Arbor. And in 1847, the state legislature transferred Michigan's capital from Detroit to Lansing. This ultimately proved terrific for Big Ten sports rivalries but debilitating for Greater Detroit.

Perhaps Greater Detroit will be forced to break its addiction to its metal-bending, auto-making economic base by going "cold turkey." The region might deindustrialize by default if the competitive superiority of Asian-based manufacturers and carmakers continues indefinitely. This prospect can already be glimpsed within the City of Detroit. Although several auto assembly and parts manufacturing facilities remain in operation, the largest employers by far are in the government, education, health care, and entertainment sectors. Employment in the last sector is dominated by the three casinos, first promoted in 1988 by Mayor Coleman Young and finally granted licenses after a 1998 referendum. As important as these sectors are to Detroit, they are not powerful engines of growth for either the city or the region because they are typically not amenable to great gains in productivity and do not primarily sell their services to customers located outside the region. They neither make the region's money go further nor do they bring new money into the region. Thus, a future based on an economy of what Peter Eisinger has called "bread and circuses" is a bleak future indeed.

Perhaps the region will be lucky and stumble upon some yet-to-be-specified, future high-tech core industry as an alternative addiction. After all, the Big Three recently have jettisoned substantial research, design, engineering, information, and marketing talents who still live in the Detroit area. Maybe this suddenly redundant but skilled pool of labor will be forced to turn entrepreneurial, and one will prove to be the Henry Ford (or should I say Bill Gates or Steve Jobs) of the twenty-first century?

Or perhaps Greater Detroit will try to modify incrementally its addiction by slowly switching to a new dope: tax incentives aimed at stealing firms from other states. Despite the mountains of evidence that this strategy rarely works in the medium run or succeeds in building a new long-term economic base, Michigan and many municipalities continue to view business tax concessions as a heroin junkie sees methadone. Two 2009 examples of heavy doses of state tax credits—one "old" economy and one "new"—are illustrative. The closed fifty-two-year-old Ford plant in suburban Wixom is slated to reopen as a $725 million project to build solar panels and storage batteries under the aegis of firms based in California, Texas, and Switzerland. Construction has started on converting another shuttered auto plant into a movie studio. Targeted tax breaks for filmmakers have already been snapped up by numerous producers who make movies featuring Detroit's "ready-made sets": antique skyscrapers, postindustrial wastelands, and large homes with owners desperate to make ends meet. So, maybe Detroit will still be a place making dreams, though dreams made out of ephemeral pixels, not heavy metal. But does anyone believe Detroit could ever seriously compete with Los Angeles, with its massive comparative advantages, for the big money segments of the entertainment industry? There may be room for a "Bollywood"— even a "Dollywood"—but a "Motollywood?"

Chapter 4

From Old World to Old South and Old Testament

We have come, over a way that with tears has been watered,
We have come, treading our path through the blood of the
    slaughtered,
out from the gloomy past, till now we stand at last
where the white gleam of our bright star is cast.
   —"Lift Every Voice and Sing," written by James Weldon Johnson in
       1900 and set to music by John Rosamond Johnson in 1905

Although written out of the experience of blacks, the sentiments expressed in "Lift Every Voice and Sing" equally apply to generations of other ethnic groups who came to Detroit seeking a better life. Despite common motivations, peopling this region tapped three distinct geographic sources. Immigration into Greater Detroit shifted from a predominantly "Old World," European stock, to an "Old South," black stock, and an "Old Testament" stock from the biblical lands of the Middle East. Only recently have substantial sources of immigration begun to diversify.

Out with the Old, in with the New

The first recorded visit of a European to this region occurred in 1669, when French trapper-explorer Adrien Joliet disembarked from his canoe. It would be another thirty-two years before Cadillac's forces built the first permanent French fortified settlement. The first generations of settlers continued to be overwhelmingly French until the British and American takeovers in the eighteenth century.

Nevertheless, one of the most constructive immigrants in the nineteenth century was a French American: Father Gabriel Richard. After completing Roman Catholic seminary in France and emigrating to the U.S. in 1792 to do missionary work with the "natives," Father Richard came to Detroit in 1804 as assistant pastor of the region's oldest Catholic parish, St. Anne's. He quickly established a school for Natives and developed what we would now call progressive "community outreach programs." These so successfully reduced long-festering tensions that dated to Cadillac's time between Natives and European immigrants that powerful Shawnee chief Tecumseh refused to fight with the British in the War of 1812 so long as they imprisoned Father Richard in the occupied city. Among Father Richard's other notable educational achievements, he imported the first printing press to Detroit to publish several periodicals, and in 1817 founded the Catholepistemiad of Michigania, which would become the University of Michigan. He also served as pastor to Catholic and Protestant parishes in Detroit simultaneously in 1807, in a notable display of ecumenical tolerance. It is deeply regrettable that Father Richard's doctrine of education and religion as vehicles for unity among groups fell on infertile ground that would soon become the impermeable rock of sectarian and racist fragmentation on which Detroit was built.

Though French and English settlers would continue to flow into Detroit (often by way of Canada), the first substantial nineteenth-century immigration from the Old World originated in Ireland and Germany. By 1830, a substantial Irish neighborhood had taken shape in an area along the river just west of downtown—Corktown (the name persists today). The neighborhood expanded rapidly after 1846 as the potato blight-induced famine in Ireland accelerated immigration. Nearly four in five of these later-arriving Irish were common laborers, twice the share of the earlier cohort. They found plenty of work in the city's sawmills, foundries, and rolling mills and as draymen for the omnipresent horse-drawn wagons, carriages, and coaches.

Germans started a sizable immigration into Detroit in 1825, focusing on the east side of downtown, north of Jefferson along Gratiot Avenue. By 1850, this neighborhood was commonly known as Germantown. Although this flow of Germans included farmers and unskilled laborers, as a group they comprised much higher shares of skilled craftsmen and professional workers. While split by Catholic and Protestant loyalties, embodied in the respective St. Joseph and St. Luke parishes, the Germans shared a clannish sense of *über* superiority that transcended mere religion.

*   *   *

It was a day on the Detroit waterfront at the foot of Woodward Avenue like so many others in 1851. Sailing vessels silently slipped past, destined for their docks just downstream, laden with lumber or iron ore. Plodding ferries shuttled passengers and railroad cars across the river to Windsor. The overnight steamship from Buffalo had just disembarked its passengers where Cadillac had landed a century and a half prior and where a century and a half later a statue commemorating the terminus of the underground railroad would be erected. The median of the city's 300-year time line intersected with ground zero for the city's generations of hopeful entrants. Those from the first-class cabins had already been swept away to their destinations in fine carriages. Passengers in steerage, especially foreign immigrants, drifted uncertainly amid the smoke, noise, and chaos of the docks, seeking relatives, friends, or other potential saviors in this strange new land.

No one took much notice of Johann Georg, the future father of the founder of Acme Wire and Iron Works, George Jacob. He was especially disoriented because it was beginning to dawn on him that this was not Chicago. Perhaps it was the lingering effects of the arduous trans-Atlantic journey from his little village in Baden-Württemberg, Altensteig, to New York City. Perhaps it was a language barrier. Boarding the steamer in Buffalo, Johann Georg had understood that it was bound for Chicago and its large German immigrant community, his intended destination. He did not understand that the steamer was also stopping in Detroit. By the time he realized his error, the steamer had departed, and he could not afford another ticket.

But being a farmer by trade and indomitable by temperament, Johann Georg figured he could succeed as well in Detroit as Chicago. So he purchased a plot of land north of Germantown a couple of blocks off Gratiot Avenue. To celebrate his new life, he lifted a beer and gave a lusty, hopeful "prost!" He may have tried an eponymous beer introduced that year by one of the German neighbors, Bernhard Stroh; his brewery would eventually not only become the Detroit area's favorite, but his beer would be widely sold outside the region.

Farming in Detroit indeed proved successful for Johann Georg, but within a few decades, the city had grown out to his land, providing him a different opportunity: residential subdivision development. He cut a two-block street through the farm, connecting Forest and Canfield Avenues; it bears his surname to this day. Several parcels were reserved for the homes of his offspring and their families. One was used for his son George Jacob's new Acme Wire and Iron Works factory. The rest were sold to other members of the burgeoning Germantown community.

*   *   *

By 1880, Detroit was overwhelmingly dominated by peoples of northwestern European extraction. According to Olivier Zunz's estimates, the single largest ethnic group, almost 30 percent of household heads, emigrated from Germany or were born in the U.S. of two German-born parents, like George Jacob. Americans born of white, U.S.-born parents comprised only 19 percent of households. Those born in Ireland or in the U.S. or Canada to two parents born in Ireland made up 16 percent; the comparable figure for the British was 13 percent. Others immigrating from Canada and whose parents were born in Canada represented another 5 percent. Those of eastern and southern European background were only 4 percent of household heads, and American blacks or mulattos were less than 3 percent. By this point, the French had slipped to only 2 percent of all households.

The white ethnic geography of Detroit was starting to change rapidly, however. A plurality of the population of Corktown were still Irish and clustered around Most Holy Trinity Church, the first Irish-Catholic parish in Detroit. But, increasingly, the second-generation Irish were dispersing and not being replaced. Instead, American-born Protestants of various backgrounds were moving in. On the east side, Germantown kept its flavor through 1900, with a majority of the area's German-origin households still residing there. But, like the Irish Americans, the German Americans were spreading into new territories, in the Mid-town section of the near east side north of Division Street, on the west side in areas formerly dominated by the Irish, as well as in newly built areas along Michigan Avenue on the city's fringes. Yet it was the upsurge of Polish immigration that most significantly redrew the map of white ethnic settlement.

By the early 1890s, the Poles had formed two distinct enclaves, one on the near west side and a much larger one on the near east side adjacent to and interspersed within Germantown. Detroit's first Polish Catholic church, St. Albertus, touted as the largest in nineteenth-century America, was consecrated in 1885 at the corner of St. Aubin and Canfield Avenues. Within a few years, the burgeoning Polish immigrant population and schisms within the parish led to two more east-side Polish churches being built within less than a mile of each other along Canfield Avenue: Sweetest Heart of Mary in 1888–89 and St. Josaphat in 1889–90. All three still stand today, though virtually no one of Polish background lives in the neighborhood any more. The highest Detroit-area concentration of contemporary Polish descendants—and the port of entry for new Polish immigrants—is a couple of miles to the north: the municipality of Hamtramck, completely surrounded by the City of Detroit as it annexed greedily in the decades around the turn of the twentieth century.

Though virtually halted by World War I, by 1920 immigration from eastern and southern Europe had transformed the face of Detroit and its neighborhoods, as Zunz documented. At 20 percent, Poles comprised the largest segment of the city's foreign-born population, followed by British Canadians (19 percent), Germans (10 percent), Russians (9 percent), British (9 percent), Austrians (6 percent), Italians (6 percent), and Hungarians (5 percent). Belgians, Dutch, Scandinavians, Greeks, and French Canadians each had only 1 or 2 percent. The Irish, who had made up a third of the city's foreign-born stock in 1850, were only a little over 2 percent by 1920.

But this surging Old World flow that in all its richness had shaped Detroit's demography for a century was about to be reduced to a trickle by xenophobic national politics. Congress established immigration limits in 1921 (the Emergency Quota Act) and 1924 (the Johnson-Reed Act). They set a quota of new immigrants from any country to 2 percent of that group already living in the U.S. as of the 1890 census. This system implicitly favored prospective immigrants from northern and western Europe relative to those from southern or eastern Europe and other continents. Yet relatively few from the older sources of immigrants wanted to move to Detroit during this period, and people from other lands were effectively barred from doing so. Southern blacks (and some whites) had already been migrating to Detroit in growing numbers; thanks to politics—war and regulations—they would now have Detroit's door open to themselves alone.

* * *

The late nineteenth-century buzz in Germantown was almost audible, the smug smiles omnipresent. Detroit's rapid industrialization had favored the skill sets that many residents of the community possessed. Though Germans held few top positions of power and prestige (these being reserved for native Anglos), they were prosperous, established, and hopeful, starting to believe that Detroit was *their* city. They dominated many industries by 1880, comprising a majority of workers in the marble, stone, and tobacco sectors, in bars and saloons, and more than a third of those in the clothing, lumber, chemical and drug, and foundry and machine shop sectors.

A robust second generation of American-born children was appearing. Immigrant Johann Georg could now dote on his new grandson, George Jacob, II, born in 1883 in his father George Jacob's house on the family's newly urbanized farm compound adjacent to Acme Wire and Iron Works. In 1888 Emma, his grandson's future wife, and Bruno, the father of his grandson's future daughter-in-law, were born in Germantown.

The community was anchored by a host of cultural-social institutions. Arbeiter Halle was the home of the German Workingmen's Aid Society, a voluntary organization providing health and life insurance for its members, as well as halls for meetings, political rallies, and dances and—most importantly—a beer garden. The Harmonie Society had a sumptuous, multistory club on John R Street downtown on a triangular-shaped square produced by the Woodward Plan, lending its name to the district in perpetuity. The building held musical rehearsal and performance spaces for men's and women's choral groups, gaming rooms, a bowling alley, restaurants, and, of course, a beer hall. The highlight of the Harmonie's social calendar was its masquerade, where a series of historical tableaux were staged, complete with lavish costumes and music. Dozens of such social clubs dotted Detroit's east side, annually joining in a day of parading and partying through Germantown. By 1891, these festivities were so significant that all major employers granted their German-American employees an excused absence or a half-day holiday. Small wonder that an 1893 *Detroit Free Press* article on Detroit's social life remarked, "Germans are by nature an amusement-seeking, sociable race. . . . They have their beer, too; one must admit that there would be something lacking without it."

By the end of the nineteenth century, 85 percent of Detroit's German-American community could speak English. It is thus a testament to their cultural conservatism that not until 1890 did a small group of parishioners from St. Luke's German Lutheran Church break away and incorporate as First English Evangelical Lutheran Church. New congregants included Johann Georg's family, George Jacob's family, Bruno's family, and Emma's family. This "modern" congregation proved so popular that it built a large church on the corner of Mt. Elliot and Mack Avenues in 1910 and a massive parish hall with full-size gymnasium and swimming pool two decades later. George Jacob and by now his four adult sons donated to the new sanctuary dozens of wrought iron candelabra they had fabricated at their Acme ironworks, which they proudly bolted to ends of the pews. There they stood for generations, unwitting symbols of so many rigid parishioners of iron wills and stiff necks.

The congregation was not without its tribulations, of course. Infant and maternal mortality were still high by modern standards and showed no respect for economic status, not even for the prosperous founder of Acme Wire and Iron Works and his son. George Jacob and his wife, Amelia, lost their first son as an infant; in his memory they named their next son the same in 1883: George Jacob II. Twenty-four years later, George Jacob II's wife, Bertha, gave birth to a healthy first child, Marvin, but she died soon after. Community ethnic social networks came to the rescue. Two years later, George Jacob II married Emma, a robust twenty-one-year-old member of First English Lutheran Church. The deal was undoubtedly sealed because, as a teenager, she had worked in one of the local factories rolling George Jacob's favorite brand of cigars. Their union produced two more congregation members: Ruth in 1910 and, quite unexpectedly in 1921, George Milton. In 1909 the congregation celebrated both George Jacob and Emma's wedding and that of another twenty-one-year-old parishioner, Bruno. Quite unusually (and likely with some communal dismay), Bruno married an outsider: Helen, a fetching twenty-one-year-old of Scottish heritage.

Self-initiated efforts at "Americanization," like forming First English Lutheran Church, came none too soon, as the 1917 U.S. declaration of war on Germany raised a storm of anti-German sentiment against the community. The story of Carl Schmidt, head of the house of Traugott Schmidt and a prosperous international leather merchant, illustrates how Detroit's German Americans had to prove their patriotism. Schmidt's frequent business trips to Germany before 1917 raised suspicions. But he demonstrated his loyalty by endowing an entire battlefield hospital in France, operated by staff from Detroit's Harper Hospital. Other, less wealthy Schmidts changed their names to "Smith" and conspicuously bought Liberty bonds. Sadly, suspicions about anything German were rekindled during World War II, producing odd adaptations. The circa-1931 Dakota Inn Rathskeller German restaurant on John R Street contributed to this "de-Germanization" effort by changing the nightly required music. They expunged the offensive lyrics of Franz Josef Hayden's tune "Deutschland über Alles" and paired it with "God Bless America."

The Big Switch

While Old World immigrants poured into Detroit, the city's black population remained miniscule. At the first Detroit census in 1820, blacks comprised only 5 percent of the population; by 1830 the figure had risen to 6 percent. For the rest of the century, the black share dropped consistently, however, to less than 2 percent by 1900. In a city of over 285,000, there were only about 4,000 black residents. They worked primarily in service industries, as barbers, waiters, hotel porters, or house servants. They lived scattered across the city, with few discernible pockets of concentration. Many lived among the Russian Jews and Germans on the east side.

This all changed in the big switch of immigration from Old Europe to the Old South. With coming of World War I, the thirst for industrial labor simultaneously intensified as the traditional wellspring of that labor was drying up. In the decade from 1910 to 1920, Detroit's black population grew a staggering 614 percent—from 5,741 to 40,838—more than any other northern city. This era has been labeled "The Great Migration." A Detroit Urban League survey in summer 1917 reported that "1,000 Negroes a month" were arriving; by 1920, the League updated the estimate to 1,000 *per day*. Indeed, the 1920s generated almost a *tripling* of the black population to 120,066—again the highest growth rate of all large cities. Most arrived via train, their first glimpse of Detroit being the spectacular, marble-clad concourse of Michigan Central Station.

One of those immigrants in 1921 was Dr. Ossian Sweet, whose effort four years later to break the residential color line would prove iconic. But he was not the only black immigrant of this era who packed potent foreshadowing in his or her suitcase along with clothing. Berry Gordy, Sr., migrated from Sandersville, Georgia, to Detroit in 1922. A year later, another Sandersville native arrived, Elijah Poole, who would become Elijah Muhammad of the Nation of Islam. Decades later, Elijah convinced Malcolm Little to move to Detroit, where, in the 1950s, Little worked on a Lincoln-Mercury assembly line as upholstery trimmer. He quit in 1953, two years before Berry Gordy, Jr., would work the same line, while dreaming of his own record company. A few years later, Malcolm Little changed his name to Malcolm X and made the Black Muslims a household name in 1960s America. Berry Gordy Jr.'s Motown record label had an even a bigger impact. William Young also arrived from Alabama in 1923 with his young son Coleman in tow. All these participants in the Great Migration came filled with optimism, but soon reality set in, as they would be exposed to the black-white tensions spreading like a virus across Detroit.

> I'm goin' to get me a job, up there in Mr. Ford's place,
> Stop these eatless days from staring me in the face.
> When I start making money, she don't need to come around,
> 'Cause I don't need her now, Lord.
> I'm Detroit bound.
> —"Detroit Bound Blues," anonymous composer, sung
> in the South during the Great Migration

> Certain [Detroit] companies . . . have actually taken active steps to increase the gap between the two [racial] groups of workers and aggravate the social situation. For instance, one of the largest factories in the city separated its colored employees from its white employees in its lunch-room with a large iron chain. There are other factories which have attempted to enforce segregation in their wash-rooms and toilets by posting signs reading "This side for whites," "This side for Negroes."
> —Forrester Washington, head of Detroit Urban League, 1920

The jobs that drew this massive black population influx were not just traditional service jobs. For the first time, factory jobs—although the least-desirable ones—were opening up to black males. They often were segregated into particular job classifications, both to avoid interracial workplace tensions and because only the most desperate immigrants would accept these jobs. So, at Dodge, black workers risked respiratory illness and asphyxiation by endlessly spraying paint on auto bodies; at Ford, they slaved in the lethal, oven-like environments called foundries.

Nevertheless, from a southern black perspective, the apparent economic advantages provided compelling reasons for migrating to Detroit. The typical auto factory job paid $6 a day in the 1920s; it might take months for a sharecropper to accumulate that much. No details are available for Detroit or Michigan, but the median wages for blacks in the East North Central states during this era were about double that of blacks living in the South.

By 1920, a prototype black ghetto was forming, concentrated on the near east side along Hastings Street. Unflatteringly, it came to be called "Black Bottom." Landlords there found it profitable to subdivide old dwellings into ever-smaller, undermaintained quarters, producing the most overcrowded, unhealthy living conditions the city had ever experienced. A quarter of the dwellings had only outhouses. Pool halls charged for the privilege of sleeping on the pool tables overnight. With increasing numbers of neighborhoods closed to them, black migrants had little choice but to occupy the appalling, mushrooming slums.

Regardless of occupation, all blacks were forced to live in this area; by 1920, the makeup of the ghetto was overwhelmingly laborer. The first, 1924 directory of the Detroit black community identified only 35 physicians, 24 dentists, 24 lawyers, 26 nurses, 15 pharmacists, 29 public school teachers, and 8 policemen, of an estimated black population of at least 65,000!

Black Bottom would be the core of Detroit's continuously growing black community for decades to come, as southern migration resumed with a fury after the Great Depression ended. Detroit's black population grew only 2 percent from 1930 to 1940. Then, in an eerie replay from a quarter-century earlier, war-induced labor demands led to the Second Great Migration. Between 1940 and 1950, the region's black population more than doubled, from 171,000 to 358,000. This second migration wave did not cease for three decades. Through both migration and fertility, Greater Detroit's black population rose another 201,000 during the 1950s, 198,000 during the 1960s, and 125,000 during the 1970s.

Though housing and health conditions remained terrible in most of the Black Bottom through the 1950s, the area had achieved some regional cachet through its noted entertainment district along Hastings Street, called "Paradise Valley" by the late 1930s. There the Forest Club, Chesterfield Lounge, and Flame Bar hosted musicians such as Josephine Baker, Nat King Cole, Lionel Hampton, and Sarah Vaughn, who played before enthusiastic, multiracial audiences.

Physical expansion of the black community—north along the east side of Woodward, east into the quickly dissolving former German and Polish areas, and on the near west side along Tireman Avenue—permitted more spatial separation of its social classes. The burgeoning disposable income of black industrial laborers during World War II spawned a host of black-owned businesses in Black Bottom. As a herald of this new black middle class, the Cotillion Club opened in 1949. This social club for black male businessmen and professionals would become a major force in local politics. Its patrons engaged in many activities similar to the posh white clubs that excluded them, including a highly publicized debutant ball. Given the members' proclivity toward conspicuously elitist, bourgeoisie behaviors in general and their penchant for marrying fairer-skinned women in particular, the more proletarian segments of the black community called the Cotillion Club's members and pretenders "The E-lites" (pronounced EE-lights).

The Flavors of the Middle East

Though southern blacks remained the dominant in-migrant group for the mid-twentieth century, Greater Detroit also saw a notable flow from the Arab lands of the biblical Old Testament. First to arrive in substantial numbers around 1900 were Arabic-speaking Maronite Christians from Lebanon and Syria. Most settled on Detroit's near east side and worked in auto factories along Jefferson Avenue; later they were followed by Chaldeans, a Catholic ethnic group primarily from Iraq. While the original setting for surging 1960s and 1970s Chaldean immigration centered on a stretch of Seven Mile Road between John R Street and Woodward Avenue, most now live in Oakland County. Many Chaldean entrepreneurs filled gaps left by fleeing shopkeepers after the 1967 civil disturbances and still comprise a dominant force in small-scale Detroit retailing. Today, roughly a third of Greater Detroit's 300,000 Arab Americans claim Lebanese/Syrian ancestry and another third, Iraqi/Chaldean ancestry.

Muslim Arabs arrived in Detroit a few years after their Christian counterparts, primarily from Palestine/Jordan and Yemen. An often-told story claims that a chance meeting between Henry Ford and a Yemeni businessman set off a chain migration from Yemen to Ford's Highland Park factory during the 1920s. Now approximately 25,000 Greater Detroiters claim Palestinian/Jordanian heritage, and another 15,000 have Yemeni heritage.

People of Arab descent today provide a remarkable flavor to Greater Detroit that distinguishes it from other U.S. regions. The Chaldean Catholic Diocese of America estimates that there are about seven times more local Chaldeans in Detroit than in the rest of the U.S. combined. Greater Detroit's Arab Americans comprise the biggest metropolitan concentration outside the Middle East, except for Paris! The single largest concentration is in Dearborn, where roughly one-third of the population claim Arab heritage. Warren Avenue, stretching from the western edge of Detroit well into Dearborn, is famed for its colorful collection of Arabic stores, restaurants, and entertainment venues.

Detroit gave me my first America.
19 years-old & scared I watched cars flow over John Lodge
Expressway
and decided that they followed a law The Law of Cars
by which blue cars follow blue cars and red cars red cars and
    so on—
I stood over the bridge there that cold March evening of 1966
in my emigrant green thin nylon Romanian coat
& shivered watching the car river
wondering why I had come
who I was
was I always going to be this skinny
was I ever going to get laid?

. . . relentlessly nervously walked
without peace over the big boulevards and into strange
neighborhoods
& past the burnt shells of factories
looking for the center of the city
wondering where the center of the city should be
because I could not imagine a city without a center—
that was inconceivable to me—
a center where everyone met, talked & maybe found love—

& when I asked people pointed me to shopping centers
and malls and central offices
& more shopping centers
& there was no sign of people meeting & talking in one place
No sign of love—

—"Detroit Love Song" by Andrei Codrescu

New Immigrants, New Gateways

Old Testament lands were not the only sources of significant postwar immigration, however. Only eight residents born in Mexico were counted in the 1900 Detroit census. By 1920, several thousand Mexicans had moved into many neighborhoods of the near east side, Corktown, and southwest Detroit and Dearborn, many moving from their prior work in Michigan's sugar beet fields. During and after World War II, Mexican immigration intensified so much that Mexicans constituted a majority population in several neighborhoods by 1980. This area, centered on the commercial strip along Vernor Avenue in southwest Detroit, became known as "Mexicantown." In the 1990s, Mexicantown expanded to encompass fifteen census tracts stretching from Corktown on the east to the city limits on the west, from the river on the south to Michigan Avenue on the north. It was the only area in Detroit to register population increases during the decade. Many of its residents now attend the Spanish-language masses at St. Anne's Catholic Church, the same parish served by Father Gabriel Richard three centuries earlier.

Southeast and South Asia has also been an important source of recent immigration into Greater Detroit. Since 1990, the region's Asian population—primarily Bangladeshi, Chinese, Indian, Japanese, Korean, Pakistani, and Vietnamese—has more than doubled, to 120,000. No clearer symbolic evidence of a group's arrival is a visible presence on Belle Isle, one of the city's prismatic place icons. So, now throughout the summer, there are Asian festivals, and one can find several cricket matches in progress on any given Sunday morning.

To a remarkable degree, newer immigrants have by and large bypassed the City of Detroit as a regional gateway. Middle Eastern Muslims and most Asian groups have moved from abroad directly to suburban Detroit, though most Mexicans, Chaldeans, and Bangladeshis have not. This geographic

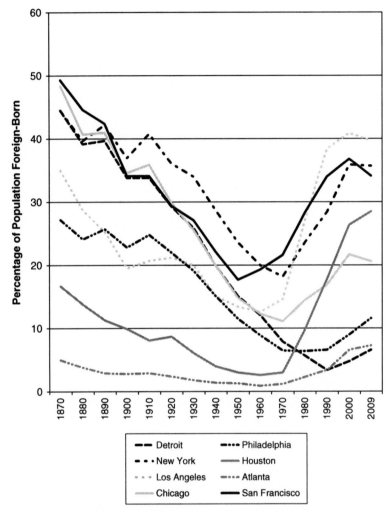

Figure 13. Percentage of population that is foreign-born, City of Detroit and selected cities, 1870–2009.

pattern is as unusual as it is significant for Detroit's fortunes. As Figure 13 shows, toward the end of the nineteenth century Detroit had one of the highest percentages of foreign-born populations in the nation. In 1870, San Francisco had the highest at 49 percent; Chicago had 48 percent; and Detroit had 45 percent, the same as New York City! Over the next few decades,

San Francisco and Chicago's percentages fell to match those in Detroit closely, while New York City's surged to the highest in the nation, a position it held until 1960. The shares of foreign-born residents in most U.S. cities continued to decline steadily from 1870 until 1960 or 1970, when substantial new immigration pushed their figures upward again. This occurred early and dramatically in San Francisco and Los Angeles and later but noticeably in Chicago and Philadelphia. Even cities that previously had a historically low foreign-born percentage, like Houston and Atlanta, saw their rates shoot up after 1970. Not so the City of Detroit; it finally saw its first miniscule increase—1.4 percentage points—in the foreign-born population from 1990 to 2000, and by 2009 another 1.8 percentage points. But by this point, every other major city surpassed Detroit, typically by a whopping margin, even those that historically had lagged far behind Detroit's immigrant character. Compared to the rest of 2009 metropolitan America's 12.5 percent foreign-born rate, the City of Detroit's puny 6.6 percent figure shows that it failed to make itself a sufficiently attractive port of entry for the world's immigrants, to its serious detriment.

The Face(s) of Detroit: Ironic Visage

Today the faces of Greater Detroit reflect centuries of immigration from the Old World, the Old South, the Old Testament lands, and more recently from Mexico and Asia. Yet behind this superficial diversity lies a distinctively simple but powerful demographic pattern. Greater Detroit's residential composition is overwhelmingly white (68 percent) and U.S.-born (91 percent), disproportionately so compared to the U.S. overall. And if one is not white in Greater Detroit, one probably is black. The region's share of blacks (23 percent) is almost double the national average. By contrast, the region's shares of Hispanics (4 percent) and Asians (3 percent) are only one-fourth and three-fourths of their respective national averages (see Figure 14).

Thus, in Greater Detroit to an exceptional degree, the demographic story can be simply portrayed in black and white terms. While acknowledging the diversity of national origins of the European immigrant streams and the inevitable intergroup tensions this mixture engendered, these divisions were substantially erased in the aftermath of World War II under the amalgamating banner of whiteness. Few contemporary immigrant groups wield sizable power in any parts of the region. The notable exceptions are Dearborn's

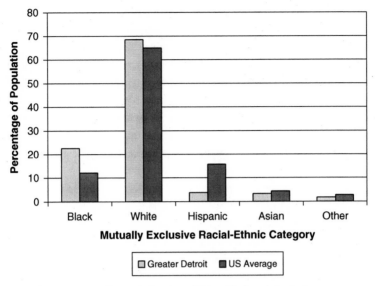

Figure 14. Percentages of population in self-identified racial-ethnic groups, Greater Detroit and U.S., 2009.

aforementioned Middle Eastern-origin groups, though they often divide politically on the bases of national origin and religion. Hispanic immigrants, though spatially concentrated now in Detroit's southwest sectors, are effectively disempowered by the at-large electoral system of the city. Throughout the last century, the primary poles of demographic diversity and accompanying power struggles have remained black and white. Why is this?

Following World War I and the 1921 and 1924 immigration acts, Greater Detroit's source for labor switched drastically from Europe to the American South, at exactly the moment when its demand for labor was one of the nation's highest. Consequently, many white and black southerners (more of the latter) moved to Detroit in unprecedented numbers, this movement peaking during World War II. This big switch in the source of labor coinciding with a peak labor demand proved ironic in multiple ways.

This changed nature of immigration to Detroit meant that "Old World" prejudices about ethnicity were overlaid by even-more intractable "New World" prejudices about race. While the South had by this time reestablished a rigid social order of racial inequality and segregation through "Jim Crow" laws, in Detroit the ground of neighborhoods, schools, and factory floors was up for grabs. Racial struggles over various turfs would prove violent and still remain largely unresolved.

Add to this the ironies of historical timing. The first wave of post-World War I racial turmoil was still cresting when it crashed on the economic insecurity of the Great Depression. The troubled waters were further roiled by the violent 1930s labor-capital strife that often took advantage of and intensified racial enmities as a weapon in the class struggle. Just as this was being sorted out came another major upset in social order—World War II—when a new immigrant tsunami from the South broke over the city, flooding the streets with hatred.

Greater Detroit's newest immigrants, from the Middle East, Mexico, and Asia, have made innumerable positive contributions to the region's culture and economy. With a few notable exceptions, they have also ruptured the traditional immigrant geographic pattern of using the central city as their entry point, instead moving directly to the suburbs from abroad. They have, thus, unwittingly intensified the core's abandonment and further pried apart the city–suburb gaps that are a regional hallmark. Nevertheless, compared to the rest of America, postwar immigrants have had numerically a much less significant influence on Greater Detroit. The region's foreign-born population is 30 percent smaller than the nation's overall. It is ironic that a place built on international immigration from 1701 through the turn of the twentieth century has had comparatively little since the 1920s. How new immigrants will respond to, and further shape, Greater Detroit's ironic demographic legacies remains to be seen.

Chapter 5

Who Will Feast on the Fruits of Labor?

They have taken untold millions that they never toiled to earn,
But without our brain and muscle not a single wheel can turn,
We can break their haughty power, gain our freedom when we learn
That the union makes us strong.
Solidarity Forever!
—"Solidarity Forever," anthem of the U.S. union movement
written by Ralph Chaplin in 1915; sung to the tune
"Battle Hymn of the Republic"

The stage that is Greater Detroit's featureless plain has now been set. The antagonists have taken their places: the capitalists and the laborers of different racial backgrounds. How will the plot play out? In Greater Detroit, the story line developed historically through two closely intertwined subplots of conflict, one involving organized labor versus capital, the other black versus white.

Many axes of tension have undoubtedly characterized Greater Detroit during its history. Examples include national origin, religion, and income. Yet I would argue that the dual dialectics of the capital-labor struggle and the black-white struggle shaped what Greater Detroit has become, and constrains what it might become, far more than any others. The rest of this book aims to build this case.

The drama of capital and organized labor in Greater Detroit played out in four main acts. The first occurred from the dawn of the city's industrialization into the 1920s, taking the guise of episodic advances and retreats in craft unionism. The second act consisted of pitched battles between industry-wide unions and the auto companies in the 1930s. The third involved 1950s and 1960s cooperation between these forces and mutual (albeit fleeting) prosperity. The last act, since 1970 still painfully limping toward a finale at a workplace nearby, entails the progressive evisceration of the industrial unions and their capitalist antagonists alike.

The common thread running through these four acts has been that the labor-capital dialogues typically do not involve polite discussions. They've been naked tests of power, raw and often violent. These acts have usually produced winners and losers: sometimes two losers, never two winners. This style of zero-sum economic play continues to dominate the region's psyche and polity to this day.

It did not take industrial Detroit long to demonstrate its penchant for acting out labor-capital disputes in irresolutely antagonistic and public ways. The so-called "Trolley Riot" of 1891 proved the perfect prologue. The Detroit City Railway Company was a private enterprise with a monopoly over public streetcar transportation provision in the city. Its horse-drawn trolleys daily shuffled tens of thousands about along rails embedded in the city's main thoroughfares. But, like most monopolies, the Detroit City Railway Company was big on greed and small on service. Unlike as in most major U.S. cities, already turning to electric powered streetcars, the company resolutely stuck to the "tried and true." Unfortunately, this meant customers had to pay five cents for the privilege of riding trolleys insulated with foul straw that the gas-powered lamp dangling precariously from the ceiling could combust at any moment. Although the vehicles' pace was leisurely at best, riders were compensated by ample opportunities to sample the delicate and ever-changing aromas of horse manure that mounded the rights-of-way. The men who operated the trolleys were paid the princely sum of eighteen cents per day (and all the fertilizer they cared to shovel and cart home).

When workers had the temerity to form a union, the Detroit City Railway Company fired twelve of the leaders. The resulting strike threatened to bring commerce to a halt, so the firm brought in strikebreakers; the city's police force escorted them through picket lines of angry trolley drivers. But, in a remarkable display of public-union solidarity, crowds soon gathered at major intersections to support the strikers and to blockade the scab-operated trolleys with toppled lampposts, trees, and ripped-up tracks. The crowds even managed to "capture" one trolley and push it into the river.

Despite his capitalist background and prior opposition to the Knights of Labor organizing his shoe factory, Mayor Hazen Pingree was forced to side with the strikers. He even threatened to join the crowds if the company did not capitulate, which it quickly did. Despite losing this battle, however, the Detroit City Railway Company continued to win the war in the City Council, persisting as a profitable monopoly until 1922 when municipal ownership of the trolley service finally became a reality.

The Double-Edged Sword

Establishing the first permanent local trade union in 1853 (Local 18 of the National Typographical Union) opened the capital-labor conflict in Detroit. It is no accident that this organization united workers with a particular and rare skill. Such early craft unions were able to organize effectively despite employer and governmental hostility because skilled tradesmen possessed two powerful attributes: there were few in number and seemed unlikely to be replaced by scabs or machines. To preserve their own elite status, the craft unions excluded unskilled workers. This would be one of many decisions by Greater Detroit economic and political institutions to enhance their own constituency's prospects and security by degrading those of other groups.

But a recession can weaken even highly skilled workers' positions. So the national economic calamites that peaked in 1877 brought an end to most of Detroit's craft unions. From the ashes arose a new breed of union seeking to organize both skilled and unskilled workers and to establish cooperative enterprises that employed them both: the Knights of Labor. In Detroit, the union created cooperative shoe-, barrel-, and iron-making enterprises, and its membership grew from 1,500 in 1880 to 13,000 in 1886. That year the Knights staged their first nationwide strike for an eight-hour day with no decrease in pay, with some 6,000 Detroit members winning such concessions. September 9, 1886, became a de facto "labor day" in Detroit, as 10,000 unionists marched instead of showing up for work, unfurling banners claiming "Divided We Can Beg; United We Can Demand." Political blunders, factionalism, and the rise of a competitor, the American Federation of Labor, subsequently siphoned off the Knights' radicals and craft workers. The union disappeared from Detroit by 1892, heralding a return to skilled-unskilled worker divisions that would persist for over four decades.

The skilled craftsmen thrived for a while as the city's industrialization proceeded apace, and the auto industry emerged at the dawn of the twentieth century. Even without formal contracts with firms, the Machinists Union gained the power to set wages de facto by dictating "price lists" for specific jobs and codifying the detailed steps needed to accomplish them. These work rules eliminated "rate busters" who might work too quickly, excluded those without requisite skills who might try to cut corners, and sucked power from bosses who might demand productivity improvements. Firms were forced to follow these dictates; no skilled strikebreakers were likely to be found in booming Detroit. Thus, even at notoriously antiunion Henry Ford's second, Piquette Avenue, factory these work rules empowered craft union members because they still had to piece together, file, and fit engines and transmissions. Each individual auto machine was a work of handicraft art.

Ford would soon find a way to end all that. The deskilling of craft labor started in earnest when Ford's Highland Park plant assembly line opened in 1914. This division of labor effectively slipped a noose around the neck of craft union power, and by the end of the 1920s, such organizations had gasped their last breath. Division of labor meant deskilling labor, and deskilled labor was more vulnerable to automation.

Though the curtain was drawn on craft unionism, the technological weapon that capital had wielded to such devastating effect has continued to be used to attempt to weaken the power of subsequent strains of organized labor. Automating engine block production at Ford's River Rouge complex, so evocatively portrayed by Diego Rivera's 1933 mural, proved in hindsight to be fairly low-tech. In 1951 Ford moved engine block production to an "automated" factory in suburban Cleveland. There, a new series of innovations cut labor requirements 90 percent and resulted in 20,000 layoffs at the Rouge. Auto industry-wide, output per worker hour doubled in 1950–1970, even before the widespread application of robotics in the late 1970s. In 1950, automakers employed 26 white-collar workers for every 100 blue-collar workers; by 1990 this ratio had been altered by automation to 63 per 100.

Ironically, the technological sword used to decapitate craft labor proved double-edged for the capitalists. Now each small task formerly performed by a small group of workers became an essential constituent of the entire, complex chain of production, often spread across many factories. A work stoppage by a small cadre of workers could bring the entire gigantic manufacturing machine to a halt. Detroit unions would soon learn how to use this edge of the sword to slash back at the companies, with powerful and permanently scarring effects.

> Our rights to determine production schedules, to set work standards, and to discipline workers were all suddenly called into question [by the 1937 Flint sit-down strike].
>
> —Alfred P. Sloan, chairman of the Board of
> General Motors, 1937

> We'll never recognize the United Automobile Workers Union or any other union.
>
> —Henry Ford, 1937

> We'll make Dearborn a part of the United States just as we made Flint a part of the United States.
>
> —Walter Reuther, 1937

Watershed, 1937

The struggles in the second act in the Detroit capital-labor drama are epitomized by the climatic events in one watershed year: 1937. It was one of those magical moments in history when the old social order seemed malleable; everyone realized it and clamored to take a crack at being a sculptor.

All the requisite legislative and political underpinnings were in place. In June 1933, President Franklin D. Roosevelt had signed the National Industrial Recovery Act (NIRA), with section 7(a) guaranteeing workers the right to organize and bargain collectively. Though the U.S. Supreme Court subsequently struck down NIRA in its entirety in May 1935, the National Labor Relations ("Wagner") Act of 1935 restored labor's rights to organize collectively. In 1936, FDR was resoundingly reelected, as were a clutch of pro-New Deal governors throughout industrial heartland. Closer to home, Frank Murphy, Detroit's prolabor mayor, had been elected Michigan governor. Surely, he would be more reluctant than his Republican predecessors to call out the National Guard to break up strikes, a prediction that would prove true within a few months.

The requisite union leadership experience in organizing, striking, and wringing concessions from recalcitrant auto companies was also in place.

Equally vital, unions had learned to wield the double-edged sword to devastating effect through a sit-down strike. First used in Detroit in November 1936 against the auto-frame maker Midland Steel, the sit-down completely upset traditional strike dynamics. Before, strikers would array themselves around the struck facility and vainly attempt to stop strikebreakers who, typically escorted by the police, would break through the picket lines and easily resume production. With the advent of the sit-down, workers would barricade themselves in the factory, securing the idle machinery in relative comfort and security, while the frustrated police milled outside in the weather.

In December 1936, Walter Reuther, the idealistic, avowedly socialist, twenty-nine-year-old head of tiny UAW Local 174, used the sit-down to make a name for himself and the union. His target was Kelsey-Hayes Wheel Company, a key Ford supplier of wheels and brake drums. Though only 35 unionists were employed among 5,000 Kelsey employees, one of them was Walter's brother Victor. Together they organized a sit-down strike that paralyzed both Kelsey-Hayes and Ford production. Caught between pressures by Governor Murphy and Henry Ford to recognize the UAW and settle the strike and unable to secure police assistance routing the strikers from the factory from a politically intimidated Detroit mayor Frank Couzens, Kelsey Hayes eventually capitulated. Within ten days the membership of UAW Local 174 had jumped to 3,000 and the union leadership was emboldened to take on the Big Three directly.

It occurred sooner than they planned, early in 1937. On December 30, 1936, a few activists struck the General Motors Fisher body plant in Flint to protest unjustified firings. Caught off guard but sensing an opportunity, national UAW president Homer Martin and CIO president John L. Lewis rushed to organize sit-downs at Flint's more strategic Fisher No. 1 plant, which supplied bodies to Chevrolet and Buick. Though exhausted from the Kelsey-Hayes battle, Reuther repeated this tactic at Detroit's Fleetwood and Cadillac factories on January 8. GM and its allies in Flint's city government counterattacked at Fisher No. 1 with a tear gas assault by police, which was repelled by strikers throwing a hail of metal hinges from the plant roof. The defense was directed and energized by the inexhaustible exhortations of Victor Reuther in the UAW sound car—an event that would become enshrined in labor lore as "The Battle of the Running Bulls." GM's fate was sealed when Governor Murphy threw the weight of the National Guard behind the strikers, forming a cordon around the plant to insulate the strikers from the police. On February 11, GM agreed to the UAW as sole bargaining agent. The mightiest corporation in the world had been defeated, and the workers proudly marched out of Fisher No. 1 singing "Solidarity Forever." They had gained a visceral understanding of the verse:

When the workers' inspiration through the workers' blood shall
      run,
There can be no power greater anywhere beneath the sun.
Yet what force on earth is weaker than the feeble strength of one?
But the union makes us strong.

The parading Fisher No. 1 workers carried placards reading "Make Detroit a Union Town!" They soon got their wish. Within the next month, 35,000 workers struck all over Detroit, the closest to a general strike the city would ever witness. Sit-down strikes took place in four downtown hotels, three department stores, nine lumberyards, ten meatpacking plants, all the major cigar factories, and scores of smaller stores, laundries, and restaurants. Five trucking firms went on strike, often organized by a young Jimmy Hoffa. Over two dozen auto parts manufacturers were shuttered by strikes, as was Hudson Motor Car Company.

Every Chrysler Corporation local plant was struck, but most conflict focused on the massive Dodge Main complex. A week after the sit-down began, its prospect for success was dimmed by a circuit court-ordered injunction issued, prophetically, on the Ides of March. Defying superstition and Shakespearian precedence, but in an eerie recapitulation of medieval battle styles, workers assembled tons of metal parts on the factory roof to drop on the expected invaders. The justness of their cause and feistiness of their banners ("Give Us Liberty or Give Us Death" and "Injunctions Don't Build Automobiles") so inspired Detroiters that they formed a human wall around the factory complex's entire 1.9-mile perimeter, and 100,000 rallied downtown at Woodward Avenue and Cadillac Square in support. The politics of the situation was going badly for the company, and Walter Chrysler ended the strike in April by recognizing the UAW as sole representative of his workers. This particularly delighted two Douglas Frasers: Senior, the UAW Shop Committee Chairman at Chrysler's DeSoto Motors; and Junior, an apprentice metal finisher at Dodge Main who, exactly forty years later, would become UAW president.

Though things seemingly could not possibly get better for the labor movement, they did. In April 1937, the Supreme Court upheld the National

Labor Relations Act. Detroit workers were starting to get the idea that their time had come at last, through collective bargaining. A barometer of the times, Reuther's UAW Local 174 skyrocketed from 78 members in September 1936 to 35,000 by the end of 1937.

Only one major auto producer resisted all organizing efforts: the Ford Motor Company. All the union still needed was an outrage committed by Ford that would turn public opinion decisively against it. They got it on May 27, 1937. Emboldened by recent successes, Walter Reuther and three UAW associates sought to exercise their rights under the NLRA and distribute UAW recruiting literature to workers at the River Rouge plant. As they walked across the bridge over Miller Road heading into the Rouge (see Figure 6), they were confronted and severely beaten by the company's "Service Department" toughs under the command of Harry Bennett. Graphically recorded by photographers on the scene, Ford's brutality against unarmed men seeking to exercise their rights proved decisive UAW propaganda. The main casualties of what would long be known as "The Battle of the Overpass" were not bloodied Walter Reuther and his colleagues but Henry Ford and his presumption of moral superiority to the godless, socialist-infected union movement. It would take until 1941, and further fierce struggles for the final Big Three domino to fall, but the irresistible force had been applied in 1937.

> I was Edsel Ford when I was alive,
> Henry Ford's only—acknowledged—child:
> That day in the car, with the reporter, and Mr. Bennett,
> (God, what a mess the War was, poor Mr. Roosevelt, so frail)
> Father, of course, too, Mr. Bennett driving and the man asked,
>> the reporter I mean,
> Who it was Father admired the most of all the men he'd never met,
>> and he said,
>> That man right there.
> And the reporter looked at me expecting me to—what?
> Beam pleasure, I suppose. But I knew better.
> Him, I mean, Father said (he enjoyed this), hooking his thumb in
>> Mr. Bennett's
>> direction.
> At the wheel. That man right there.

(That little man, head of the Service Department—Father named it—with his

 thug operatives, and his secrets, and his guns, the only man I hated, truly

 hated. Father knew. I think Harry Bennett wanted to kill Mr. Reuther at

 the overpass that day. There were others too. Other men had died.)

It was an awkward moment, then, the poor man, the reporter, not knowing

 what to do

 With his eyes.

But I knew. I'd done it before.

Lots of times.

     —"The Passion of Edsel Ford" by Jerry Herron

* * *

Their father George Jacob may have blundered in 1903 by not investing in Henry Ford's new enterprise, but the four brother-owners of Acme Wire and Iron Works would not make the same mistake twice. Whenever one of Ford's plants solicited bids for wire work, the firm responded. In 1935, they finally succeeded, led by co-owner George Jacob II's older son Marvin. At twenty-eight, Marvin had scoped out a massive Acme proposal, and was awarded a contract for all Ford's woven wire factory window guards. These would be installed by Acme just in time for rocks to be thrown at them during UAW organizing efforts a few years later.

Marvin's younger brother George Milton worked on another Rouge contract during summer 1937. His job was to render Diego Rivera's 1932–33 fresco historically inaccurate, though undoubtedly he did not realize it at the time. *Detroit Industry* portrayed a conveyor line snaking its dangling load of auto component parts dangerously above the heads of workers. It did not portray the all-too-frequent accidents involving these parts falling from the conveyor onto the workers' unsuspecting and soon-to-be-unconscious craniums. Acme's contract called for installing wire mesh screens under the conveyor line to "head off" such eventualities. This installation required that sixteen-year-old George Milton work on a high ladder, exposing him to approving gazes (and sometimes pinches) of passing female Ford workers. Whether George Milton viewed this as a fringe benefit or work hazard is unclear.

Because he was the co-owner's son, George Milton had no sympathy for unions and probably viewed with disdain the rash of sit-down strikes infecting Detroit. Perhaps he even secretly admired Henry Ford's ability to hold off the unions. On his ladder, George Milton likely paid no heed to the young black labor organizer working below him on the Rouge shop floor in 1937. Even if someone had mentioned his name to George Milton, why would "Coleman Young" have rung a bell?

> My first memories are of walking a picket line.
> Somewhere I sit on the steps of a downtown building.
> I am very small.
> We are singing Solidarity Forever. My mother
> keeps me away from angels and Madonna pictures
> and fears the nun's fervor in my eyes.
> She is not Catholic.
> Her big dare was to cross a picket line,
> drop, secretly,
> a stink bomb, perfect and round,
> crushing in its paper bag.
> The department store crowd
> scattered and screamed
> and she loved angels but thought
> she was one.
> She talked about freedom and dignity;
> I saw solitary riverside
> where I turned myself into a mermaid.
> My mother sang, "Just like a tree a-standing by the water,
> we shall not be moved."
> We were serious in those days.
> She took me to see the Diego Rivera mural at the art museum,
> car-factory workers full of sweat and muscle strain.
> She said rich didn't believe
> working people worked that hard.

I look at the angel pictures.
We both mean it.

—"Serious Childhood" by Judith Roche

Capital Fights Back

Though 1937 produced an unprecedented array of union victories, Detroit's capitalists viewed this as a temporary setback in a longer-term struggle. Capital surely used a technological sword to disempower labor, although this cut both ways. But automakers did not stop at technology. They used a vast arsenal of subtle and blunt weapons—including racism, violence, and local government power—to maintain control over the workplace and the profits it generated. The problem was that its continued use of this weaponry had unintended and long-lasting side effects for the region that still adversely affect both labor and capital.

Racism existed before the Big Three. But the auto companies shamelessly played the race card when it suited their purposes, and it always seemed to. They understood that it was tougher for a racially fragmented, mutually suspicious workforce to sing "Solidarity Forever" on key and in unison.

Henry Ford undoubtedly wielded the race weapon most comprehensively and insidiously. As part of his 1914-era "Americanization" project to teach white European immigrants to assimilate, the civics text used in his classes was blatantly racist, reflecting Ford's beliefs in racial hierarchy and the propriety of segregation. The 1917 *Ford Guide* noted that "yellow races . . . have been called half-civilized because they have not got ahead as well as white people. . . . [Blacks] came from Africa where they lived like other animals in the jungle. White men brought them to America and made them civilized." No wonder there was tacit, if not rousing, approval among white workers when Detroit employers segregated factory lunchrooms, toilets, and social activities beginning with the Great Migration.

Ford assiduously cultivated some leading black ministers, contributing money to their powerful churches and, in turn, soliciting their help in recruiting "respectable" (docile, loyal) black workers. Ironically, this effort began in 1919 with the Rev. Robert Bradby, pastor of Second Baptist Church, the same congregation that a century earlier was famed as the terminus of the Underground Railroad. Now it and a few other black churches would become the terminus of the overground railroad from the South, effectively the gatekeepers of opportunity. For his part, Ford delivered an unprecedented number of (least-desirable, segregated) industrial jobs to Detroit's black community—by the mid-1920s, roughly a tenth of Ford's workforce was black. What he got in return was fealty to Henry Ford and the Republican agenda. Ford's paternalistic system was called by B. J. Widick "plantation politics," and it would impede the development of independent black politics for decades to come. So powerful was Ford's grip on Detroit's black community that the local NAACP and Urban League, departing from their organizations' national stances, remained vigorously anti-union through the 1930s. Bethel African Methodist Episcopal Church was forced to cancel a scheduled appearance of nationally known black unionist A. Philip Randolph because Ford threatened to fire congregants he employed. It took the persistence of the Great Depression to start swinging blacks in Detroit toward the union cause. One of the first cracks in black solidarity was wedged open in 1936 by the Detroit chapter of the National Negro Congress; one of its noted activists was Coleman Young. Yet, even up to the ultimately successful 1940–41 UAW organizing effort at Ford, a coalition of black ministers advocated the company position, touting Henry Ford as "the Negroes' friend."

Ford's patronage secured not only black political support but also their muscle and blood. As early as January in the watershed year of 1937, Ford's Service Department began recruiting brawny "loyal" black employees at the Rouge, arming them with blackjacks for the upcoming struggles. It was an interracial group of Ford Service Department thugs who would participate in the Battle of the Overpass four months later. After a general strike to secure union recognition was called for 50,000 Rouge workers in April 1941, the Service Department hired 2,000 black strikebreakers and ordered them to attack the picketers arrayed on Miller Road. A group of 800 blacks assaulted the UAW lines three times on April 3. Though ultimately repelled, they left an indelible mark of distrust among the union faithful. Ford's heavy-handed playing of the race card backfired politically, however, as both the Detroit Urban League and NAACP switched support from the company to the union. Deep racial rifts in the psyche of Detroit's working class remained, however, exposing fault lines. With the UAW firmly in place by 1941 representing both white and black workers, Henry Ford clearly had no further use for his cynical, self-serving black paternalism. He ceased financial support for the City of Inkster and for black ministers in Detroit and began aggressively discriminating against new black job applicants. During the wartime production escalation in the second half of 1942, the number of white employees at Ford grew by over 30,000, while the number of black employees actually declined.

Companies' use of violence in the war against labor did not always have a racial flavor. Long before race was used as a proletarian wedge, employers' private police (often working with city police and even state troops) were used to quell labor rallies, protests, and strike actions. The situation was so dire in the early days of Detroit union organizing that, in December 1885, the budding Knights of Labor organized its own self-defense force armed with Winchester rifles, "The Detroit Rifles." Danger did not end when union organizing activities intensified in the 1930s. An aura of workplace suspicion, intimidation, and physical threat prevailed. GM employed fourteen detective agencies to spy on union organizers. Chrysler had forty professional labor spies infiltrate the workforce and compile lists of stealth union members.

Yet the Big Three prize for violence again goes to Ford Motor Company. Henry Ford hired disreputable Harry Bennett, who built his plant security force on a core of 800 former boxers, ruffians, and gangsters recruited heavily from Michigan's prisons. Their intentions were obvious in the murderous treatment of unemployed "hunger marchers" at the Rouge gates in March 1932 and in their brutalizing of UAW organizers at the Battle of the Overpass four years later. The hubris of the Service Department was highlighted on April 9, 1938, when one member and another tough tried to kidnap Walter Reuther at gunpoint from his home; they were thwarted by Reuther brothers Victor and Roy and other UAW associates. By 1940 the Service Department had grown to 3,000 men with a vast arsenal of clubs, handguns, rifles, and tear gas. The physically failing Henry Ford had given Bennett so much power that he arguably was the dictator behind the throne in a fascist industrial ministate. Within Ford plants, fear reigned: there were spies and stool pigeons everywhere; discovered union sympathizers were beaten and then fired, notwithstanding NLRA rules. According to a 1939 NLRB report, "The River Rouge plant has taken on many aspects of a community in which martial law has been declared and in which a huge military organization . . . has been superimposed upon regular civil authorities."

But workplace violence could not match the sheer ferocity of the battles associated with the wave of 1930s' strikes. Thirteen workers were wounded by police gunfire, and countless more beaten, during three 1937 attempts to break into barricaded sit-downers inside the GM Fisher No. 1 plant. Scores of Rouge strikers in 1941—one of them future U.S. Representative John

Conyers—were seriously injured by the strikebreakers' assaults with five-inch tie rods and heavy steel pipes. Of course, workers did not respond to such attacks nonviolently in the style of Gandhi. When Detroit police on horseback charged the picket line at the Federal Screw strike in March 1938, the well-prepared marchers removed the placards from their supports, revealing heavy clubs that were brandished with devastating effect on the cops' kneecaps. The UAW even organized its own mobile paramilitary brigades, known as the "Flying Squadrons," as a rapid-response counterforce to anti-union violence.

Though it is difficult to verify direct links to major companies, Detroit unions also had to battle with shadowy forces that served big capital's interests. The most infamous was the Black Legion, a vigilante group formed in 1933 by white male Protestants fond of wearing black robes, masks, and pirate hats emblazoned with skulls and crossbones, long after Halloween. Their avowed aim was to exterminate "anarchists, communists, and Roman Catholics," meaning a hearty slice of the union leadership. Well-publicized Detroit trials in 1936 and 1937 not only convicted many Black Legion members of murdering several unionists but revealed the dominance of their membership by foremen and police. Walter Reuther himself was ambushed by an assailant firing a shotgun into his home in 1948; his brother Victor met the same fate thirteen months later. Both would survive but were maimed. Thirty-nine sticks of dynamite were discovered outside UAW headquarters in 1949. Had not a heavy rain defused the bomb, it likely would have finished the gunmen's job.

The final weapon capitalists used effectively to fight labor was local government. Greater Detroit's local governments have bent to the will of capital in many ways. Under the banners of professionalism and efficiency replacing corruption and machine politics, big business promoted a "reformed" system of municipal government. This was institutionalized in Detroit's 1918 City Charter amendments, which called for at-large City Council elections and concentrating strong powers in the mayor. Incidentally, these reforms also made it easier for business to control the levers of local government. It was symbolically fitting that the first mayor elected under this system, James Couzens, was a former Ford Motor Company vice president. Substantively, the power of corporate interests in Detroit politics was never clearer than during the fall 1937 election. Having won a string of major organizing victories that year in many industrial sectors, unions tried to consolidate their political momentum by running a union slate for Detroit mayor and City Council, including Walter Reuther himself. The *Detroit Free Press* called the slate "The Five Conspirators . . . radical socialists . . . advocates of the sit-down strike." Republican mayoral candidate Richard Reading added a dose of red-baiting hysteria, and Father Coughlin denounced "the tyranny of labor government" on his weekly radio broadcasts. The union slate won no council seats and lost the mayor's race by over 100,000 votes.

Nowhere was the corporate influence over local government so comprehensive as in Dearborn. Ford Motor Company often used Dearborn police to defend the Rouge facility, sometimes with the deadly consequences of the 1932 hunger marcher murders. So complete was Ford's control that no police officers or Service Department employees were charged with crimes in the aftermath. Ford convinced Dearborn to outlaw the distribution of pamphlets on Company property, a legal pretext for the bloody repression of First Amendment rights at the Battle of the Overpass.

> Walter Reuther is the most dangerous man in Detroit because no one is more skillful in bringing about the revolution without seeming to disturb the existing forms of society.
> —George Romney, president of American Motors, future governor of Michigan, U.S. Secretary of Housing and Urban Development, and father of Mitt Romney, 1945

> Man, instead of being the end, becomes the mere means—a tool of production [in the auto industry]. . . . He is a cost to be eliminated the moment there is no need for his services. [The UAW's proposal for a guaranteed annual wage is, therefore,] a demand for a proper scale of moral values which puts people above property, men above machines.
> —Walter Reuther, 1955

The Treaty of Detroit and the Era of Comfortable Cooperation

It is one thing to gain the ability to organize collectively and quite another to know how to exercise the power when it comes. Because strikes were illegal while wages and prices were set by federal boards during World War II, Detroit unions had to wait until the war was over to flex their new muscles.

They wasted little time. Why should they? In 1945, an amazing 60 percent of Detroit adults either belonged to a union or were related to someone who did, compared to 31 percent nationally.

Soon after the war ended in September 1945, the UAW under Reuther's leadership targeted GM for a strike. They made three key demands: a 30 percent wage increase, ability to inspect GM's accounting records, and no offsetting increase in car prices during the length of the contract. GM's haughty response prompted a strike that started on November 21 and lasted 113 days. Arguably it was the first high-profile strike since the 1870 cycle for which unions could legitimately say they were fighting for mainstream America, not just narrow self-interest. The UAW wanted to extract profits from the GM oligopolist and its shareholders, not simply have the wage hike passed on to consumers through higher prices, leaving profits intact. This intriguing notion misfired because other major industries like steel struck at the same time but settled for much less than Reuther was asking. The UAW was eventually forced to accept only a modest raise, with neither financial transparency nor a limit of auto price increases. Soon after contract signing, wartime price controls ended, and consumer prices shot up 14 percent, wiping out the autoworkers' gains. Despite this hollow victory, Walter Reuther was elected national UAW president in 1946.

The next rounds of GM contract negotiations in 1948 and 1950 proved dramatically more successful for the union and established the foundation of what would become a middle-class standard of living for the unionized working person in Detroit and, indeed, in America. Burned by inability to negotiate wages that kept pace with inflation in the 1945 contract, the 1948 GM contract institutionalized a cost-of-living adjustment (COLA) clause that automatically raised UAW members' wages if prices rose by more than a specified amount. To ensure that productivity gains were shared with workers, the contract called for a 2 percent across-the-board "annual improvement factor" (AIF) wage increase. The 1950 contract moved to a five-year term, with more generous COLA and AIF provisions that effectively produced a 20 percent raise over five years. It also established a company-funded pension of $125 per month, and a new health insurance plan financed evenly between the company and the worker. In contrast to contracts hammered out only after protracted strikes at Ford and Chrysler the prior year, the 1950 GM negotiations were concluded quickly, in virtual secrecy. The seeming lack of contention and the benefits to both sides were so obvious that *Fortune* hailed the deal as the "Treaty of Detroit."

When Chrysler later would balk at following the bargaining pattern set at GM, UAW went on a 104-day strike. Chrysler lost a billion dollars in sales and lost its momentum in catching Ford as the number two automaker. After this, Chrysler, GM and Ford followed the UAW-set pattern at whatever Big Three firm the union chose as the "strike target" that bargaining year. This pattern quickly spread to much of the U.S. heavy industry that was unionized. By the early 1960s, the COLA principle had been incorporated into half of all union contracts, and one-third of the entire American workforce had some sort of corporate-funded pension coverage. Detroit-style unionization proved the path breaker throughout the economy.

Though a few 1950s and 1960s strikes occurred in the auto industry, a new era of cooperation had clearly dawned. The auto companies knew full well how much a strike could hurt them. They also knew how immensely profitable they were, so there was little resistance to what they might perceive as overly generous concessions to unions. Using violence and racism as anti-labor weapons also waned, though more subtle weapons would soon emerge.

Nevertheless, the postwar decades were clearly a period when Detroit's union workers finally secured a reasonable share of the economic pie. In the first decades following World War II, the auto industry was the nation's wealthiest, and the UAW made sure autoworkers received a goodly chunk of this wealth. By 1955, UAW wages of $98 per week were 31 percent higher than the U.S. manufacturing average, a 40 percent gain in real purchasing power since 1945. Between 1947 and 1960, average auto industry wages nearly doubled. What's more, these phenomenal wages were part of a larger compensation package that included company-financed pensions, medical insurance plans, sick pay, life insurance and disability insurance coverage, paid vacations, and emergency funds to be tapped in extended layoff periods to provide 95 percent of income for up to 52 weeks of unemployment. Unsurprisingly, the statistics for Greater Detroit during this era suggested nothing less than a "working-class paradise," with one of the highest home ownership rates in the nation, appropriate to union members' high wages and benefits. This unbridled prosperity and security would last less than a generation.

The Final Act

The final act in Greater Detroit's labor-capital saga began in the mid-1970s and continues to today. The curtain opened with the gasoline shortages spurred by the OPEC oil embargo of 1973. It revealed that Americans would buy fewer cars—especially big cars—during an extended period of "stagflation," and that the cars they bought would no longer solely originate in Detroit. Imported cars' share of the U.S. market jumped from 15 percent in 1971 to 20 percent in 1975 to 30 percent by 1980.

Detroit's automakers struggled throughout the 1970s to catch up in fuel efficiency, manufacturing efficiencies, and quality control. They were dealt another blow by again-rising gasoline prices triggered by the Iraq-Iran war and the Iranian revolution. The first of the Big Three to falter was Chrysler, which lost $1 billion in 1979. In an eerie *déjà vu* episode, UAW president Douglas Fraser had to find a way for employees to rescue the same firm he worked for in 1938, which then had been spared UAW's full might by Walter Reuther's successfully arguing against pressing Chrysler too hard to prevent bankruptcy. Fraser's solution: union contract concessions averaging $15,000 per worker over three years, in exchange for "profit sharing" and some job security for the most senior workers. The term "givebacks" was coined, and has been furiously minted ever since. UAW flexibility helped convince Congress to approve a loan guarantee package that secured Chrysler's future, at least for the next thirty years. The company promptly cut half its workforce, despite the givebacks. These tactics were soon mimicked at GM and Ford, to such an extent that labor costs dropped $1 to 2 billion at each company over the next two-and-one-half years.

Ronald Reagan's 1980 election may have meant "morning for America," but it meant "lights out" for Detroit. Restrictive monetary policies drove the economy into a sharp depression, and Republican-dominated congressional welfare and other social service cuts left gaping holes for unemployed workers to fall through to their impoverishment. It became known locally as the "Second Great Depression." In December 1982, Mayor Coleman Young called it "the winter of crisis."

Detroit-area factories produced fewer vehicles in 1980 than they had in twenty years. The ripple effects across the region were like tsunamis. About 130,000 blue-collar jobs in the auto, steel, trucking, and construction sectors disappeared. Those laid off were sometimes able to find local work in service and clerical positions, but at one-third the pay and with few, if any, benefits. The UAW lost 125,000 members between 1979 and 1983, 40 percent of its metrowide membership. But official statistics portray only the tip of the iceberg of desperation. On a cold, rainy Thanksgiving morning in 1982, an estimated ten thousand needy people waited patiently in line outside

Solomon's Temple Church in northwest Detroit to receive a free basket of food. In the prior few years, hundreds of autoworkers had scraped together enough to purchase new cars, heeding their companies' increasingly desperate pleas to "buy what you build." Perversely, these wheeled assets later rendered them ineligible to receive welfare benefits when their unemployment benefits expired.

Despite their success in extracting givebacks, the auto companies dusted off and updated an old weapon in their ongoing fight with labor: relocation of production. GM was the first of the Big Three to discover the benefits of scattering production facilities across the country. Unlike Ford and Chrysler, with their dominant Rouge and Dodge Main facilities, as early as the mid-1930s, GM sought redundancy by building factories elsewhere to make it tougher for a single strike to cripple the entire organization. In 1938 alone, in response to the famous 1937 sit-down strike, GM built five new plants, all far from quickly unionizing southeast Michigan. The largest was near union-free Los Angeles, built to assemble Buicks, Oldsmobiles, and Pontiacs. This trend continued through the 1970s, when GM built fourteen plants in southern "open shop" states that did not require workers to belong to unions in particular establishments. Other automakers followed suit; between 1950 and 1970, Greater Detroit's share of national auto employment dropped from 35 to 20 percent.

Of course, the UAW countered these gambits. The successful 1979 UAW strike forced all Big Three plants to be covered by the same contract, regardless of their U.S. location. So, this time the Big Three shifted production internationally. With falling international shipping costs, the international wage differentials appeared irresistible. In the early 1980s, Japanese autoworkers earned only two-thirds what UAW members did, Mexican autoworkers only one-third, Korean autoworkers less than a fifth. And these wage differentials did not count the vacation, pension, and health insurance benefits won through UAW negotiations. Outsourcing auto parts production proceeded especially quickly. Within 25 years, 77 local Delphi factories were reduced to 27, and only 19 of the 120 Visteon factories (GM and Ford spin-off parts suppliers), remained in the U.S.

At the same time that General Motors was busily developing production facilities as far as possible from Detroit and its unions, it was also experimenting with a new form of Detroit political gamesmanship that played off nervous autoworkers and the city government against working-class neighborhoods. It began in 1980, when GM announced it would close two venerable Cadillac plants on Detroit's southeast side. The company also hinted that it had a prototype Cadillac factory it was going to build, perhaps in Oklahoma, but GM was uncertain. It would not rule out Detroit "if an appropriate site could be found" for the gigantic, single-story facility surrounded by acres of parking lots. This announcement set Mayor Coleman Young's and Governor William Milliken's economic development minions scurrying about to find potential 500-acre sites within the city, as Wilbur Rich documented. None were shovel-ready, but there was one possibility. The site of the abandoned Dodge Main plant adjacent to Hamtramck could provide much of the needed acreage, but some of the surrounding multiracial neighborhood—known as Poletown—would also need to be demolished.

The Byzantine, high-decibel political shenanigans that transpired over the next year would make even the most jaded Detroiter take notice. The saga is replete with charges of "undue pressure" articulated by firebrand attorney and City Councilor Ken Cockrel, Sr., community protests and lawsuits by the Poletown Neighborhood Council, candlelight vigils in the Catholic church slated for destruction, and consumer advocate Ralph Nader gratuitously appearing to support the neighborhood and vilify GM and its lackey "Mayor Marauder" Young, who responded in kind and with more effect ("Nader the Carpetbagger"). Swirling amid the rhetorical din were a host of crucial public policy questions. Should a financially strapped city be forced to negotiate terms of a deal with the most powerful company in the world? Is it fair for the city to acquire private property involuntarily for the benefit of a private interest? Does a stable, racially diverse neighborhood have any rights to self-preservation? Is sustaining employment a compelling public interest justifying the abrogation of due process rights?

When the rhetoric died and ground was finally broken for the "Central Industrial Project" on May 2, 1981, these facts were clear. In a 5-4 vote on March 14, the Michigan Supreme Court upheld the city's position that job preservation was an appropriate use of eminent domain powers, a national precedent-setting position that held sway for thirty-five years. Approximately 4,000 residents, 150 businesses, a hospital, and several churches were displaced; compensation for property and relocation costs was paid by the city. Land acquisition, relocation, demolition, and site preparation cost Detroit $200 million. To cover the bill, the city diverted $130 million of Community Development Block Grant funds from current and future neighborhood revitalization projects, cashed in a $30 million federal Urban Development Action Grant, and encumbered future property tax revenues from the site. The city granted GM a twelve-year, 50 percent property tax abatement estimated at $120 million. In return, Detroit got $6.8 million for the land from GM after the city cleared and prepared it with new utilities; it also got about $10 million in annual property taxes (twice that when the abatement expired), and 1.5–3 percent income taxes paid by plant workers. It also got GM's projected average 3,000 jobs at the new plant, a far cry from the 10,000 provided by the two older plants being consolidated. "What's Good for GM . . ." has had a distinctly hollow ring in Detroit after the Poletown project.

*   *   *

In 1980 Marvin was hoping beyond hope that General Motors would build its new Cadillac factory in or around Detroit because it would be a potential gold mine for Acme Wire and Iron Works. A huge plant needed lots of tool cribs, room separators, window and machine guards, and innumerable other woven wire fabrications. A long time had elapsed since anything of this scale had been done in Detroit, and Acme was feeling the pinch. Though no fan of Coleman Young, Marvin breathed a sigh of relief when the Central Industrial Project was finalized. Too bad the project was going to slice up an area of the city he had frequented as a young man. But this was progress and the city desperately needed that plant! Acme desperately needed the work.

Winning a contract for the Cadillac plant's wirework was not a sure thing, however. But Marvin mustered all his skill and over half a century of company experience to develop what proved a winning bid, just as he had in 1935 at Ford's Rouge facility. Marvin retired from Acme soon thereafter. His gift to himself was a career book-ended by helping equip both one of the first great auto factories in Greater Detroit and one of the last.

*   *   *

The last act of Greater Detroit's labor-capital strife had one more scene filled with economic gains for both parties—the late 1990s during the SUV/minivan craze—but that proved only a minor tangent. Since then, the region has been mired in the "Third Great Depression," which knocked the Big Three onto the ropes and organized labor and working people it represents unconscious.

From 1990 to 2000, Detroit labor got its last, ephemeral taste of the sweet fruit of success. Inflation-adjusted average household income in the City of Detroit grew by 18 percent, to $46,000. Three years later, it slipped below 1990 standards and has been falling ever since. Since 2005 the city's official unemployment rate has remained above 25 percent and the poverty rate above 33 percent.

Even if a worker still has a union job in Greater Detroit, it likely no longer provides an expressway to the middle class. The financial travails of the Big Three auto firms and their suppliers sparked a wildfire of union concessions that drastically reduced workers' standards of living. Often, bankrupt firms have used bankruptcy court judges to obtain concessions that otherwise could not have been gotten through collective bargaining. Delphi, the giant parts manufacturer GM spun off as a separate entity, declared bankruptcy in 2006 and demanded jaw-dropping wage cuts of over 50 percent. When the UAW balked at renegotiating its existing contract, Delphi successfully petitioned the bankruptcy court to throw out the contract. Deep wage cuts at Visteon, the parts supplier spin-off from Ford, followed a similar pattern. UAW impotence was never more apparent than in the case of Detroit-based American Axle, the last major parts supplier to pay wages over $20 an hour to assembly line workers. Though profitable, American Axle intransigently proposed significant wage concessions in its 2007 contract negotiations. Despite a lengthy and venomous UAW strike, the contract ratified in 2008 called for wage cuts of up to $10 per hour for many workers.

UAW President Ron Gettelfinger (2000–2010) agreed for first time to a two-tier wage system distinguishing incoming and veteran workers in 2007 Big Three contract talks. The Big Three then bought out over 100,000 seasoned employees nationwide who earned over $20 per hour; the few who were hired as replacements earned considerably less and with fewer benefits. A significant if unheralded change, this acknowledged the demise of a powerful union company industrial structure that had produced middle-class wages for workers with modest educational credentials since the close of World War II. But it was not the last concession that would shake the foundations of industrial unionism.

The UAW had not agreed to a major wage giveback in the middle of a contract since the 1979 Chrysler bailout. Despite incessant pressures from major auto parts suppliers beginning in 2005, the union resisted, fearing this would set a precedent for givebacks to the Big Three themselves. Yet, in December 2008, the UAW relented and agreed to adjust 2007 contracts to help the automakers appeal to Congress for bailout funds. In February 2009, the UAW modified its 2007 Ford contract to save the company $500 million. In summer 2009, it was forced into even deeper concessions to Chrysler and GM as part of these firms' bankruptcy proceedings, including a six-year pay freeze for entry-level employees, a no-strike clause until 2015, and reduced numbers of job classifications; similar terms were extended to Ford in October.

The emasculation of the once-mighty UAW is now virtually complete. In 2009, its membership stood at (or, more accurately, was beaten down to) 392,000. At the end of World War II, there were over a million UAW members; at its peak in 1979, membership stood almost four times higher than today, over 1.5 million.

> These murals would have existed here,
> In Detroit, even if Diego had never painted
> Them. The sweat and the labor of this city,
> Along with the sacrificed blood
> Of its workers, would have stained
> These walls. No matter what.
>
> Not here! The politics of Detroit
> Go beyond arguing fresco vs. classic,
> Or any something vs. anything. Here we deal
> In a culture of collective energies,
> Beating union heart. Here, its always
> Work—Not talk. We know that
> Talk is cheap, but work is
> Forever. We know
> That building is more
> Essential to our survival than politics
> Is to our reality.
>
> —"Save the Frescoes That Are Us" by M. L. Liebler

Did Labor Unions Win Too Much in Detroit?

Some believe that labor unions in general, and the UAW in particular, are responsible for the fall of America's once-great industries because they financially crippled them in the competition with lean, union-free foreign companies. UAW critics point to an array of statistics indicating the extra expenses that its contracts created for auto firms. It is widely accepted that worker benefits, pensions, and health care insurance costs added $1,300–1,500 in costs for a Big Three vehicle, at least before the latest round of concessions. By contrast, comparable items cost Toyota $210 per vehicle built in the U.S. and $97 per vehicle built in Japan. Union-negotiated work rules and job classifications undoubtedly boosted costs as well. An oft-repeated illustration is found in a Chrysler "hazing ritual" for newly hired engineers. The boss hands the victim a piece of hard rubber sandwiched between a metal plate on one side and a wooden board on the other. The new engineer must get a hole drilled through it. But no worker in the plant will do it because this chore does not fit the contractual job description of either union woodworkers or metalworkers. Eventually, the new engineer returns to the boss, frustrated but wiser.

Unions needed to walk a fine line: protect against employer exploitation or protect worker incompetence; advance labor's long-run interests by collectively bargaining for wages and benefits or retard labor's long-run interests by enshrining archaic, inflexible work rules and unproductive habits and rendering their host firms uncompetitive. Retrospectively, there is no doubt the unions have sometimes fallen off this tightrope. Yet it is disingenuous to suggest that unions are responsible for Detroit's downfall, and that of the Big Three, because they extorted an unfair share of the industry's profits. In the U.S. national motor vehicle industrial sector, output per hour worked rose 84 percent from 1987 to 2003, but the labor compensation (wages and benefits combined) rose only 43 percent over the same period. Even during the last period of industry profitability, employment has been steadily cut. In the ten auto industry profit boom years beginning in 1995, Greater Detroit's auto manufacturing employment declined over 21,000.

The primary failure of unions was not economic but political. As Thomas Sugrue argues, it was the postwar American failure of liberal-labor *national politics* that forced the UAW and other unions to resort to the second-best option of getting *companies* to pay for worker pensions, health care insurance, vacations, and other progressive social policies, instead of the nation *as a whole*. The right-wing U.S. political shift starting in 1946, and extending through the 1950s, put the brakes on any discussion of moving toward a national welfare state similar to those installed in Germany and Japan, our future major automotive rivals. Companies in such places need not worry about safety net benefit costs for their workers because they are covered by the state. Detroit prospered from this union-imposed "corporate welfare state" for only a single generation, when the Big Three held unquestioned dominance over the world's biggest car-consuming market. Perversely, such legacy costs accrued over a generation of collective bargaining eventually eroded the competitiveness of its home-grown industry. Thus, Greater Detroit's economic failure is fundamentally the American political economy's failure to institute a national social support system that might enhance the economic foundations of all U.S. industries in today's globalized competition.

The Metropolis of Dialectical Extremes

Greater Detroit is a place of dialectical extremes. It is a place where extreme capitalism was countered by extreme unionism, which in turn was countered by extreme racism, violence, automation, and relocation by the capitalists. The local unions and capitalists, in turn, were both countered by extreme competition from foreign capitalists. Detroit thus epitomizes the dialectic of conflict between countervailing forces armed with powers of shifting potency: mechanization, collectivization, decentralization, and globalization. The dehumanizing, undemocratic Fordist assembly line gave workers a motive to revolt. It also gave them a way to do so effectively: a strike by one key parts supplier, fomented by a radical minority, could halt an entire industry. As effective strikes and fat contracts took their toll, the Big Three reacted by replacing labor with machinery and moving to non-unionized parts of the U.S. and, eventually, overseas. But financial legacies of UAW concessions persisted long past the "fat days" when the Big Three was an oligopoly with little foreign competition. Because these legacy costs could not be outsourced or automated, in a regime of rampant global competition, they threaten to cut down the fruit tree that Greater Detroit's capital and labor have feasted on for generations.

This extreme dialectic between labor, local capital, and foreign capital has rendered Greater Detroit a place of promises made/promises broken. The working class flocked to Detroit in the twentieth century, believing in the promise of opportunity. After World War II, members of the UAW and the other Detroit industrial unions were "promised" a middle-class standard of living, a pension, and health insurance, with minimal education and less professionalism. Today, with all the bankruptcies, layoffs, contract givebacks, two-tier wage systems, and evaporating UAW membership, this promise has been resoundingly broken. In 2005, only 48 percent of all Greater Detroiters with less than a bachelor's degree held middle-class jobs; this put the metropolitan area in the bottom fifth nationally for access of the less-educated to jobs that provide a middle-class standard of living. It is thus not surprising that a Gallup-Healthways Well-Being Index released in March 2011 showed that the congressional district with the nation's lowest overall emotional and physical quality of life was located in Detroit.

"The Union Makes Us Strong! Solidarity Forever!" has morphed from a hallowed premise to a hollow promise. What happens to a metropolis when its citizenry believe they have been victimized by broken promises regarding how they earn their daily bread? How do they respond by this fundamental act of disrespect?

> Thank God
> there are still young men
> who wear biker jackets
> and straight-legged jeans
> and drag down Telegraph
> in the Base Line Eight
> in Motor City.
>
> Young men
> who still live at home
> or above funeral homes
> Delray-way or by the Bridge
> or in Lithuania-Town
> who work in tool-and-die
> or on the line
> for nine bucks an hour
> and fly at lunchtime
> on beer and the big H.
>
> Young men
> who still touch children
> and the right kind of women,
> who are healthy as cats
> and whose nails are dirty
> because they still know

how to fix their own cars,
whose hips are small
under rolled-up T-shirts
because they don't dine
on gourmet food and wine.

Young men
whose hair is still wild
in braids as long as Samson's
whose flaming beards
mark them metro prophets
who watch and wait
and gaze intensely
these thin young men
in Detroit City.

—"Motor City Men" by Christine Lahey

Chapter 6

Turf Wars

I have a dream this afternoon that one day right here in Detroit, Negroes will be able to buy a house or rent a house anywhere that their money will carry them.
>—Martin Luther King, Jr., in his original "I Have a Dream" speech, Cobo Hall, Detroit, June 23, 1963

People movin' out, People movin' in
Why, because of the color of their skin.
>—"Ball of Confusion (That's What the World Is Today)" sung by The Temptations, 1970

Lust for Land, the Preamble

Immediately on pulling his canoe ashore at the narrowest point of the Detroit River, Monsieur Cadillac established a precedent that would define this place for centuries to come: grab some land and then defend it to the death. The log stockade called Fort Pontchartrain du Détroit was not only a deterrent aimed at the British. It was a symbol of security seeking: others coveted the space a person occupied, so it needed protecting. Detroiters have been walling themselves off, literally and figuratively, from the feared "other" for three centuries since.

Intense competition over turf has been Detroit's hallmark from its inception. While the city was still in its infancy, Cadillac thought it a good idea to have more Native American groups encamped nearby, apparently believing this would expand the post's trading networks and make him a richer man. Unfortunately, having invited the Fox group from Wisconsin to resettle in Detroit, he paid scant attention to potential social tensions that might follow. Indeed, when over 1,000 Fox arrived at the gates of Fort Pontchartrain in the summer of 1711, the established Huron, Ottawa, and Potawatomi groups were not pleased. Cadillac had deftly departed for Louisiana by this time, leaving the new commander, Joseph Guyon du Buisson, to deal with the nasty little problem of allocating turf. As intergroup tensions mounted the next year, Commander Guyon du Buisson's imaginative response was to revoke Cadillac's invitation, apparently without offering complimentary vouchers to cover return transportation to Wisconsin. Understandably, the Fox responded by attacking the fort and laying siege for nineteen days. In a resolution suggestive of Detroit-style justice, the Fox were eventually slaughtered and driven off with the military aid of the Huron, Ottawa, and Potawatomi, who wanted their turf back. Only a hundred Fox made it back to Wisconsin. Detroit has had trouble attracting out-of-state tourists ever since.

This was hardly the only example of how lust for land dominated Detroit's formative days. In 1793, the new U.S. president, George Washington, sent peace emissaries to Native American groups in the Northwest Territories. Despite the end of Revolutionary War hostilities, the British still occupied most of the territory, including Detroit, and thwarted any U.S.-Native reconciliation efforts. In response, Washington sent troops under the direction of General Anthony Wayne, who defeated a combined British-Native force from Detroit on August 20, 1794, at the Battle of Fallen Timbers, just southwest of Toledo. Their military position now untenable, the British abandoned Detroit on July 11, 1796. Two days later, U.S. colonel John Hamtramck and 400 troops arrived, joined a month later by victory-flushed General Wayne. In 1868, Wayne would be posthumously honored for his heroism by attaching his name to a newly founded Detroit college. Detroit was finally under American control thirteen years after the Treaty of Paris ended the Revolutionary War, guaranteeing that future turf battles would be homegrown. And did they continue!

Understandably discontented with their lot in Canada, the British continued to covet the lush Michigan turf; and the War of 1812 gave them one last chance to attain this prize. They captured Detroit on August 16, 1812. But their hopes for an expanded Canada were dashed in September 1813, as a U.S. flotilla under Commodore Oliver Hazard Perry's command defeated the British fleet in Lake Erie, and U.S. troops recaptured Detroit under General (and future President) William Henry Harrison's command. A month later, Harrison appointed Lewis Cass both governor and military commander of Michigan Territory, a position he held until 1831. When Cass and his family arrived in Detroit on October 24, 1815, the town was awed by their opulent carriage. Thinking this inappropriate, Cass quickly sold it. Unfortunately, his rejection of ostentatious wheels set no precedent for future Detroit politicians; Mayor Kwame Kilpatrick's penchant for a publicly funded posse of Cadillac Escalades is the most recent egregious case.

Lust for land proved so strong in southeast Michigan that it even got in the way of statehood. In 1835 Michigan's admission to the Union was delayed (two years, it turned out) due to a border dispute with Ohio over a narrow strip of land from Lake Michigan to Lake Erie that included the town of Toledo. Feelings ran so high that Michigan sent militia to the disputed territory, but no casualties resulted. As it turned out, Michigan clearly had the issue resolved in its favor; it not only did not have to take Toledo, but got the entire Upper Peninsula as well!

Defending White Neighborhood Turf

The lust for land so evident in early Detroit proved a tepid foreshadowing of the rabid black-white turf wars that would characterize twentieth-century Detroit. This competition was distinguished by the remarkably comprehensive turf defense system whites erected and the viciousness by which its protagonists carried it out. Given the personal insecurity spawned by the auto industry's cyclical nature and the capitalists' racially inflammatory actions discussed earlier, both groups sought to reinforce identity and self-esteem through turf, to acquire or preserve status, power, and resources. This chapter shows how Detroit whites defended neighborhood and school turf against black encroachment.

Greater Detroit's white residents developed an intricate, mutually reinforcing, tripartite system to defend residential turf, involving the federal and local government, the real estate industry, and homeowners. The federal government provided a foundation for racial segregation through its mortgage market and public housing policies. Though nationwide, these policies took particularly pernicious forms in Greater Detroit, as David Freund demonstrated. For example, the federal Home Owners Loan Corporation

(HOLC) began in 1933, aiming to stabilize a faltering housing market by making long-term mortgages available to a million Americans—but it did so on a racial basis. Following long-held real estate biases, HOLC was concerned that home values in anything but an exclusively white residential neighborhood would decrease, thereby threatening the value of its loan collateral. So, the corporation mapped neighborhoods in each city and graded the "security" of properties in each: A, B, C, or D. In 1930s Detroit, about three-fourths of all neighborhoods fell into the first three categories, where federal lending was permitted. The mean number of blacks residing in the two top-graded Detroit neighborhoods was zero; in grade C neighborhoods, it was 0.3 percent. A 1939 HOLC survey of Detroit was not subtle in describing neighborhoods as having a "Negro concentration" or "developing as a Negro colony;" all such were given D ratings. Though HOLC ceased making loans in 1936, its practice of racially grading neighborhoods carried over to mortgage insurance programs instituted by the Federal Housing Administration in 1934 and, later, the Veteran's Administration. The insurance provided through these programs made it possible for private lenders to offer mortgages with low down payments and extended repayment terms at fixed interest rates, thus opening the door to homeownership for millions . . . as long as they were white. Because they continued to use the original HOLC neighborhood-grading scheme for decades, the FHA/VA programs focused private mortgage resources exclusively on white neighborhoods (either existing or to be developed). In a classic "catch-22," nonwhites need not apply for FHA/VA-backed mortgages because, by definition, any neighborhood they might buy into would be rendered ineligible by their action. By 1940 over 44,000 mortgages in metropolitan Detroit had been backed by FHA insurance; none were issued to blacks.

These federal mortgage market policies left Detroit an indelible marker. It is a six-foot-high, half-mile-long concrete wall that runs along the alley between Mendota and Birwood Streets, just south of Eight Mile Road (see Figure 15). As recounted by Thomas Sugrue, it was built in 1941 by a white real estate developer who wanted to build a new subdivision adjacent to the longstanding black subdivision located near the Eight Mile-Wyoming intersection. When the developer was initially told that his homes here would not qualify for FHA mortgage insurance as part of a racially mixed neighborhood, the solution was obvious. His wall would emphatically distinguish his intended white neighborhood from the existing black neighborhood. FHA mortgage insurance was then provided for his subdivision.

Figure 15. The Eight Mile-Wyoming wall.

Not only was the homeownership market infused with federal segregationist policies, so was public housing supplied to the needy. Detroit's turf
struggles over public housing are clearly revealed in the case of the Sojourner Truth Homes. Faced with a rapid expansion of defense production,
and an associated 1941 influx of southern black and white workers, federal
and local public housing officials faced a major dilemma. They needed to
keep workforce peace, yet shortages of decent housing for blacks were critical
precisely because there were so few options for them outside the desperately
overcrowded and unhealthy Black Bottom neighborhood. Their solution was
to build a modestly sized public housing complex in a Detroit neighborhood
of white homeowners just north of predominantly Polish-occupied Hamtramck. It would be named after the famous black abolitionist because black
Detroiters were to live there. There was a certain logic to this choice: Polish-
black relations up to this time had been tolerably friendly, and Conant Gardens, a pocket of black-owned businesses and homes, was located a few
blocks from the proposed site.

This "certain logic" evaporated instantly when the proposal was unveiled in June. Thomas Sugrue recounts that white homeowners protested through their newly formed "neighborhood improvement association" and, ironically but understandably, blacks from Conant Gardens objected to the "lower-class" influx into the area. The FHA advised that neighborhood mortgage money would disappear were the project to go forward, prompting the local congressional representative and the Detroit Housing Commission to withdraw their support, save for its one black member, Rev. Horace White. Federal housing authorities waffled, first approving the project for black occupancy in January 1942 but quickly reversing the decision. This prompted a huge outpouring from Detroit's black community, which formed the Sojourner Truth Citizens' Committee, whose efforts were soon supplemented by an interracial coalition of liberal Protestant churches, the UAW, and other unionists. Their effective lobbying and nightly picket lines in front of City Council and Housing Commission offices finally convinced Mayor Edward Jeffries, the Commission, and the Council to back black occupancy of the project. In light of this local endorsement, federal public housing officials personally told the large delegation of Sojourner Truth Citizens' Committee leaders who had traveled to Washington that, despite white protests, blacks would begin moving in February 28.

On February 27, the Ku Klux Klan organized a cross burning on the site of the project. The improvement association widely distributed an unambiguous flyer:

HELP THE WHITE PEOPLE
Keep this District White

- - - - -

MEN NEEDED
To Keep Our Lines Solid
Come to Nevada and Fenelon
Sunday and Monday

- - - - -

We Need Help
Don't be Yellow—Come Out
We Need Every WHITE MAN
We Want our Girls to Walk on the Street, Not Raped

The recruiting proved successful, as hundreds in a jeering white mob attacked the arriving black tenants the next morning, overturning their moving vans. The police responded by arresting the people moving in, while the crowd ransacked their scattered belongings. Responding to this outrage, hundreds of black youths arrived to battle whites and the police, prompting the Commission to again withdraw its support for black occupancy, arguing that this would foment a "race war." Mayor Jeffries, undoubtedly still sniffing the tear gas needed to disperse an unruly white mob outside his office, eventually backed away as well, blaming "extremists on both sides." Thanks to continuing pressure from the Sojourner Truth Citizens' Committee, the aggressive public support of national UAW president R. J. Thomas, and First Lady Eleanor Roosevelt's personal intervention with the president, Washington officials held firm. Black tenants began living in the project in April 1942.

This was an uncharacteristic conclusion to a Greater Detroit public housing controversy. The Federal Public Housing Authority made no secret of its policies to have one exclusive racial group occupy its developments, even when a preexisting neighborhood's interests were not involved. This became patently clear in 1942, when the public housing developed for war workers near Ford's new Willow Run B-24 bomber plant in suburban Ypsilanti was allocated to whites only. Black plant workers would be accommodated in other (farther away) developments to be built near black-occupied Inkster, despite protests of black leaders.

Local politicians in Greater Detroit soon learned it was dangerous to come down on the wrong side of the public housing issue. Some were slower learners than others, such as Detroit's incumbent Mayor Eugene van Antwerp. In 1949 he supported the progressive idea of building a dozen public housing complexes in the outlying areas of the city. He finished a weak third in that year's mayoral primary for his troubles.

Dearborn mayor Orville Hubbard, on the other hand, was a quick study, as extensively documented by David Freund. From the start, he adamantly opposed the Federal Public Housing Authority's 1944 proposal to build public housing for black workers near Ford's Rouge complex. Though the racism was thinly veiled indeed, official Dearborn rhetoric spoke of the need for "sound development practices" that would "protect property values" from "inharmonious land uses" and threats to "health, safety, and public welfare." Mayor Hubbard was a wizard at cloaking racism with the American flag. His draft resolution presented to the City Council to protest the proposed public housing flourished a states-rights rhetoric that would have made any Jim

Crow southerner proud. Among the rationales he provided were the following:

> Whereas [the FPHA's actions] will be a direct interference with and an invasion of the right of the City of Dearborn . . . to determine its housing needs; . . . Whereas the war is being fought to maintain and continue our American Way of Life and we want to keep Dearborn a desirable place in which to live; . . . Whereas we have the right and want to choose our own neighbors . . . and resent being forced to accept the dictates of some bureaucrat in Washington that we must accept a federal housing project for Negroes when we refuse to build a like project for our own race.

Mayor Hubbard later revealed his deeper concerns when he spoke darkly of "The Negro Housing Project" bringing to Dearborn "racial differences where there now are none," and warning about white homeowner resentment that might spawn "bad riots," as they had with the Sojourner Truth Homes two years earlier. The electorate must have shared these concerns because they reelected him time and time again.

Local governments in Greater Detroit, on behalf of their white citizens, employed several techniques to maintain the color line, including zoning, occupancy restrictions, and harassment. Local zoning codes were often used as subtle but effective weapons in interracial turf wars. A case in point was the Schoolcraft Gardens Housing Cooperative, a nonprofit organization that wanted to buy land in western Detroit to provide decent, affordable, nonsegregated housing. The Cooperative started in 1947 when group of families bought a 70-acre plot at the northwest corner of Schoolcraft and Lamphere; they planned to build a rowhouse subdivision with 400 to 500 homes, including playgrounds, a shopping center, and a community center. A Detroit City Council committee studied the proposal and recommended the site in question be rezoned from R-1 to R-2 to permit the desired plan. Work progressed until the Tel-Craft Association, a nearby Telegraph and Schoolcraft Road homeowners' group, petitioned the Council to return the zoning to R-1. The City Planning Commission initially denied the petition, as did the entire Council. But a week later, a month-long series of local newspaper articles (*Redford Record* and *Brightmoor Journal*) began alleging the "socialist" Co-op was stirring up conflict with its proposals for "unrestricted racial housing" and "bi-racial housing." One story suggested that the site was chosen for being on the route between Detroit and a new horse race track in Livonia, implying a scandalous brew of gambling and misogyny would soon infect the area. The City Council, having been bombarded with letters from Tel-Craft supporters, held a second hearing within a month after the first. Three weeks later, the Co-op's first site plan for phase 1 was submitted for the required (albeit rubber stamped, typically) Council vote prior to granting the building permit. One councilman instead introduced a resolution to rezone the site back to R-1, and yet another public hearing was set for the next month. After that meeting, the Council narrowly voted to retain the R-2 zoning and grant the building permit. But in its divided state, the Council was unable to overturn Mayor Al Cobo's subsequent veto. The path-breaking cooperative project died, with the original investors losing substantial sums.

Even if proposed developments were not explicitly designed for nonwhite occupancy like the Schoolcraft Gardens Housing Cooperative, the vague threat that they could be proved sufficient for municipalities to block their construction. Again, Dearborn provides a transparent example. In 1948, the John Hancock Life Insurance Company proposed building a $25 million rental complex of 600 duplex units on Ford Motor Company land. The Springwells Park Development, described as a "garden community" and "model town-within-a-town," easily secured Dearborn Planning Commission approvals and seemed headed for quick City Council approval until Mayor Hubbard played the race card. Though vehemently denied by project officials, Hubbard asserted, in perhaps an intentional double entendre, that the development "would change the whole complexion of the population." Rents would be so low, the mayor argued, that while some residents "would be the kind of people we are eager to welcome, some people would not. Anybody can afford rentals." The Hancock proposal was put before a public referendum in November. On the day of the vote, Mayor Hubbard deployed city department heads and staff to polling places to distribute leaflets braying, "Keep Negroes Out of Dearborn! / Vote NO / Protect Your Home and Mine!" A 60 percent majority defeated the Hancock proposal.

Dearborn was hardly an isolated case of Greater Detroit suburbs blocking new developments they thought might crack open the door to racial integration. In a well-publicized and explicitly racist 1970 feud with the federal Department of Housing and Urban Development (HUD) and its secretary, George Romney, Warren voted to return already allocated urban renewal funds because they came with "fair housing" strings attached. In 1978, a federal judge ruled that Livonia could not spend $150,000 in HUD community development block grant funds because it had not complied with the federal fair housing requirements. In 1982 another federal judge ruled that Birmingham had refused a permit to build low-income housing because it did not want poor blacks living in the city. These cases represented only a few tips of the turf-defense iceberg; in 1975, the Detroit NAACP documented how twenty-six Detroit suburbs had filed federal grant applications, despite policies that revealed "systematic patterns of racism."

The most infamous example of defending turf through municipal occupancy controls was the Grosse Pointe "point" scheme (or, preferably, the Pointe scheme), as documented by Kathy Cosseboom. Private detectives working for the Grosse Pointe Real Estate Brokers and Grosse Pointe Property Owners Associations investigated all prospective homebuyers and filled out questionnaires that included the following items:

> If not American born, how long have the applicants lived in this
>   country?
> Is their way of living typically American?
> Are the husband's immediate associates typical?
> Are their friends predominantly typical?
> Appearances—swarthy, slightly swarthy, or not at all?
> Accents—pronounced, medium, slight, or not at all?
> What is the husband's position as distinguished from his
>   occupation?
> How does this position stand in the public's estimation?
> Dress—neat, sloppy, flashy, or conservative?
> Grammar—good, fair, or poor?

The maximum possible points (pointes?) on this questionnaire were 100; 50 were the minimum needed to gain entry into Grosse Pointe if you belonged to a preferred group. Those of Polish heritage needed at least 55 points; Greeks needed 65; Italians needed 75; Jews needed 85. No points were awarded blacks or Asians. When the Michigan attorney general exposed this scheme in 1960, a representative of the Grosse Pointe Real Estate Brokers Association publicly defended the point system, asserting that it kept up property values and 95 percent of residents supported it. Though this system did not prevent Grosse Pointe from becoming the well-known home of several Mafia bosses, it undoubtedly did command strong public support. Despite a noble, decade-long effort by a dedicated group of reformers to enact an open housing law, the ballot initiative was only brought to a vote in one of the five Grosse Pointe communities, Grosse Pointe Farms, in 1969. It was resoundingly defeated (59 percent majority) exactly one year after the federal Fair Housing Act was passed.

*   *   *

George Jacob, II, son of the Acme Wire and Iron Works founder, had done very well for himself during World War I and the ensuing "Roaring Twenties." So, in 1926, he packed up his wife Emma and their three children, Marvin, Ruth, and George Milton, and left the old Germantown house on Moran and Canfield, only a half block from his factory. His destination was a new brick, two-story home on Yorkshire Road in Grosse Pointe Park. Commuting to work and First English Lutheran Church was much farther now but was made bearable by his fine new automobile.

George Jacob's move was only a few miles away geographically but was psychologically worlds apart. Leaving the old German community meant a symbolic end of ethnicity. He would think of himself now as an American, a *white* American. And as a white American, he understood that *you are where you live.* In Detroit's old ethnic enclaves, people of all classes lived together because they shared some bond of national origin or religion. But in modern Detroit, space fractured along the fault lines of social status. Moving to Grosse Pointe symbolized that a person had "made it." George Jacob probably never realized that his future Polish-American neighbor next door needed to "make it" even bigger (that is, get more "pointes") for the privilege of living beside him.

Now that George Jacob and his other accomplished white neighbors had reached a place of prestige and privilege, its exclusive character had to be maintained at all costs. "After all, if some socially inferior *they* were able to be my neighbor, what would it signal about *my* social status?" they worried. This singular motive to preserve white status privilege by demarcating white-only turf was not a Grosse Pointe exclusive; it was a hallmark of white neighborhoods up and down Detroit's status hierarchy. Despite many differences, they could all agree on one thing: the inferior quality of their neighbors would be particularly fatal to their self-image built shakily on pretensions of prestige.

*   *   *

They can't get in here. We watch it. Every time we hear of a Negro moving in—for instance, we had one last year—we respond quicker than you do to a fire. That's generally known. It's known among our people and it's known among Negroes here.
—Dearborn Mayor Orville Hubbard, quoted in a 1956 Montgomery, Alabama, newspaper article, "Why No Negroes Live in Dearborn."

If zoning and occupancy restrictions proved unsuccessful in keeping blacks out or if blacks had already lived there a long time, municipalities always had one more weapon at their disposal: harassment. Ferndale, a suburb adjacent to Detroit along Eight Mile Road that we visited as we drove along the Woodward Avenue corridor, is an improbable but potent illustration. Today, "Fabulous Ferndale" is noted for its tolerance and diversity but not so seventy years ago, as David Freund showed. In the twentieth century's first decades, a white landowner named Henry Stevens made a tidy sum selling small, unimproved lots to blacks in the then-unincorporated territory that would become Ferndale. Even though far from anywhere and without public sewer, water, lighting or paved streets, at least this area was not defended by whites. By 1926, an estimated 4,000 blacks lived there in tents and informal, self-built dwellings. But by 1940, white-occupied neighborhoods sprang up nearby and dominated Ferndale's politics. Thus, the blacks had to be convinced to go, through concerted efforts of public and private intimidation. With the city's tacit support, the Ku Klux Klan burned a ten-foot cross in the yard of a black-owned home on March 9, 1940, while a mob pelted the house with rocks. When it soon became clear that not all blacks would be bullied out of Ferndale, a second-best strategy was adopted: ghettoize them in the original area sold off by Stevens. In July 1941, the city built an eight-foot-high, half-mile-long brick wall to divide the black and white sectors of town. The affront this represented to the sensibilities of civil libertarians was best expressed by the Rev. Horace White, a black state representative and member of the Detroit Housing Commission. "This is the only place in the world, except under Hitlerism, where groups are being segregated in a sort of ghetto," he lamented. During the following months, Ferndale's long-time black residents reported numerous acts of harassment by neighbors, the police, even the mail carriers (who requested moving their mailboxes out of the "n _ _ _ _ _ side of town"). The "wall of spite" (as some black Ferndale residents called it) and the quiet apartheid policy that it represented—punctuated by acts of blatant harassment—broadcast what whites wanted. These signals eventually took their toll. By 1950, only 178 blacks remained within the suburb of over 29,000 whites.

Local governments did not act alone in trying to hold the color line. Throughout the region, they were buttressed by a host of longstanding and codified real estate industry practices. Because whites constituted the vast majority of regional housing consumers, and whites did not care to live with blacks, the real estate industry concluded that only complete segregation would maintain white-owned home values. This was "confirmed" by independent real estate appraisers, who routinely downgraded property values in a neighborhood with even a single black family. The industry logic led to the inevitable conclusion that, as agents of home owners who must keep their financial interests paramount, it was their *professional duty* to maintain segregation. As enshrined in their Detroit association's written code of conduct since 1924, it was a breach of professional ethics "to introduce inharmonious elements" into a neighborhood. So a segregated real estate profession developed in Detroit and across the nation, with "realtors" serving the needs of those buying and selling homes in the white community and "realtists" doing the same in the black community. Black or white agents would "steer" their clients toward home listings in neighborhoods where the client's racial group predominated. Paradoxically, regardless of their race, agents could convince themselves that this was in their clients' best interests: whites did not care to live with blacks and could not get FHA/VA-backed mortgages if they did; blacks should not have to face the harassment in white neighborhoods and would not get FHA/VA-backed mortgages in any event.

If local governments and real estate agents couldn't protect their turf from "them," homeowners had still more weapons at their disposal. Restrictive covenants forbidding particular future uses or kinds of occupants were attached to property deeds and became a common practice in Greater Detroit in the early 1920s. Sensing whites' insecurities, developers led the way in using restrictive covenants as a marketing tool. A major developer crowed as it opened its new, deed-restricted west-side subdivision, "We have carefully restricted this section to include only the kind of people you would be glad to have next door." Until 1948, all new Detroit-area subdivisions were similarly restricted to Caucasians. The deeds precisely specified who such people were: those who had less than ⅛ Negro blood.

A close reading of some of the restrictive covenants reveals how white Detroiters equated racial minorities with other sorts of noxious land uses. A covenant filed by the Bonaparte Heights subdivision, for example, prohibited "the production or sale of spirituous or malt liquors" and the manufacture of soap, candles, glue, starch or gunpowder, tanneries, and slaughterhouses. At the end of this long list of undesirables, the covenant added, "nor shall any lot be occupied by a colored person."

In older neighborhoods, forming restrictive deed covenants was a bit trickier because a majority of property owners had to sign a covenant petition to the local government before it became binding. Homeowners Associations and Neighborhood Improvement Associations were often formed to organize the task of obtaining the requisite signatures, often aided by local real-estate agents who helpfully provided moral support and templates of model covenants. Once executed, these covenants had the force of law.

At least they did until 1948. In the mid-1940s the McGhee family purchased a home in northwest Detroit, unaware of the racially restrictive covenant attached to the property's deed. The neighbors sued to have the restriction enforced and the sale nullified. The legal struggle went all the way to the U.S. Supreme Court, where the case was bundled with a similar one involving the Shelley family in St. Louis. On May 3, 1948, the Court found in the case of *Shelley et ux. v. Kraemer et ux. McGhee et ux. v. Sipes et al.* that local governments could not enforce such racially restrictive covenants because doing so would violate the Fourteenth Amendment's equal protection clause. The McGhees' case was argued by Thurgood Marshall, who in 1954 would successfully argue the landmark *Brown v. Topeka Board of Education* school segregation case, and later become a Supreme Court justice. Paradoxically, the case revealed how pervasive racially restrictive covenants had become as a way to hold the color line. Three of the nine Supreme Court justices had to recuse themselves from the case because they owned homes with restrictive covenants! Ironically, one of the three was former Detroit mayor and Michigan governor Frank Murphy, who, as a trial judge in 1925, had come to prominence in another Detroit case involving the color line; the defendant was Ossian Sweet.

*   *   *

The sixteen years of marriage since their vows in First English Lutheran Church had proven happy ones for Helen and Bruno, despite their differing ethnic backgrounds. Their union had been blessed by the births of Karl, Louise, Robert, Helen, and Elizabeth. Bruno's Delicatessen Shop at 10 Broadway Market downtown distinguished itself by distributing folders "printed for the purpose of aiding the busy housewife in preparing quick meals and appetizing luncheons" using the store's products. It eventually became locally famous for its chicken pot pies. Indeed, business was so good that it allowed Bruno and Helen to buy a new house on Hurlbut Street, a few blocks north of Waterworks Park off Jefferson Avenue. This is where the family was gathered as usual for a weekday breakfast on September 10, 1925. Karl had already departed for Southeastern High School and the twins Bob and Louise were preparing their lunches under Mother's watchful eye before the short walk to Howe Elementary School. Betty, who had just turned three, and Helen, who would turn four in a month, chattered over their breakfast cereal. All were startled into silence by Bruno's sudden exclamation, "Gott im himmel!" All listened intently as he read from the front page of the *Detroit Free Press*:

ONE SLAIN AND ONE SHOT BY NEGROES
VICTIM'S WIFE IN COLLAPSE, IS NEAR DEATH
It was announced that Assistant Prosecutor Edward H. Kennedy, Jr. would recommend warrants charging murder against the 11 Negroes now under arrest in connection with the outbreak last night at 2905 Garland Avenue. . . . Shots poured without warning and seemingly without provocation last night at 8:30 o'clock from the second story windows of 2905 Garland Avenue, into which Dr. and Mrs. Ossian M. Sweet, a Negro couple, had moved Tuesday, cost one man's life, put another in the hospital with a bullet in his leg, and called out 200 heavily armed police reserves, detectives, and regular policemen

from every precinct, as well as an armored car. . . . In describing the shooting, [Police Inspector Norton] Schuknecht said there had been no demonstration previously.

In June, Bruno had heard rumors circulating about a "Negro" (his wife Helen would never permit the word n_ _ _ _ _ to be used in her presence) family buying a home on Garland, the next street over from Hurlbut. He was not inclined to believe these rumors because, if true, they would have been too unsettling. Most of his life's savings were tied up in his house, and he could not afford to lose them "because of some uppity n _ _ _ _ _ who didn't know his place." Daughter Helen seemed more interested in the rumor that this Negro family had a daughter about her age. Ever the gregarious child, Helen eagerly anticipated the arrival of any new playmate in the neighborhood. Even better, this new girl would be an *unusual* playmate, judging by the comments her father was making, only a few of which she understood.

Now the rumors had proven correct, and Bruno's mind was swirling. His first thought was of the good fortune that his impetuous son Karl was otherwise engaged in his weekly bowling league the night before and came home via Jefferson, instead of Charlevoix where the trouble was. Bruno could easily imagine the robust fifteen-year-old joining a crowd surrounding the Negro's house, as he fancied himself a macho stud. Next it crossed Bruno's mind that Howe Elementary School was diagonally across the street from where the trouble was. Surely, he said to his wife Helen, it would be for the best if the twins could stay home today. Finally, Bruno realized that one of his neighbors, Leon Breiner, was dead. As his anger rose, he wondered aloud what Breiner's widow and two children would do now. "But at least the filthy Negro murderers have been arrested," he concluded with conviction, adding silently, "and they won't be moving in here . . . or anywhere else for that matter."

*   *   *

Two days before this breakfast at Bruno and Helen's, Ossian and Gladys Sweet had finally decided to start moving into the tidy, two-story bungalow at 2905 Garland Avenue that they had purchased for cash in June. As explained

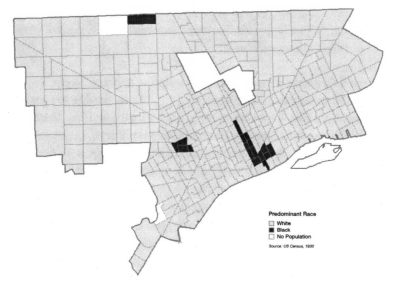

Figure 16. Black- and white-majority neighborhoods in the City of Detroit, 1930.
Ossian Sweet house marked by X. Map courtesy of Jason Booza.

by Kevin Boyle, the Sweet family was well aware that there might be trouble because they were moving three miles farther east than the accepted color line (see Figure 16). Indeed, that summer alone five other black families had purchased homes in the white east side, and all were greeted by angry mobs. It was, therefore, prudent for the Sweets to both leave their daughter, Iva, with Gladys' parents, and for Ossian's two brothers and four other male friends to accompany them to the house . . . along with firearms and ammunition.

Their worst fears were realized on their first night in their new home, when hundreds of whites hurled rocks and insults at the home. Urged on by the Waterworks Improvement Association, thousands gathered the second night and the home bombardment intensified, while 17 Detroit police watched impassively. One stone crashed through a window and struck Dr. Sweet. When his brother and another friend arrived at the home by taxi they were set upon by the mob amid shouts of "Get the n _ _ _ _ _!!" As the mob surged forward, Dr. Sweet's other brother fired two shots from the home's upper window; they struck one man across Garland in the leg and another man in the head. At this point, the police stormed the home and, meeting no resistance, arrested all the occupants and charged them with conspiracy to murder and assault with intent to kill.

The fledgling National Association for the Advancement of Colored People latched onto the Sweet case to set a clear legal precedent that defense of one's own home from a mob was justifiable self-defense, not murder. To argue its case, the NAACP hired the nation's most famous defense attorney, the Johnny Cochran of his day, if you will: Clarence Darrow. Darrow had burnished his reputation the prior July in his famously flamboyant, if ultimately unsuccessful, defense of Tennessee biology teacher John Scopes for teaching the theory of evolution, despite state laws to the contrary. Darrow, an incisive cross-examiner, exposed the blatantly fabricated and inconsistent testimonies of the white witnesses and police at the Garland Avenue scene, revealing their unbridled racial prejudices. Judge Frank Murphy had little choice but to declare a mistrial. He probably averted a conviction. Upon hearing the Judge's declaration, one juror blurted out, "I don't give a god damn what the facts are, a n _ _ _ _ _ has killed a white man and I'll be burned in hell before I will never vote to acquit a n _ _ _ _ _ who has killed a white man." In the subsequent retrial in Judge Murphy's court, only Dr. Sweet's brother who pulled the trigger was charged with murder. He was acquitted.

The case of the Sweet family was concluded. Yet it left unresolved the fundamental question of which "right" would take precedence in Detroit: blacks' rights to reside and own property wherever they wished or whites' right to live with whom they wanted and with their property values maintained. The white power structure of 1925 Detroit gave lip service to the former rights but de facto privileged the latter. Too little has changed in near-century since; turf still counts.

> When any person moves into a new neighborhood, it becomes by law the duty of the police agencies to protect that man or woman in his life and property. . . . But the duties which are ours legally, differ materially from what we, as sensible men, know are the causes which resulted in the recent murder, and which, if they are unchecked, may cause equally shameful incidents in Detroit's future history. In that connection I must say that I deprecate most strongly the moving of Negroes or other persons into districts in which they know their presence may cause riot or bloodshed. I express this personal feeling, which is perhaps beyond the proper province of an executive officer, sworn to enforce legal policies which are different, but I do it in the

hope that some official expression can prevent a recurrence of the tragedy of Wednesday evening. . . . It does not always do for any man to demand, to its fullest, the right which the law gives him. Sometimes by doing so he works irremediable harm to himself and his fellows. . . . I shall go further. I believe that any colored person who endangers life and property, simply to gratify his personal pride, is an enemy of his race as well as an incitant of riot and murder. . . . [Nevertheless], it lies with you [Police Commissioner Frank Croul] and members of your department to protect fully the life and property of all persons without regard to creed or color. And in addition to those laws, there are laws against inciting to riot.

—Detroit Mayor John W. Smith, in an open letter printed
in the *Detroit Free Press*, September 13, 1925

The weapon of racial harassment did not, of course, begin and end with the Ossian Sweet incident. Indeed, the geography of Greater Detroit's evolving color line might well be mapped by plotting the coordinates of hate crimes over time. In 1917, a black family starting to move into a Harper Avenue apartment, just north of Black Bottom, was met by two former city councilors leading a mob, which proceeded to load the family's possessions into trucks, take them back to Black Bottom, and dump them unceremoniously on the street. In 1956, a black secretary for the Royal Oak Township School Board was attacked in her home by three white men, who bound, gagged, and beat her; a death threat was left on her door the next night. In 1957, in northwest Detroit, a black divorcee was threatened by a mob of 300, and forced to sell the home she had bought to the local neighborhood improvement association. In 1961, a black family purchased a home in the "copper canyon" neighborhood on Detroit's far west side, so named for its large concentration of homes owned by police. The day before they were to move in, their furnace was tampered with and caused a major fire; two months later after repairs were made, the house was firebombed. In a less threatening but motivationally revealing incident, a black minister bought a home near Marygrove College in 1960 and received a hysterical call from a woman who said, "I cannot understand how in the world you can stand in the pulpit and preach about the love of Jesus and know what you are doing to our property values!"

The list of such incidents is, sadly, much longer than can be repeated here. But one more is noteworthy because it illustrates whites' blind fear and unquestioning, rabid commitment to turf defense. On Labor Day 1963, two black men and a pregnant black woman were spotted moving furniture into a Dearborn home owned and occupied by Giuseppe Stanzione. The rumor quickly spread that he had sold the place to these blacks, whereupon a mob of 600 descended on the home, throwing stones, bottles, and eggs and vandalizing Stanzione's car. The Dearborn police on hand—including the chief, deputy chief, and safety director—did nothing as the violence escalated, despite twenty calls from the terrified Stanzione inside. The furor abated only after Stanzione's attorney brandished a copy of the deed, proving that the home had not been sold. No, Stanzione had merely rented his house to a *white* man who, in turn, had contracted with two black men to move his furniture; one mover brought along his pregnant wife. *OOPS! Sorry! Never mind!* No, instead the response from politicians and citizens across Greater Detroit was a blizzard of letters and telegrams praising the vigilant citizens and government of Dearborn.

To be fair, parts of the white power structure in Detroit took courageous positions to further fair housing rights of black home-seekers. The former head of the Detroit Housing Commission during the Sojourner Truth Homes controversy, and from 1962 to 1964 Police Commissioner, George Edwards tried valiantly to nudge a recalcitrant police force to respect civil rights. Detroit City Councilor Mel Ravitz sponsored open housing legislation in 1963. Yet those focused on defending turf prevailed. Ravitz's proposal was defeated by a council vote of 7-2. As if to make their position even clearer, in 1964, the City Council passed a resolution giving homeowners the right to refuse to sell to anyone they wished, despite being warned by the City Attorney of its illegality. The unyielding prejudices of the police force would be exposed many times over the ensuing years.

Redrawing the Color Line

Holding the color line meant, of course, a "captive" market in the relatively few neighborhoods that black families could occupy. In turn, this meant that property owners in such districts could reap unconscionable profits while supplying overcrowded, undermaintained, unsanitary quarters. This set the stage for the incremental, spasmodic expansion of the color line into adjacent, previously white-occupied neighborhoods through a process of "blockbusting." Real estate agents (both black and white, and usually outside the orbit of their professional associations) would target a white neighborhood and employ racial scare tactics to frighten whites into selling quickly at deflated prices, "while your home is still worth *something*." Having completed the white panic sale, the blockbuster would then quickly negotiate a resale of the same property at an inflated price to a black buyer, desperate to escape the confines of Black Bottom. This sale further frightened white neighbors, and the contagion of panic spread until the neighborhood tipped exclusively to black residents.

This periodic but rapid reconstruction of the color line at the edge of existing black neighborhoods led to a remarkable and distinctive pattern of racial change in Detroit, as first documented by Robert Sinclair and Bryan Thompson. Figure 16 shows the racial geography of the City of Detroit in 1930, the earliest year for which census tract racial data are available. The tiny black enclaves in western Detroit along Tireman Avenue and at the aforementioned Eight Mile-Wyoming location are clearly visible. But the main black community was strung along Hasting Street in Black Bottom, just northeast of the downtown. Woodward Avenue formed its knife-edge, three-mile western border. In the next twenty years Detroit's black population doubled, and the color line was redrawn accordingly (see Figure 17). By 1950, blacks were allowed to settle a bit farther north and east than before, but the line at Woodward still held. Blacks were then a majority in the neighborhoods immediately north of Hamtramck where the Sojourner Truth Homes had been opened for black occupancy in 1942. By 1970, blacks and whites had achieved rough numerical parity in the city, and the color line was redrawn correspondingly (see Figure 18). The western wall of Woodward was breached just south of Highland Park, as black families spilled into the Dexter-Davison neighborhood once primarily occupied by Jews. Blacks constituted a majority through vast swaths of the near west side, all the way to Eight Mile Road, with Hamilton, Livernois, and Wyoming forming major north-south commercial spines of the rapidly expanding black community. The contiguous upper-income neighborhoods of Palmer Park, University District, Sherwood Forest, Green Acres, and Palmer Woods managed to secure the color line on their southern and western flanks at McNichols and Livernois Roads. Black settlement on the east now extended almost to the municipal line of Grosse Pointe Park. Viewed as time-lapse photography, the changes portrayed in Figures 16–18 must have represented the scariest sort of horror film to white homeowners, who could easily foresee a day when their neighborhood would be "engulfed." This either made them intensify their efforts to defend their turf or abandon the field and head for

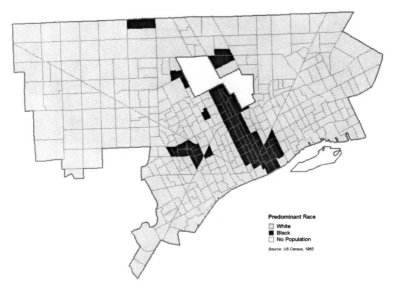

Figure 17. Black- and white-majority neighborhoods in the City of Detroit, 1950. Map courtesy of Jason Booza.

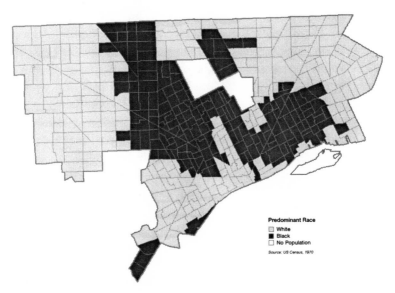

Figure 18. Black- and white-majority neighborhoods in the City of Detroit, 1970. Map courtesy of Jason Booza.

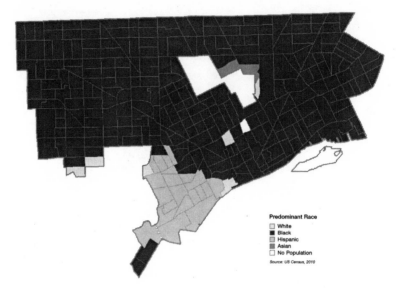

Figure 19. Black-, white-, Asian-, and Hispanic-majority neighborhoods in the City of Detroit, 2010. Map courtesy of Jason Booza.

greener (that is, whiter) pastures. The latter response increasingly predominated, as one by one the previously common turf defense weapons were ruled illegal. Detroit's black population grew only modestly in the next thirty years but came to predominate in virtually all the city's neighborhoods as whites fled *en masse*. The lopsided racial geography by 2010 appears in Figure 19. Non-Hispanic whites remained a majority in only six neighborhoods, one being the Midtown area around Wayne State University. In eighty years, the City of Detroit was completely transformed demographically as the color line kept being redrawn. Today it has not disappeared; it has merely been redrawn again, but outside the city limits.

The potent lines separating black and white communities in Greater Detroit today are easily visible in a demographic map of the region, as in Figure 20. One of the color lines on the northeast separates Detroit from Warren along Eight Mile Road. But equally clear lines are drawn between Detroit and Livonia on the west, Dearborn on the southwest, and Grosse Pointe on the east. No wonder that, for decades, Greater Detroit was the most segregated metropolitan area in America. Over 74 percent of the black residents of the region would need to switch homes with white residents to achieve an even distribution of population in 2010.

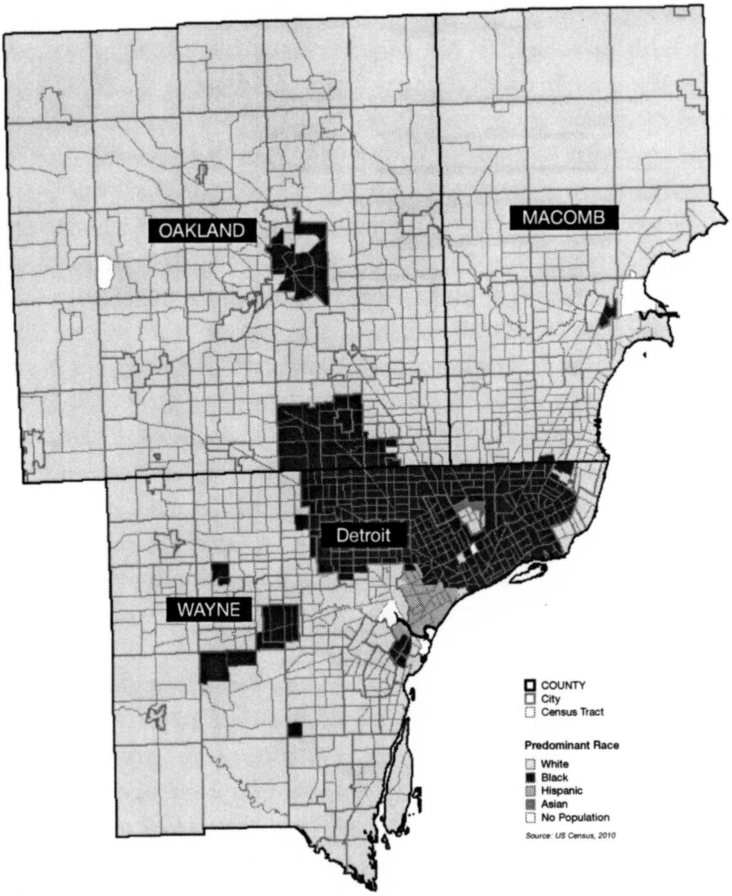

Figure 20. Black-, white-, Asian and Hispanic-majority neighborhoods in
Metropolitan Detroit, 2010. Map courtesy of Jason Booza.

Defending White School Turf

Defending white neighborhoods for social status and housing value preservation had a logical corollary: defense of white schools. White children were
also valuable resources that needed to be protected from the presumed
corrupting influence of ill-mannered, misbehaving, and academically
underachieving black children. White Detroiters have believed this for a
long time.

Blacks in Detroit got their first school (for black students only, of course) in 1841. Even after the Civil War ended in 1865, the city fought to maintain its aptly (if unimaginatively) named "Colored Schools 1, 2 and 3," arguing that white parents were so prejudiced the school board could not contemplate racial mixing of students without violence. The intransigence of the city stood in sharp contrast to a state law passed in 1867 stating, "All residents of any district shall have an equal right to attend any school therein." The political climate in post-Emancipation Proclamation Detroit had changed, however, to the point where blacks began to challenge the color line in schools. Most notable was Joseph Workman, a black porter, who wanted his ten-year-old son to attend a nearby school instead of the distant "colored school." School officials refused, so Workman sued. In its decision in *Joseph Workman v. The Board of Education of Detroit*, the Michigan Supreme Court ordered the racial desegregation of all Detroit schools in 1869. Writing for the majority, Chief Justice Thomas M. Cooley said, "It cannot be seriously argued that with this [1867 state] provision in force, the school board of any district . . . may make regulations which would exclude any resident of the district from any of its schools, because of race or color, or religious belief."

Despite this precedent that "you can't be serious in arguing for school segregation," a century later the Detroit Board of Education was found guilty of doing exactly this, as Eleanor Wolf showed. An NAACP investigative team documented numerous actions after World War II and continuing into the early 1960s, where the Board tried to maximize school segregation. These included redrawing attendance boundaries, siting new schools, enacting transfer policies allowing white children to opt out of majority-black schools, and busing black children away from predominantly white schools.

Since 1964, this segregationist legacy began to be thwarted by a labor-liberal coalition that formed a slim majority on the Detroit Board of Education. The group sought to desegregate Detroit schools voluntarily before an anticipated, inevitable court battle. To say that racial tensions were high at this time would be a drastic understatement. In the few schools that were desegregated, black students expected harassment on a regular basis. But defending school turf took on a decidedly uglier turn on September 19, 1969, at Cooley High School on the city's northwest side. A group of Ku Klux Klan members were staging an anti-integration rally across the street from Cooley, when a group of racist teachers and police briefly took control of the school. After pulling the fire alarm to evacuate the building, they locked the students out. The teacher conspirators led the police to a supply of pickaxe handles kept in the school. The cops then emerged, forcibly isolating groups of black students and beating them until they were forced to flee into the waiting arms (clubs, chains, and knives, not body parts) of Klansmen.

In the wake of the Cooley outrage, in April 1970, the Board of Education reformers were finally able, on a 4-3 vote, to force through an integration plan for fall 1970. Their proposal involved redrawing the school catchment area boundaries, not busing. This outraged most white Detroit parents, who not only saw the prospect of "their" lily-white high schools having more black students but also resented that some of their children would now be attending traditionally black high schools. They took their revenge through a successful referendum campaign by the Citizens Committee for Better Education, which put the recall of the Board on the August primary ballot. This election ousted the reformers en masse. The local furor convinced the Michigan legislature in Act 48 not only to overrule the Board's plan but also to decentralize the school system, so black and white "communities" could assume more control over their de facto separate and unequal segments.

Despairing that the desegregation plan had been voided and that an even more segregated alternative than the status quo had been legislated, Superintendent Norman Drachler and several liberal Board staff convinced the NAACP in New York to bring legal action on behalf of a group of black parents. In 1971, Federal District Judge Stephen Roth found the Board guilty of violating Michigan and federal statues against government-sponsored acts of segregation. The ruling was simple compared with his challenge of finding an effective desegregation remedy for a district that had 53 percent black children, and that would not trigger white flight from the system. He ordered the pooling of black and white students *across the entire metropolitan area* into 17 moderately sized new districts, each cutting across existing municipal lines and containing a segment of the central city. The suburban school districts argued that *they* had not been found guilty of illegally segregating students (a fatuous point since few if any had *any* minority students due to residential segregation patterns!), so they should not have to participate in any remedy. Though the U.S. Sixth Circuit Court of Appeals upheld Judge Roth, the U.S. Supreme Court in August 1974 decided 5-4 in favor of the suburban view in the landmark *Milliken v. Bradley* case. Thus ended any hope for effective desegregation of northern schools generally, not just

Detroit's. By giving the suburbs a free pass to preserve de facto segregated schools, *Milliken v. Bradley* forged an ironclad link between whites' desires to defend their neighborhoods and their schools. It all but mandated flight from the City of Detroit for prejudiced white parents of schoolchildren.

A Detroit-only interschool busing plan eventually went into effect, with predictable consequences. Within fifteen years, Greater Detroit had the most black-white school segregation in the nation's largest fifty metropolitan areas: over 88 percent of black students would need to switch districts to achieve desegregation. At the same time, school segregation by income also intensified; this produced a remarkable concentration of not only black students but of black students from poor families. The average black student in Greater Detroit in 2005 went to a school that had 93 percent black students and over 76 percent were from poor families (the second highest in the nation behind New Orleans); the comparable national poverty average for black students is 64 percent. Even more shocking is the disparity between this 76 percent and the poverty figure for white students in Greater Detroit: 21 percent. White parents have to a large extent successfully defended their school turf against not only black but also poor students.

> In *Brown v. Board of Education*, . . . this Court held that segregation of children in public schools on the basis of race deprives minority group children of equal educational opportunities and therefore denies them equal protection of the laws under the Fourteenth Amendment . . . .The Court today takes a giant step backwards . . . notwithstanding a record showing widespread and pervasive racial segregation in the educational system provided by the state of Michigan for children in Detroit. . . . School district lines, however innocently drawn, will surely be perceived as fences to separate the races when, under a Detroit-only [desegregation] decree, parents withdraw their children from the Detroit city schools and move to the suburbs in order to continue them in all-white schools. The message of this action will not escape the Negro children in the city of Detroit.
>
> —Justice Thurgood Marshall, in his dissent to
> *Milliken v. Bradley,* 1974

> [The *Milliken v. Bradley* decision] represents a formula for American Apartheid. . . . I know of no decision made by the Supreme Court of

the U.S. since the Dred Scott decision . . . which is so fraught with disaster for the country.

—Federal Judge George Edwards, former head of the Detroit
Housing Commission, Detroit City councilor,
and Detroit police commissioner, 1974

The Segregation Machine

Beginning in the 1920s and continuing essentially unchanged for over a half century, a vast social machine operated throughout Greater Detroit. In the best Detroit assembly line tradition, this machine was efficient and vertically integrated and used a division of labor to replicate its output over and over and over. Its product was racial segregation.

The workers employed by the segregation machine included bureaucrats, bankers, real-estate agents, elected officials, police, and white homeowners. They could all justify doing their part in the production process by pointing to the work of the others. Federal FHA/VA administrators justified refusing to insure mortgages in integrated or black neighborhoods because appraisers assured them that property values were depressed in such areas. Real estate agents steered prospective white buyers away from integrated neighborhoods for the same reason; what's more, their children might be forced to go to school with "inferior" black children. Banks rationalized not lending to black homebuyers because appraisers told them their collateral would be devalued by the very act of a black family purchasing it; besides, even the federal government would not insure integrated and black-occupied areas. Home appraisers knew that the entrance of blacks into a neighborhood would reduce property values because the flow of home mortgages would quickly dry up and prospective white buyers would disappear. They also knew that integrating the local schools would drive down property values. That this interlocking system created a gigantic self-fulfilling prophecy probably escaped the attention of the individuals and institutions that invested so much in creating and perpetuating the segregation machine.

From the perspective of the white homeowner and the local governments and school boards that represented them in Greater Detroit, the segregation machine was invisible. All they saw was its vile output, a trifecta of "facts" that seemed the natural order of things: (1) when blacks moved into an all-white neighborhood or started attending local schools, its status fell and home values declined; (2) the neighborhood or the school in question quickly became predominantly black; (3) predominantly black neighborhoods were not well maintained, predominantly black schools did not educate students well, and both harbored a variety of social problems. For these whites and white governments, there was a compelling *rational interest* in maintaining the color line. It was not just a matter of irrational racial prejudices or fears, though there were plenty of those. The segregation machine was maintained by a "white protection racket," though a different sort than the gangster kind. White homeowners needed to *protect* the value of their major asset. White parents needed to *protect* the socialization and security of their children in the neighborhood and at school. Municipalities needed to *protect* their property tax base and the reputation of their schools. All were drawn by the white protection racket into lubricating the segregation machine, through acts of exclusionary zoning, restrictive covenants, harassment, and, ultimately, flight from the city.

The competition over turf that led to creating the segregation machine was hardly unique to Greater Detroit. Yet it assumed an especially virulent, violent guise in Detroit for three reasons. First, Detroit's capitalists intentionally stoked white racial prejudices as a way to weaken union organizing efforts. Second, Detroit had an exceptionally large share of white homeowners from early in the twentieth century, people who would adamantly protect the value of their main asset, even if not personally prejudiced. Third, Detroit suffered bad luck during a crucial period from 1920 to 1945. At the two points when its firms most desperately needed more workers—the 1920s and the 1940s—this labor had to come from the Old South due to limits on immigration. This meant that "New World" prejudices replaced "Old World" prejudices after 1921. Yet, while the Old South had established a rigid, comprehensive social order of racial inequality through segregationist Jim Crow laws by the 1920s, in Detroit neighborhood, school, and factory floor turf was up for grabs. Add to this another cruel irony of historical timing: none of this interracial turmoil was settled when the Great Depression's economic insecurity consumed all races, ratcheting up competition another notch. Just as the Depression waned, Detroit was beset by violent labor-capital strife that took advantage of and intensified racial resentments. Then as this upheaval was settling, World War II brought yet *another* major upset to the social order, when even *more* new black and white immigrants from Old South crowded into the city. This unfortunate history meant that Greater Detroit's segregation machine could maintain its irresistible momentum into the present.

Today, real estate agents still engage in acts of racial discrimination to hold the color line. Research sponsored by the U.S. Department of Housing and Urban Development in 2000 used carefully matched white and black investigators who posed as apartment- and home-seekers, and then compared their treatment after inquiring about the same advertised property. The study found that blacks in Greater Detroit encountered discrimination 11 out of every 100 times in seeking rental accommodations, and 16 out of every 100 times they sought homes to buy, both well above national averages. It also revealed especially pervasive steering of home seekers away from certain neighborhoods and toward others on the basis of race. As one agent remarked to a white investigator while showing him around a white suburb of Detroit, "[another area] is different from here; it's multi-cultural. . . . I'm not allowed to steer you, but there are some areas that you wouldn't want to live in." This problem was highlighted by a similar 2005 investigation that revealed that a Grosse Pointe-based real estate office steered black homebuyers to Detroit but less-well qualified whites to white suburbs.

Most whites in Greater Detroit still harbor deep-seated fears about integration, which creep out in a variety of subtle and not-so-subtle ways. For example, in September 2005, the Livonia Planning Commission held a public hearing on Walmart's application to build in the city. Realizing that Livonia was adjacent to Detroit and that Detroit had no Walmarts, several citizens voiced opposition, charging that blacks would come to Livonia to shop and work and, before you know it, the city would become a "ghetto." Though city officials stepped forward to denounce such explicit racial fears, the reality of such fears was incontrovertible. Earlier that summer, 3,000 residents of the Grosse Pointes signed a petition to force their school board to re-register all 9,000 students in the district and require iron-clad proof of residency. Whites also evince such fears in searching for housing. In Greater Detroit, whites overwhelmingly search for housing in areas with few blacks in residence or nearby. When a 2004 regional survey asked white Detroiters to show on a map all the places they searched for a home or an apartment in the last ten years, the five most popular areas were Sterling Heights, Warren, Troy, Dearborn, and Mt. Clemens, all with miniscule black populations. Finally, whites show their fear through continuing acts of harassment of any who dare to cross color lines. In 2005 alone, racially motivated vandalism, fire-bombings, cross-burnings, and lynching threats were reported in Trenton, Taylor, Troy, and Warren. The most recent documented case of a cross-burning was in August 2009. The white protection racket is alive and well in Greater Detroit.

They drag my daddy out the car, beat him, told him no shit
come in here. This after 14 hours at the Bessemer, and he was
so thirsty he need a damn drink, that's all . . . Please be seated
take a number I'm sorry we can't help your kind
if you don't want to help yourself . . . All the time I'm in this
big house starin' at white babies, white babies wondering
what my own kids be doing . . . They may work here, but they'll
never fuckin' live here. This is Dearborn, buster, not some
backwater goddam southern town . . .

—"Uprising" by Dennis Teichman

The Turf Wars Have Been Won

For a century, turf has been fiercely guarded by whites in Greater Detroit, where visible and invisible walls were secured with a vast institutional infrastructure and individual acts of violence and avoidance were common. Even though these turf wars continue, the outcome is clear: whites have won. The century-long battle to protect what they perceive as their interests has been largely successful. Greater Detroit's neighborhoods and schools have the nation's highest degree of black-white segregation.

The region essentially is characterized by a black-occupied central city surrounded by a white-occupied suburban ring, as seen in Figure 20. Only the suburban enclaves of Pontiac in central Oakland County, Southfield in southern Oakland County, Inkster in western Wayne County, and Ecorse-River Rouge in southern Wayne County represent minor exceptions. The 2010 census figures show that Detroit is 83 percent black and 8 percent white; its suburbs are the reverse: 83 percent white and 10 percent black. Take out the suburban black clusters in Inkster, Pontiac, and Southfield and the figures become starker. These numbers reflect two distinct turfs, separate and unequal. A local joke pokes fun at this distinctive pattern but does not challenge it. "Metro Detroit is like a Krispy Kreme: blacks live in the hole in the middle and whites live on the outside where all the dough is." How ironic that the place that gave the nation Motown, the first black-white crossover music, remains so racially segregated.

Chapter 7

Wrestling for Pieces of the Proletarian Pie

> The best things in life are free, but you can keep 'em for the birds
> and bees;
> Now give me money, that's what I want . . .
> —"Money," sung by Barrett Strong, produced by Motown Records
> and co-written by Berry Gordy, 1959

Workers in Greater Detroit not only battled over turf but engaged in a fierce, sustained, and often violent economic competition delineated by ethnic or, more powerfully and perpetually, racial categorizations. This competition was naked, and groups organized to win it. As illustration, during World War I, Detroit's black leadership widely circulated a poem among blacks who for the first time had higher-paying industrial jobs opened to them as the white foreign labor pool dried up:

WHY HE FAILED
He watched the clock,
He was always behind hand.
He asked too many questions.
His stock excuse was "I forgot."
He was not ready for the next step.
He did not put his heart into his work.
He learned nothing from his blunders.
He was contented to be a second-rater.
He didn't learn that the best part of his salary was not the pay
  envelope—SUCCESS

In case the message of requisite industrial discipline in a cutthroat environment was missed, the flyer conveniently summarized: "Note: By not paying strict attention to the above details you may not be able to keep your job after the war is ended and foreign labor is again available." Certainly, trying to improve the quality of your labor is a laudable way to compete. However, intragroup economic competition in Detroit more often took three other, less laudable forms. They can be summarized as the 3Rs: robbery, renewal, and riot.

Competing with Robbery

It would be miserable affectation to regret the progress of civilization and improvement, the triumph of industry and art, by which these [Northwest Territory] regions have been reclaimed, and over which freedom, religion, and science are extending their sway. But we may indulge the wish, that the blessings had been attained at a smaller sacrifice; that the aboriginal population had accommodated themselves to the inevitable change of their condition, produced by the access and progress of the new race of men, before whom the hunter and his game were destined to disappear. But such a wish is in vain. A barbarous people, depending for subsistence upon the scanty and precarious supplies furnished by the chase, cannot live in contact with a civilized community.

—Lewis Cass, War of 1812 general, first governor of the
Michigan Territories, Secretary of War under Andrew
Jackson, major landowner in Detroit, and namesake of
Cass Avenue in Detroit, 1830

Ah, yes, the precedent-setting principle for interracial economic struggle in Detroit was established long ago: If you do not accommodate to our attempts to exploit you, we will push you away, take your land, and then demonize you to justify it!

The U.S. and various Native American groups in the Northwest Territories signed dozens of treaties before Michigan's 1837 statehood. In each, the U.S. essentially stole land from the original inhabitants. The first act of robbery relevant to the area around the fort and village of Detroit occurred in 1785, but the most comprehensive rip-off came in 1795 under the guise of the Treaty of Greenville (Ohio). Here General Anthony Wayne "negotiated" with Ottawa, Chippewa, Potawatomi, and a half dozen other native groups to cede lands in northern Ohio and Indiana and the territories that would become the Detroit metropolitan area. The Michigan territory stolen by General Wayne bore a remarkable congruence with the U.S. Bureau of the Census-defined Detroit metropolitan statistical area two centuries later:

> The post of Detroit, and all the land to the north, the west, and the south of it, of which the Indian title has been extinguished by gifts or grants to the French or English governments; so much more land to be annexed to the district of Detroit, as shall be comprehended between the River Rosine [now Raisin, in Monroe], on the south, Lake St. Clair on the north, and a line, the general course whereof shall be six miles distant from the west end of Lake Erie and the Detroit River.

Fresh from his victory over the English and Native American forces at Fallen Timbers near present-day Toledo, General Wayne was on a testosterone rush and in no mood to negotiate seriously. He dictated the terms for this land grab: $20,000 worth of blankets, utensils, and livestock to the Native Americans, plus $9,500 in future payments.

Unfortunately for the Native Americans, the United States proved to be a repeat offender. In the 1807 Treaty of Detroit, Native Americans ceded southeast Michigan for the token sum of $10,000 and an annual payment of $2,400. This seemed to be a good deal to the Native Americans because they retained the right to hunt and fish in the area. How abundant the hunting and fishing for the natives would become once the land was cleared of forests and converted to farming by the Anglo settlers was left unspecified in the treaty.

But this was a paltry prelude to the even bigger 1836 land heist: the Treaty of Washington. This treaty resulted in the U.S. gaining title to the northwest corner of Michigan's lower peninsula and most of its upper peninsula—fully 37 percent of modern-day Michigan, while drastically reducing the acreage set aside for "Indian reservations." This treaty was negotiated by Henry Schoolcraft, a scholar of Native American lore and "Indian Commissioner of the U.S.," for whom a community college in the Detroit area would be named in the twentieth century. This robbery was accomplished in the most genteel fashion. Representatives of several Native American groups were present in Washington, D.C., for these negotiations. They were pressured to stay there for two months while the Senate debated and amended this treaty, all the time being wined and dined and, in one noted case, clothed with a replica of the suit worn by President Andrew Jackson. Unbeknownst to the tipsy Native American signers, the Senate had unilaterally modified key terms they had negotiated with Schoolcraft. The Senate knew Michigan would never become a state unless it stripped all the resources from its Native Americans. What Schoolcraft originally negotiated merely as a bad deal for the Native Americans thus evolved into highway robbery. It set the precedent for "Indian removal." Those principles were still being practiced a century and a half later, with the word "Negro" substituted for "Indian."

The contentious issue of black-white economic standing in Detroit is older than the Republic. Whites learned quickly that the most effective way to rob competitors' resources was to steal their freedom and the fruits of their labor through the vehicle of chattel slavery. A Detroit census of 1779 showed 138 slaves among the 1,880 residents; a whopping 23 percent of Detroit households held slaves. By 1782 this figure had increased to 26 percent. These statistics are particularly ironic inasmuch as buying and selling slaves was never permitted in the city because the Northwest Territory, designated by U.S. Ordinance of 1787 (the Northwest Ordinance), was a slave-free sector:

> There shall be neither slavery nor involuntary servitude in the said [Northwest] Territory . . . provided always that any person escaping into the same, from whom labour or service is lawfully claimed in any one of the original states, such fugitive may be lawfully reclaimed and conveyed to the person claiming his or her labour or service aforesaid.

Michigan territorial governor Arthur St. Clair thought this meant that slaves could still be owned in the state so long as they were purchased in states where slavery was legal. In 1807, none other than hallowed Judge Augustus Woodward provided support with an egregious legal decision *In the matter of Elizabeth Denison et al.* Four slaves tried to use the habeas corpus proceedings to claim that their owner had no right to detain them, based on the 1787 Northwest Territory Ordinance. Judge Woodward agreed that the Ordinance forbade slavery in the region but argued that this was nullified by a phrase in the 1794 Jay Treaty that ended the War of Independence: "All settlers and traders shall continue to enjoy unmolested, all their property of every kind." Predictably, Judge Woodward ruled that "property" included slaves and ordered the four slaves returned to their owner. Concerns over property and perpetuating white privilege defeated concerns over justice—a continuing theme in Detroit established over two centuries ago.

As if rulings from the court were insufficient to secure whites' upper hand in the economic competition, the early Michigan legislature passed several discriminatory laws. The Act to Regulate Blacks and Mulattoes, and to Punish the Kidnapping of such Persons (a.k.a. the "Black Codes") of 1827 was the most notorious. The Black Codes ostensibly protected free blacks but actually restricted their flow into the territory. After the Erie Canal opened, many white Detroiters feared that hordes of free blacks would move in from the East, undercutting their wages and stealing their jobs. Thus, the Black Codes required blacks moving into Michigan to present a court-attested certificate that they were free, register with the local court, and post a substantial $500 bond guaranteeing their "good behavior." Few blacks could muster the funds for such a guarantee.

But free blacks in Detroit did not throw in the towel, despite these rulings and laws. In 1806, 1828, and 1833, they organized angry and ultimately successful demonstrations that frustrated attempts by slave hunters to return runaways to their masters. The events in June 1833 were the stuff of pulp fiction. In 1831 Thornton Blackburn and his wife Ruth escaped from their Kentucky slave master and came to Detroit via the Underground Railroad. Two years later, the Blackburns were tracked down by their owner who, invoking the Fugitive Slave Law of 1793, convinced cooperative Wayne County Sheriff John Wilson to confine them in the Wayne County Jail before extradition. In case legal precedent proved unpersuasive, the slave owner greased the palm of the sheriff with $50. Mrs. George French, a respectable free black Detroiter, appeared at the jail wishing to comfort the distraught Mrs. Blackburn. In the privacy of the cell, the ladies exchanged clothing. Soon "Mrs. French" walked out of the jail and eventually to freedom in Windsor, thereby establishing the First Pillar of Detroit Law Enforcement: *In the eyes of the law all blacks look alike.* Sheriff Wilson's embarrassment proved short lived, however.

The following day a crowd of free blacks gathered around the jail demanding Thornton Blackburn's release. As the sheriff and slave owner tried to move Blackburn to the jail coach, the crowd pressed in threateningly. Blackburn convinced the sheriff to allow him to address the crowd to calm them, but in the process someone slipped him a gun, which he brandished dramatically and threatened to shoot anyone who impeded his escape. At this highly charged moment, some white onlookers rushed forward to assist the sheriff. In the ensuing melee, Sheriff Wilson was shot and later died; Blackburn was spirited away by Daddy Walker on horseback. Being a local, Walker first headed out Gratiot Avenue to fool pursuers, before doubling back to River Rouge and a waiting rowboat to Canada and a joyful reunion for the Blackburns.

White Detroit did not take kindly to this outrageous display of black initiative, to put it mildly. Mayor Marshall Chapin appealed to troops garrisoned in Fort Wayne to quell the mounting interracial violence; they spent two weeks restoring order in the city. This was the first of four instances in which federal troops had to be called into Detroit to quell racial violence, an unenviable American record that still stands today. The mayor also devised an effective way to stifle the subsequent march that local blacks planned to protest the heavy-handedness of the troops and white citizens. Invoking the Black Code, Mayor Chapin threatened that anyone demonstrating would need proof that he or she was free, knowing full well that few had such documentation because it was so expensive. Thus the Second Pillar of Detroit Law Enforcement was established: "Guilty until proven innocent." This dictum and its implied threat led to an exodus of free blacks from Detroit to Canada. Thus, the black community's victory in the "Battle for the Blackburns" eventually assumed a hollow character. Seething Detroit whites would later call this the "First Negro Insurrection." Little could they have guessed what was coming.

Holding slaves in Michigan finally was abolished by the state constitution as a prelude to statehood in 1837. Yet the 1835 constitutional convention abolished slavery while denying blacks the right to vote or otherwise participate fully in Michigan society. Ironically, the author of the constitutional amendment to abolish slavery, John Norvell, a Democratic delegate from Wayne County, took the lead in fighting against full racial equality, revealing his deep prejudices in the process. He argued,

> Why then should we invite within our limits; why hold out inducements to the migration hither, of a description of population confessedly injurious, confessedly a nuisance, to the community? It would not be denied that the Negro belonged to a degraded cast of mankind. We did not take them as equals to our homes, to our tables, to our

bosoms. . . . Nature has marked the distinction. Society has, in all
ages, recognized and sanctioned it.

Delegate Norvell's statements were typical of the white community's sentiments, sentiments that would prove stubbornly resistant. In 1868, Michigan proposed a new state constitution that prominently included a provision
for black male suffrage. It was defeated in every ward in Detroit, with working-
class wards providing the strongest opposition. Despite winning the Civil
War in which Michigan's Union forces suffered mightily, Detroit could not
abide blacks competing at the ballot box. This had to be forced down Detroiters' throats by the Fifteenth Amendment to the Constitution in 1870, which
expanded suffrage to all males. The uncivil war between the races has been
fought ever since in Detroit, though the weapons have evolved.

Competing with Renewal

One by one, the nineteenth-century weapons available to Detroit whites to
maintain their edge in the economic competition—slavery, residential reg-
istrations and behavioral bonds, voting rights—were rendered illegal. What
was there to do in the twentieth century but go back to the future and dust
off a weapon that had been used so effectively against the Native Americans
in the eighteenth century? However, now it would be called "urban renewal"
instead of a "treaty," though token cash payments masking a land grab remained its core feature.

In 1930, this rehabilitated weapon was introduced in northwest Detroit's
Fitzgerald neighborhood, where Marygrove College was located. The Detroit
Board of Education wanted to build a new junior high school (for whites), but
there were no vacant parcels of sufficient size. So it used the unusual presence of three black-owned homes in a row on Roselawn Street as justification for condemning the entire area for demolition. The Board's logic was
unassailable, given the real estate practices and public prejudices of the
time. The Board could acquire this land most cheaply, thus economizing on
the taxpayers' monies, because the three black-owned homes devalued the
property in the environs from the normal $8,000 to only $7,000. Moreover,
the Board would perform a community public service by removing this
"blighting influence." Ironically one of the homes that fell to the wrecker's

ball was owned by Roy Turner. Turner was the rigger and head of the all-black crew who erected the majestic statue of the Virgin Mary that sublimely greeted guests entering Marygrove College. Fitzgerald's "Negro removal" prototype proved a paltry precedent, as this weapon of mass destruction wiped out the historical black community's core over the next three decades.

*   *   *

By the 1930s, it had come to be known as "Paradise Valley," for reasons no one can recall for certain. The Valley was centered on Adams and St. Antoine Streets in the heart of the Black Bottom neighborhood. It was home to establishments selling music, food, clothing, booze, policies, and rooms, some of them containing women. Policies were a form of lottery gambling; one played by buying three numbers ranging from 1 to 78 for five cents. Hitting your daily number meant a payoff of $25. The Valley was well known to both Bruno's son Karl and George Jacob's son Marvin, though for different reasons.

Ever the party boy after his work was done at Acme Wire and Iron Works, Marvin enjoyed the Paradise Valley music club scene. He had an all-star cast of entertainers from which to choose. Count Basie, Cab Calloway, Duke Ellington, Ella Fitzgerald, and Billie Holiday were Valley regulars, playing to racially diverse, enthusiastic, boozy audiences.

Even though he was new to the Detroit Police Department, Karl knew Paradise Valley's reputation as a haven for illegal gambling twenty-four hours a day. He also knew that the cops would look the other way if blackjack and poker were involved, so long as the cops got some "consideration." What he did not know then was that the Valley's policy operation was at the center of a web of corruption spreading all the way to City Hall and police headquarters. Mayor Richard Reading, the superintendent of police, the former Wayne County Sheriff, Joe Louis's manager, and numerous policy operators and beat cops were convicted of graft conspiracy after a sensational trial in June 1942. The free publicity generated by the Reading trial made the owners of the pleasure emporia of Paradise Valley smile all the way to the bank.

The Valley was the Detroit black community's cash cow and its artistic soul. It was as nationally renowned as it was locally infamous in the 1930s and 1940s. Within twenty years, it was completely and intentionally wiped out; nothing has since replaced it.

> The cracks
> in sidewalks, walls, roofs, smokestacks,
> have broken too many backs already
> for we to be saying "yes"
> attack on our territory.
> The helicopters
> are now steady landing
> on the miracle
> of some many still standing.
> But we,
> veterans of domestic and foreign wars,
> don't need no more walls
> in our Valley
> don't want our backyards
> turned into alley
> will not be roped in
> by yet another Lt. Calley
> proclaiming:
> "We destroyed the village to save it"
> Mother wit won't allow it
> and we who live here
> avow it for true:
> This valley become the Bottom
> Black and blue
> will be Paradise again
> no matter who,
> with whatever "new"
> thinks they have the right
> to come through.
>   —"Message from the Meridian" by Michele Gibbs

World War II was over, and the City of Detroit was physically and psychologically exhausted. Its factories, neighborhoods, and workers had run 24-7 for four long years. Thoughts of a fresh start, of "renewal," abounded. But darker thoughts and longer memories of local events from the wartime period did, too. Their convergence would prove politically irresistible, as June Thomas has shown.

The Detroit Plan was introduced with much fanfare in 1946 by Mayor Edward Jeffries, who had already learned the hard political lessons of racial turf wars during the 1942 Sojourner Truth Homes controversy. The plan proposed condemning and then acquiring at city expense about one hundred acres adjacent to downtown along Gratiot Avenue, along the same route that Daddy Walker used to shepherd Thornton Blackburn to freedom 113 years earlier. The plan called for demolishing all blighted structures and clearing the site for new development. It foresaw a $2 million cost to the city, which purportedly would be recaptured when the parcel was sold to developers and new property tax revenues from the site were realized. The site was indeed blighted; for decades, poor black immigrants had been forcibly overcrowded there into aged structures that were systematically undermaintained by their slumlords. The site was the heart of the Black Bottom neighborhood.

Condemnation of the Gratiot site started in February 1947 but was soon stopped by a flurry of legal suits. This condemnation, acquisition, clearance, and resale of a site to private interests represented a radically new policy. In an eerily prescient foreshadowing of its 1980 Poletown industrial redevelopment ruling, the Michigan Supreme Court upheld the city's plan in October 1948. Further legal challenges were brushed aside with the passage of the federal Urban Renewal Law in July 1949, which codified Detroit's scheme.

The Gratiot urban renewal project's fate took center stage in Detroit's 1949 mayoral election. One candidate, Democratic City Councilor and former Housing Commissioner George Edwards, favored construction of public housing on the cleared site. His Republican opponent, Albert Cobo, promised that the property would be used for private business interests. Mr. Cobo surmised from incumbent Democratic Mayor Eugene Van Antwerp's embarrassing primary election loss that support for new public housing replacing black-occupied dwellings demolished by urban renewal was political suicide. He was correct. After Cobo's resounding victory, he stacked the Housing Commission with his cronies, who reversed the prior Commission's plans for twelve new public housing developments around the periphery of the city. Thereafter, Detroit would de-emphasize public housing, and it would not be used as replacement housing for those displaced from urban renewal sites. By 1953, Mayor Cobo's wrecking balls had demolished 700 buildings in Black Bottom, displacing 2,000 black families without building any replacement housing.

The Gratiot project eventually expanded to 129 acres cleared before anything was built on the site. For whom would it be? Certainly not for poor black families, but what about middle-class black families who also had been displaced? City planners drew and redrew plans to find some density and design compromises between the city (advocating single-family units attractive to upper-class whites) and Washington urban renewal officials (demanding some consideration for those displaced). The first compromise plan involving moderate-density dwellings was forwarded in 1952, but no developers bid because they thought that "moderate density" meant "Negro occupants." Other failed plans followed until, in 1955, the nonprofit Citizens Redevelopment Corporation was granted control of the entire parcel. The corporation devised a mixed-income, mixed-density, mixed-tenure plan and secured a non-Detroit firm, Cities Redevelopment Inc., as master developer. The chief designer was internationally renowned Ludwig Mies van der Rohe, who contributed his iconic International Style architecture. The first buildings were occupied in newly christened Lafayette Park-University City in fall 1958. Though a few middle-class blacks were among the occupants, the problem of finding replacement housing for the poor and working-class blacks displaced during the prior decade was never resolved by the higher-end Lafayette Park.

Urban renewal eventually mushroomed to cover vast tracts of the former black community, picking off the few remaining areas that had escaped demolition for the construction of the I-75 Fisher Freeway and its I-375 feeder into downtown. The same year that Lafayette Park finally opened, the city completed its plan to demolish the vestiges of Paradise Valley and three thousand surrounding homes. This site became home to Wayne State University's vast new hospital and medical school campus. Only a last-minute suit by the NAACP forced the plan to include a token number of affordable housing units and three churches. Today, these modest structures sit forlornly on a narrow strip of polluted wilderness along Beaubien Street, wedged between the Fisher Freeway and the gigantic Detroit Medical Center complex, mute totems of a lost world. As the urban renewal dust settled at the close of 1963, the Detroit Commission on Community Relations estimated that this weapon of mass destruction had leveled 10,000 structures and displaced over 43,000, of whom over 70 percent were black.

As might be expected, other local jurisdictions were quick to emulate Detroit's success with "Negro removal." Dearborn mayor Orville Hubbard had his own problem for which urban renewal was the solution. In the 1950s, a community of Muslim Arabs had arisen in a section of Dearborn known as the South End, just east of Ford's Rouge complex. Mayor Hubbard made it well known that this area was inhabited by undesirable "white n _ _ _ _ _," and he wanted them gone. His technique involved a new twist on the renewal weapon: systematically deny owners in the area permits to build or renovate homes and badger the Federal Housing Administration into restricting mortgage insurance in the area. As the South End's housing market predictably dried up, Mayor Hubbard's officials stepped in and bought up Arab-owned houses at bargain-basement prices. These were quickly demolished in accordance with the expressed goal of converting the area to industrial uses. A class action suit raised by the South End Community Council, headed by Arab American Alan Amen, challenged these heavy-handed actions. In August 1973, federal judge Ralph Freeman found in favor of the council, stopped further destruction of the community, and gave the 350 homeowners already displaced the right to sue the City of Dearborn for the difference between the price paid by the city and true value in an open market. It was the only local case where a racially motivated urban renewal program was stopped before the community in question had been irreparably lost.

A less felicitous outcome occurred in Hamtramck. In 1965, the city proposed a civic center. It chose a site bordering Detroit that coincidently had Hamtramck's main concentration of black residents. The demolitions ended up reducing the black population of the city from 14.5 percent in 1960 to 8.5 percent in 1966. Though a legal suit was filed in 1968, the damage had already been done. In 1971, federal judge Damon Keith ordered that Hamtramck build homes for the displaced black families. The city appealed, then dragged its heels when Judge Keith's ruling was upheld, until finally agreeing to construct 200 replacement homes and 150 senior units in 1981. The senior units eventually opened on one part of the cleared site in the late 1980s. But the plan for the replacement homes was not settled until 2003, by which time many of the original plaintiffs were dead. By 2000, Hamtramck still had no majority-black neighborhoods, despite having such on all but one of the census tracts bordering Detroit. It never built a civic center.

The white power structure used urban renewal as a weapon of mass destruction in the interracial competition over economic resources and created collateral damage to the white working class of Detroit, though the whites probably never realized the connection. Mayors Jeffries and Cobo placated white voters by aggressively pursuing urban renewal concentrated on black-occupied neighborhoods, while pledging not to build replacement public housing on renewal sites. These and other area mayors knew that winning postwar politics in Greater Detroit meant loudly opposing aid and housing opportunities for blacks, while simultaneously downplaying the inescapable mathematics of where black families displaced from urban renewal sites would live. Urban renewal and failure to build replacement housing meant more black population pressure on white-occupied neighborhoods. It helped fuel the blockbusting and rapid racial transitions of these neighborhoods. Ironically, Detroit's white working class cheered urban renewal at the same time it was intensifying the racial assault on their home turf. There is little wonder that, during the 1950s, the number of majority-black-occupied census tracts in Detroit increased from 24 to 83, according to Bob Sinclair.

Urban renewal, like union-busting race-baiting, revealed how the competition within racial segments of the proletariat, though real, was often a smokescreen for competition between the proletariat as a whole and the capitalists. In the case of urban renewal, what seemed like a populist political maneuver to benefit white working-class homeowners in fact worked against their interests, instead favoring white real estate developers, business interests, and a few upper-income white homebuyers. It was yet another example of how racial divisions were used by the powerful classes to exploit both white and black classes below them. This same dynamic persists today in the "Housing Disassembly Line," explained later.

Competing with Riots

> Henceforth all hostilities shall cease; peace is hereby established and shall be perpetual.
>> —General Anthony Wayne, concluding the Treaty of
>> Greenville ceding Detroit to the U.S., 1795

Perpetual peace is perhaps the least apt description one might make of Greater Detroit's social relationships over the centuries since General Wayne's optimistic pronouncement. Detroiters always embraced interracial violence as a means of economic competition. The mindset has been "Perhaps if you can't get local government to be your proxy force to win the competition, you can take things into your own hands. If you can violently eliminate the competition, intimidate them to stay in their place, or grab a piece of their loot—go for it." Yes, competing through riot has a long and sordid history in Greater Detroit.

On New Year's Day 1863, the black community of Detroit gathered in the Second Baptist Church on Monroe and Beaubien Streets to celebrate the recent Emancipation Proclamation. How fitting that this joyous occasion should be marked in this church, which for so many years had served as the terminus for the Underground Railroad. That proclamation proved illusory within two months. Some white working-class Detroiters were spooked by newspaper reports that newly emancipated slaves would soon stampede to Detroit and take away their jobs. Others were upset that, with the Civil War going badly, President Lincoln called for 300,000 more troops. They anticipated being drafted because they could not afford the official price of $600 to buy their way out. Their resentment was not directed at the government, however, but against blacks because they were the "cause of the war." Thus, competitive fear and anger conspired to create a highly flammable situation awaiting only a spark for conflagration.

That spark came on March 6, when William Faulkner, a local mulatto restaurateur, was found guilty of molesting two nine-year-old girls (one white and one black). The conviction was based solely on the verbal testimony of the white girl, with no other witnesses or corroborating physical evidence. As news of the verdict spread, white (primarily Irish immigrant) dockworkers surrounded the county courthouse and demanded that Faulkner be turned over to them for lynching. The Wayne County sheriff, seeking to avoid the fatal precedent of his deceased predecessor during the 1833 Thornton Blackburn incident, prudently called for federal troops at Fort Wayne to escort Faulkner from the courthouse to the jail on Beaubien Street. The crowd of several thousand hurled whatever objects came to hand at the troops. Desperate and badly outnumbered, the troops returned the favor by shooting into crowd, killing one.

Enraged that Faulkner had eluded their clutches, the mob took vengeance on the nearby black community. Described the next day by the *Detroit Advertiser and Tribune* as "crazy with whisky and prejudice," they destroyed almost half the six-block area between Crogan, Brush, Congress, and Beaubien Streets. Thirty black-occupied and often owned buildings went up in flames before troops could restore order. The city fire marshal, W. M. Champ, admitted that he had not allowed his men to turn on their fire hoses at the height of the firestorm because the mob had threatened to cut the hoses if they were used; Marshal Champ thought it more prudent "to preserve city property." He did see fit, however, to hose down white-occupied homes adjacent to burning black-occupied ones, ostensibly "for the greatest good for the greatest number."

The white riots of 1863 spawned multiple ironies. Two black citizens were killed, one by fire and the other beaten to death by the white mob. The latter victim's name was Joshua Boyd, an escaped slave who had arrived in Detroit only a few years before, seeking a better life. William Faulkner served seven years in prison before the white girl he was accused of molesting recanted her testimony; she admitted that the two girls had fabricated the incident to avoid being punished for coming home late. The heaviest riot damage centered on a stretch of Lafayette Street between Brush and St. Antoine. In this vacuum settled a nascent Greek immigrant community. Remnants of this ethnic enclave (mainly restaurants and pastry shops) survive to this day as the popular "Greektown" entertainment district. In the middle of Greektown still sits the Second Baptist Church. The city's vulnerability to such lawlessness, and the uncertainty of securing federal troops, led the City Council to establish the Detroit Police Department. Protecting the city from racial unrest remained its *raison d'être* for the next century, though a century later the Department had become more a cause of racial unrest than its solution.

*   *   *

The University of Detroit's aeronautical engineering program was demanding: a cooperative arrangement in which the student studied for six months and then worked at a company for six months putting classroom ideas into practice. Being the star junior student in the class of 1944, George Milton had secured a plum placement: the Ford B-24 bomber factory at Willow Run. There he would develop his skills by designing a strategically trivial but ergonomically vital crew bed that nestled between the cockpit and the bomb bays. This job was infinitely safer and more comfortable than his prior work for his father George Jacob's Acme Wire and Iron Works under contract at the Rouge complex. George Milton relished the intellectual challenge of the aircraft job but despised the commute: over an hour with good traffic from his parents' Grosse Pointe Park home on the far east side to Willow Run on the far west side, even though the last few miles were driven on the new-fangled, four-lane, divided road dubbed "Bomber Highway." At least he was able to drive, instead of taking an ill-fitting combination of trolleys and buses, blessed as he was with a special ration of gasoline coupons because of his "critical defense job."

These ration coupons also allowed George Milton a wide range of recreational opportunities, most of them involving Helen. He had been swept away by Bruno and Helen's second daughter since they met at Luther League, the teen social group at the First English Lutheran Church. Against his mother Emma's advice, he stuck with Helen through her bout of tuberculosis and long confinement in the Northville sanitarium. But it was the summer of 1943 and those bleak days seemed far behind them; Helen had recovered, and they were engaged. Once freed from "the san," as Helen called it, the young couple spent many a languid hour on Belle Isle, listening to an open-air band concert, canoeing or "necking" in the back seat of George's dad's car. Ah, the perks of those gasoline ration coupons!

Future son-in-law George was warmly embraced by Helen's family. Bruno made a habit of asking him and Bruno's oldest son Karl to "come down to the basement to help with an engineering problem" when he arrived to pick up Helen for a date. The "problem" was inevitably solved by consuming a shot of whiskey and a cigar, while complaints were aired about the difficulty of finding quality ingredients to produce Bruno's increasingly famous chicken pot pies, what with wartime rationing and all. With a couple of whiskeys in him, Karl grimly reflected on the increasingly alien, tension-filled city he was experiencing as a motorcycle cop with the Detroit Police Department. He warned George to keep off Belle Isle, as it seemed to be turning into an interracial battleground. There was an upside to all this upheaval, however. Theaters, bowling alleys, and grocery stores extended their hours of business to accommodate the life styles of the three-shift wartime proletariat. This was a boon to Karl, for he could now engage in his favorite sport—bowling—at any hour of any day, regardless to which police shift he was assigned.

*   *   *

Detroit workers seem to hate and suspect their bosses more than ever. Detroit manufacturers have made a failure of labor relations. . . . Too many of the people in Detroit are confused and embittered and distracted by Hitler. . . . Morale is the worst in the country . . . the city could blow up Hitler or blow up the U.S.
—"DET Is Dynamite," *Life Magazine*, August 1942

Unless some socially constructive steps are taken shortly, the tension that is developing [in Detroit] is very likely to burst into active conflict.
—Federal Office of Facts and Figures confidential report to President Roosevelt, April 1942

Let us drag out into the open what has been whispered throughout Detroit for months—that a race riot may break out here at any time.
—Walter White, national director of the NAACP, in a speech in Detroit, June 1943

Detroit Mayor Edward Jeffries ridiculed the *Life* article; he was either woefully optimistic or willfully uninformed. According to the War Manpower Commission, a half million new residents had moved into Detroit between June 1940 and June 1943. Detroit became a city of strangers, with cohesion and collective social control as scarce as gasoline. Detroiters felt pride at being the presidentially proclaimed "Arsenal of Democracy," but also resented the stressful working and living conditions that this designation carried. They were tired: tired of regularly working 48-hour weeks; tired of waiting in long lines for everything; tired of living in cramped, often squalid conditions; tired of adjusting life to evening and night-shift work; tired of scrambling daily to find someone to care for the kids; tired of having more money in their pockets than ever before but little to spent it on; tired of having to rub elbows with people who were so different from "folks back home" and "did not know their place." It's no wonder that Detroiters soon started grimly referring to their city as the "Arsehole of Democracy."

Defecation began on June 20, 1943. Nearly 100,000 black and white Detroiters gathered on Belle Isle to escape the heat and humidity. For most, it was their only day off work, and they were not about to let anyone get in the way of their well-earned Sabbath. Minor interracial incidents were reported throughout the day at the Belle Isle police station, everything from arguments over public barbecue grills to charges of assault. Things finally got out of hand when traffic backed up near sunset as the crowd tried to get home and crammed the narrow MacArthur Bridge (see Figure 8). The particular triggers remain in dispute, but a full-scale black-white brawl erupted, soon joined by 200 white sailors from the Brodhead Naval Armory at the foot of the bridge on the Detroit shore. Fictitious yet flammable rumors about the mêlée spread like wildfire through both black and white communities. At one all-night movie house, the Roxy on Woodward Avenue, someone started a rumor that blacks had raped a white woman on Belle Isle and that blacks were rioting all over the city. White moviegoers began to accost black ones. At about the same time, someone announced at the popular Forest Club in Black Bottom that whites had thrown a black woman and her baby off Belle Isle's MacArthur Bridge and that police were beating blacks there. Patrons poured onto Forest Avenue and began taking out their frustrations on passing white motorists. Five thousand whites gathered that night on the MacArthur Bridge, trying to pick off black stragglers from the island, while simultaneously some blacks started to break windows and burn white-owned stores on Hastings Street in Black Bottom.

Daybreak on Monday, June 21, illuminated racial mayhem on Woodward Avenue in the heart of downtown, with whites pulling blacks from trolleys and autos and beating them. The frenzy was symbolized in a nationally circulated press photo showing a black World War I veteran being held by police as a white man struck him. Mayor Jeffries estimated later that day that the white mob grew to an overwhelming 100,000, and admitted the police could not or would not control the situation. He reluctantly asked the governor to request federal troops. By the time troops arrived and order had been restored, nine whites and 25 blacks had been killed, hundreds had been injured, 500 whites and 1,300 blacks had been arrested, and $2 million in property damages had been incurred. As staggering as the riot of 1943 was, it was but a tepid preamble to the events starting on another hot Sunday two dozen years later.

As described by Suzanne Smith, the venerable, 4,000-seat Fox Theater on Woodward Avenue downtown was *the* place to be on Sunday afternoon July 23, 1967. This was the venue of the "Swinging Time Review," a regional variant of Dick Clark's trendy *American Bandstand* TV show, broadcast live by CKLW in Windsor, the region's hip station. Hometown heroines Martha and the Vandellas were the closing act. They were on a roll, with their string of Motown hits "Nowhere to Run," "Jimmy Mack," and "Heatwave." The show did not disappoint, and by the time Martha and the Vandellas took the stage, the crowd was drenched in sweat and joy. But as the singers were about to launch into their biggest hit, Martha Reeves was pulled offstage and informed that this would be their one and only song. Rioting was breaking out all over the city, and they needed to evacuate the theater. As the disappointed crowd filed out, it left the world of Fox's dance frenzy and entered a different sort of frenzy. Did the audience members take any note of the symbolism of the climactic song they had heard that afternoon: "Dancing in the Street"?

The trouble began during the wee hours of Sunday morning, when Detroit police tried to bust a "blind pig," an illegal drinking and gaming parlor, located at Twelfth and Clairmount Streets. As documented by Sidney Fine, police were surprised by the size of the crowd; they arrested all 82 black patrons but had to hold them outside a long time before sufficient police transport arrived. The delay allowed a large and increasingly hostile crowd to gather around those arrested. Taunts and slurs eventually turned to rock throwing. By 5 a.m., looting had begun along Twelfth Street from Clairmount on the north all the way south to the Henry Ford Hospital complex at Grand Boulevard, then west to Linwood in the vicinity of New Bethel Baptist Church. By noon, looting spread east along Mack and Kercheval Avenues, and arson began in already looted areas. At its height, disturbances spread west all the way to Grand River and McNichols, northwest to Livernois and Eight Mile, north into Highland Park and Hamtramck, and east almost to the Grosse Pointe border. Desperate and none-too-hip-or-literate white merchants scrawled "Sold Brother" on their storefronts in a vain attempt to ward off Soul Brother looters and firebombers.

That Sunday afternoon, as the Fox concert was underway, Mayor Jerome Cavanagh called the State Police and National Guard for help. On Monday, Governor George Romney requested federal troops. The next day 4,700 paratroopers from the 82nd and 101st airborne divisions arrived and quickly quelled disturbances in the east side areas they had been assigned. By contrast, unrest and killings persisted on the city's west side, patrolled by 9,200 poorly trained and trigger-happy Michigan national guardsmen and Detroit police. On Wednesday, the police gunned down innocents at the Algiers Motel. On Friday, President Lyndon Johnson appointed the Kerner Commission to probe the causes of urban unrest in places like Detroit.

Unlike the 1943 riots, during 1967 there was little interracial violence among citizens; instead, most of the violence occurred between black citizens and police and National Guard forces. Nevertheless, the toll was higher on every count: 33 blacks and 10 whites dead; 467 injured; 7,231 arrested; $80 million worth of damaged property; 17,460 police and soldiers involved. In an understandable fit of hyperbole, Mayor Cavanagh remarked that his city "looked like Berlin in 1945." He could not have pictured in his worst nightmares what it would look like forty-five years later.

In the wake of the 1967 disturbances, there were a variety of laudable if largely ineffective public and private efforts to reknit the shredded civic fabric. Racial polarization was beyond repairing through rhetoric and tokenism, however. Emblematic of the two worlds Detroit had become was the Police Department, which was 95 percent white, though blacks constituted 35 percent of the city's population. A 1968 *Free Press* poll showed vast differences in how white and black police officers saw the racial situation in Detroit. A majority of white police thought that housing and job opportunities were equal for blacks and whites, that the police treated blacks fairly, and that blacks were favored in schools. By contrast, only 3 percent of black officers thought blacks had equal housing opportunities or were favored in school, 8 percent thought they had equal job opportunities, and 87 percent thought the police treated blacks unfavorably.

> He saw Fords and Chevys, the carcasses
> of carmakers' assembly lines,
> torched and overturned by the narrow lots
> of warehouses stacked along the river;
> the discount drug stores and gas stations
> being looted, neon signs spreading their dust
> over the ground like ashes of the dead,
> and he saw onlookers hiding behind
> newspaper boxes staving off the fury
> of the exhausted crowd with a *Free Press*.
> He was one of those bystanders who watched
> the fires from the bus stop, waiting for
> the transfer to Dearborn to go home from work,
> and though the burning will finally calm
> and disperse and drift, he understood
> this night, which burst forth like a fever,
> would last forever. He saw the storm of history

hurl the past onto the citizenry of Detroit,
piling wreckage upon wreckage, like
coal slags that rise above the horizon.

—"Angelus Novus" by Hayan Charara

The events of the hot summer of 1967 were the first civil disturbances to come with their own, locally produced soundtrack. First came "Dancing in the Street" by Martha and the Vandellas. Though released in 1965, its continuing popularity and obvious (if unintended) symbolic relevance to 1967 Detroit is inescapable. Then, The Supremes' "The Happening" reached the top of the pop charts in May 1967. It was the last single produced by The Supremes; Florence Ballard was released that spring; henceforth, the ensemble was known as Diana Ross and the Supremes. Later that summer, after the disturbances, the group was enlisted to create an upbeat musical video extolling the good features of Detroit and encouraging charitable giving, titled "It's Happening." As if the irony of the song's title were insufficient, the sponsoring agency was the Community Torch Drive. "The Happening" was pushed off the top of music charts in June 1967 by yet another Detroit artist's song, which resonated much more profoundly with the psyche of Detroiters. The artist was Aretha Franklin. The song was "Respect."

The Old Boy walks from Canfield and Woodward
to Mansfield, Highland Park Ford Plant,
with Herman Davis and Sam Rustin, looking
to find Mr. Henry's man, Marshall,
who could say these boys are alright.

Pickup men take your number and duck
between alleys and houses, not to get caught.
If you hit, you hope he'll hop to your door
with the money.

Trying to be the temporary weather-boy,
you look at the sky, scratch your head,
dig in your ass, shuffle at the same time,
waffling through a minefield of eggshells.
You got rhythm.

Jabberwocking through the pains of being colored.
Dancing sometimes, even jitterbugging
through a Strauss waltz. Friday night, rent party.
Eva's again? After we could get to fish fry
at Wimpy's. Up all Saturday night.

Pray a little on Sunday. Stand on tiptoes,
straining to peer on the other side of death, singing
the edges of despair "Swing Low, Sweet Chariot."
Monday, start to be colored again.
                    —"Growing Up Colored" by Murray Jackson

From Fraternity to Fratricide

Detroit's three primary vehicles of interracial economic competition—
robbery, renewal, and riot—were employed with surprising intensity given
its highly unionized environment. Surely, Detroit's strong unions could re-
strain this competition, uniting the proletariat with the rhetoric of common
class interests against those of the capitalists. Sadly and crucially, they could
not, despite some valiant efforts. Instead, unionism in Greater Detroit has
a long history of foundering on the treacherous shoals of racial solidarity
before reaching the safe harbor of class solidarity.

Racial cleavages were apparent from unionism's earliest days. Late in the
nineteenth century, the National Labor Union, the first such national organization, established its headquarters in Detroit. Its leader, Richard Trevellick, argued that blacks should be allowed as members and be paid wages
equal to those of whites for the same work. Trevellick's brave proposals were
soundly defeated by white unionists. The subsequent success of the Knights
of Labor in Detroit meant an entrenchment of unionization for whites only.
By the time of the first Great Migration, some Detroit unions were refusing
admittance to blacks, including the Amalgamated Association of Street
Railway Employees, fabled opponents of the transit monopoly. Others admitted blacks to their ranks but consigned them to marginalized, black-only
locals. The Carpenters Union permitted some blacks to become tradesmen
but refused to allow any members to work under black foremen.

No wonder that most blacks had little sympathy for the union movement and often sided with capitalists in advocating "open shop" rules. This

first became clear during the 1921 Timken Axle Company strike, when the Detroit Urban League had little trouble recruiting blacks to work as strikebreakers. The exclusive Detroit Athletic Club's white Waiters' Union employees went on strike in 1921, only to find to their dismay that the management fired them *en masse* and hired only blacks to replace them. Thus, discriminatory and segregated unions undercut their own effectiveness by encouraging black, nonunion members to become strikebreakers because this was the only way they could gain access to many occupations.

This racial schism within the labor fraternity persisted through the glory days of union organizing, even when some unions like the United Auto Workers adopted explicitly integrationist rhetoric and recruiting tactics during the 1930s. As was apparent from the segregated union-sponsored dances and picnics, the UAW was unable to convince a majority of its white members that interracial solidarity was crucial for union success, especially when attempting to organize at Ford Motor Company. The UAW also faced a hard sell convincing potential black recruits that union seniority rules would do more than reify existing racial segregation of occupations. Tellingly, in the key 1937 city election when the UAW ran (unsuccessfully) its vaunted "labor slate," the NAACP supported the opposition candidates, citing the segregated UAW social events as the rationale.

With the advent of wartime production and accelerating labor migration from the South, Detroit unions faced an increasingly difficult challenge building racial solidarity in the ranks. Discrimination in the hiring, job classification, promotion, and seniority assignment of blacks was rampant, even when shops were unionized. When firms tried *not* to discriminate, white workers often protested to retain their privileges by walking off the jobs. In 1941, such "hate strikes" took place locally at Curtis Aircraft, Hudson Motors, and Packard Motors; in the spring of 1942, at least half a dozen more occurred. The most infamous occurred in June 1943, when 25,000 white UAW members at Packard ceased their production of Rolls-Royce engines for Patrol Torpedo boats and aircraft. Their rationale was that the firm had promoted three black workers into a department that previously hired only whites. The UAW leadership vigorously opposed this wildcat stoppage, arguing that Ku Klux Klan agitators were to blame. Though they offered no proof, there was no denying that a southern-accented voice over a loudspeaker inflamed strikers with commentary like "I'd rather see Hitler and Hirohito win than work beside a n_ _ _ _ _ on the assembly line." UAW president R. J. Thomas was booed down when he urged strikers to return to work. In Detroit, race not only trumped union solidarity, but it even trumped patriotism. No sooner did the Packard hate strike end than the hate riots started on Belle Isle.

To its credit, the UAW leadership usually *said* the right thing regarding race relations, even when it was unpopular to do so. In the aftermath of the 1942 Sojourner Truth Homes riots, UAW President Thomas bravely and effectively criticized the city and police and marshaled influence in Washington to resolve the situation in favor of black occupancy. In April 1943, the UAW organized a mass march down Woodward Avenue to protest discrimination in war plants. It culminated at a Cadillac Square rally where 10,000 heard UAW vice president Walter Reuther proclaim that the union would "tell any worker who refused to work with a colored worker that he could leave the plant because he did not belong there." In what came to be known as the "Cadillac Charter," the audience ritualistically committed themselves to fighting discrimination. This ritual, like so much other integrationist rhetoric, would prove a weak levee in the face of the flood of hatred that would burst through in the coming months.

Unfortunately, when it came to *actions*, the UAW record was more mixed. The UAW had a fatal blind spot when it came to fighting discrimination against black women. Efforts to alleviate wartime labor shortages by recruiting women focused almost entirely on whites, yet this never was a major rallying point for unionists. By the end of 1942, with the war already a year old, thousands of black women had taken factory training courses but could find no jobs. There were no black women workers at Chrysler's Highland Park or Dodge Main plants or at GM's Cadillac plant; Hudson and Packard employed a dozen black women between them. Ford was infamous for hiring white women at Willow Run, while turning away equally skilled black women. A federal report in the summer of 1943 estimated that 25,000 black women represented the city's "largest neglected source of labor." It is thus no accident that the iconic poster "Rosie the Riveter" was portrayed as a white woman.

It also became clear that UAW and other major union leaders were not interested in power sharing arrangements with rising black leaders or in taking strong actions in support of issues that primarily concerned black rank-and-file workers. The black community responded institutionally in several ways. One of the first was the multiunion National Negro Labor Council, formed in Detroit in 1951 and led by Coleman Young, which organized local councils to fight job discrimination and enhance black political success within their various unions. This was succeeded by the Union Leadership Council in 1957, organized by 13 black labor activists in Detroit with similar aims as the NNLC. It became a hotbed for political debate, strategizing and mobilizing in an effort to extend black political representation in unions and local government. But the most radical, influential, and polarizing black responses within the union movement of Detroit appeared in the late 1960s.

The 1960s were not just famous for protests against civil rights injustices and the Vietnam war but also local grievances (often with racial overtones) on factory shop floors to which unions were slow to respond, as Heather Ann Thomas documents. In May 1968, 4,000 UAW workers conducted an unauthorized wildcat strike at Dodge Main to protest assembly line speedups. Though white workers were the main participants, black workers received a disproportionate share of disciplinary actions, with Chrysler firing several black strike leaders. These fired leaders decided to form DRUM, the Dodge Radical Union Movement. DRUM wanted to address grievances against *both* capitalists and the UAW hierarchy by organizing black workers nationwide as the "vanguard of the revolutionary struggle in the country." Its constitution declared, "We must gear ourselves in the days ahead toward getting rid of the racist, tyrannical, and unrepresentative UAW as representation for the black workers, so that with this enemy out of the way we can deal with our main adversary, the white racist management of Chrysler Corporation." DRUM's media mouthpiece was a newspaper aimed at black community concerns, the *Inner City Voice*, subtitled "The Voice of Revolution." The *ICV* front pages in summer 1968 used unmistakable imagery to lambast the "white racist and bigoted foremen . . . snapping the whip over the backs of thousands of black workers" and "the double-faced, backstabbing UAW . . . [that] in many cases is unwilling to press forward the demands and aspirations of black workers." DRUM members adopted the bongo drum as their symbol. Imagine what UAW President Walter Reuther thought—did he feel that DRUM's young radicals disrespected his longtime advocacy for civil rights, or did he empathize by recalling his own youthful experience of socialist solidarity while helping retool a Soviet tractor factory in Gorky?

Equivalent "RUM" organizations sprouted all over Detroit: at UPS, the *Detroit News*, Cadillac, and major employers of health care workers. An exceptionally revolutionary RUM was organized at Chrysler's Eldon Avenue gear and axle plant, widely known for having the industry's most inhumane and dangerous working conditions. The Eldon Radical Union Movement

(ELDRUM) loudly accused the Chrysler Corporation of murder after each death of a black worker in an industrial accident. One worker at this factory was James Johnson, whose violent reaction would soon spotlight the plant's inhuman working conditions. The League of Black Revolutionary Workers was incorporated in Detroit in 1969 to champion these local RUMs' cause. Its seven-member board included Kenneth Cockrel, who would famously defend the New Bethel Church internees in 1969 and James Johnson in 1971, and as a city councilor in 1980, would fight Mayor Coleman Young over the Poletown industrial redevelopment project.

Detroit's black grassroots union movement was more than just antira-cism/antiwhite union revolutionary rhetoric. DRUM urged workers to carry out their own job actions in protest, bypassing standard UAW-sanctioned grievance procedures. The precedent was set at Dodge Main in July 1968, when black workers struck to publicize their (repeatedly ignored) demands for a black plant manager and equal pay. The DRUM-organized pickets gathered at 5 a.m. before the first shift, some wearing brightly colored African-style robes and dancing in the street to the bongo beat. The sights, sounds, and revolutionary polemics alienated many conservative white workers, thus rendering the anticivil rights, anticommunist, antiblack rhetoric of presidential candidate George Wallace even more appealing. Martha Reeves may have insisted that her song was only about partying, but "dancing in the streets" undoubtedly took on a prismatic political *cachet*, for both good and ill.

Grassroot wildcat strikes, typically led by revolution-spouting black UAW workers—not sanctioned by the UAW hierarchy—grew more prevalent over the next five years. However, the August 14, 1973, wildcat strike at Chrysler's Mack Avenue stamping plant proved the tipping point. The strike was called because numerous safety problems leading to documented deaths and dismemberment on the job had not been corrected through the standard union channels. In a flashback to 1937 tactics, two workers began a sit-down strike and soon were joined by hundreds more. Perhaps blind to the legitimate grievances because of the radical politics and race of the wildcat organizers, the conservative, white UAW hierarchy addressed the crowd of curious workers outside the plant in terms usually reserved for management. UAW Executive Committee member and future UAW President Doug Fraser belittled the sit-downers as "agitators" and told reporters that the UAW had pledged that "*these people* were not going to take *our* union and the plants where we represent workers." Thus it was not surprising that the UAW did not object when 60 Detroit Police Department troopers in full riot gear, led by police commissioner and just-defeated mayoral candidate John Nichols, burst into the plant and arrested the sit-downers on August 15. Enraged workers descended on their local union hall and shouted down the international union leaders telling them to return to work. The next morning, union leaders from locals all over Detroit devised a strategy to keep these "uppity workers" in their place, inflamed by incendiary rhetoric ("they're a bunch of punks [and] we are not going to let them destroy everything we've built") spouted by the International UAW leadership. Armed with baseball bats, pipes, and other miscellaneous weapons, mainline UAW leaders went in groups of 250 to each of the Mack Avenue plant's four gates to attack the DRUM-UAW picketers. It was a surreal scene that would have made Harry Bennett's Service Department at Ford Motor Company proud. Even more egregiously, UAW leadership told the press that "they were on call 24 hours a day" to go to any other plant that workers might disrupt without their permission!

Though they lasted barely five years, the RUMs succeeded in getting Chrysler to hire more black foremen and supervisors and the UAW to hire more black staff. All UAW locals in Chrysler's five east side plants elected black presidents by the mid-1970s. These proved pyrrhic victories, as hard economic times and plant relocations took their toll on Detroit auto employment. Sixty percent of the workforce at Chrysler's Dodge Main was black by 1971 when it closed; all the other plants where RUM had success soon followed suit.

These fractures in the racial solidarity of the UAW never fully mended; the union still limps. As recently as 1995, a black UAW official in Detroit named Oliver French grew so frustrated by what he perceived as union discrimination against him that he murdered two white UAW officers and wounded two others. Unlike James Johnson, Oliver French was convicted. The mushrooming of a radical black political infrastructure in reaction to an entrenched, conservative, white union bureaucracy was understandable. Yet, like so much of the dialectical evolution of Detroit, it had an undesirable side effect. Once again, a wedge was driven between racial factions within the proletariat. Ironically, this time it was driven by blacks' grievances against UAW unresponsiveness and white union bureaucrats' ensuing overreactions, not by capitalists.

Deep in the gloom
Of the oil-filled pit

Where the engine rolls down the line,
We challenge the doom
Of dying in shit
While strangled by a swine . . .
. . . But now we stand
For DRUM's at hand
To lead our freedom fight,
And now 'til then
We'll unite like men . . .
For now we know our might.
And damn the plantation
And the whole Chrysler nation
For DRUM has dried our tears,
And now as we die
We've got a different cry
For now we hold our spears!
UAW is scum
Our thing is DRUM!
—Anthem of the Dodge Radical Union Movement, 1968

The Arsenal of Discrimination

For centuries, Detroit's working people, divided into different racial and ethnic camps, competed relentlessly and ruthlessly for a larger share of the economic pie being baked by the region's economy. Over the years, the competition was characterized by robbery, renewal, and riot, all blatantly discriminatory. From the current perspective of whites, the game is over; they for the most part have "won" a superior economic position compared to blacks.

The economic situation of the average black person in Greater Detroit has deteriorated relative to the average white person since the end of World War II, by almost every measure of interracial inequality. From 1950 to 1970, the poverty rate among blacks in Greater Detroit stayed roughly twice that of whites, but thereafter the gap progressively widened to the point where, since 1990, poverty rates for blacks have remained over three times as high. The median family incomes of metropolitan area blacks in 1950 were 72 percent as high as the median incomes for white families. Blacks' relative position eroded by 2009 to the point where their median income was only 50 percent that of whites. Even at the peak of Greater Detroit's 1990s boom, only two-thirds of working-age black males were employed, compared to almost nine-tenths of white males.

Unions in general and the UAW in particular were unable and sometimes unwilling to close these racial gaps in the proletariat, despite their power to wrest gains from capitalists. To be sure, the UAW was notably successful in reducing interracial wage differentials within its membership and job segregation in the auto plants. But the UAW never built a powerful interracial political coalition that coalesced when facing the combined threats of neighborhood racial change, school integration, and erosion of property values. These political mobilization efforts were impeded both by many white rank-and-file members with their own racial prejudices and fears and by an increasingly conservative leadership that saw any dissident labor movement with leftist tendencies as a threat, especially if led by black workers. Thus, it was ironic but powerfully symbolic that, at the same time the UAW reached its zenith in national membership, its Detroit leaders were violently crushing wildcat strikes led by radical black DRUM-UAW members. It turned out that those bongo drums on the Detroit picket lines were not only beating African rhythms, but they were beating a death knell for American liberalism: the end of any hope for a then-powerful union movement to heal interracial wounds with working class-union solidarity expressing itself as a unified, potent political force in local and national struggles against business interests.

Even when it had traffic flowing at maximum legal speeds, Detroit's blue-collar freeway to the middle class had a fast lane (reserved for whites) and a slow lane (reserved for blacks). This freeway is now closed for unscheduled repairs, with no certain date for reopening. Greater Detroit is stuck in a working-class traffic jam where no one is getting ahead, yet all stay in their separate and unequal lanes. All drivers are frustrated, envious, resentful, and deeply afraid of each other. And how those horns do blow!

Many of Detroit's prominent citizens are buried in Elmwood Cemetery, the rolling, wooded, 84-acre enclosure a mile east of downtown. In stark contrast to most of its counterparts, the ground of Elmwood has been open to all races since its opening in 1846. Notables resting there include Fannie Richards, the city's first black school teacher; Cora Brown, Michigan's first black state senator; and Coleman Young. Jacob Howard, a white U.S. Senator from Michigan during the Civil War, is a lesser-known occupant of Elmwood Cemetery, although he drafted the Thirteenth and Fourteenth Amendments to the Constitution that abolished slavery and established the governmental equal protection clause so vital for securing civil rights. On first seeing Senator Howard's gravesite, one is struck by a broken obelisk on the tomb. It is tempting to register disgust at this apparent desecration of the resting place of one who should be celebrated as a local hero. Closer inspection reveals, however, that the break is intentional. The senator wanted it that way, to symbolize a task unfinished.

Chapter 8

Feasting on Fear

Crime is increasing, Trigger happy policing
Panic is spreading, God knows where we're heading
— "Inner City Blues" sung by Marvin Gaye in 1971

Greater Detroit is gripped by deep-seated fears. It is a place where everyone has a gut feeling, "*They* want what I have, and will stop at nothing to take it." This is understandable, given the never-ending, no-holds-barred competition between its ethnic and, especially, racial groups.

Three distinct elements of Greater Detroit feast on this fear. They secure money or power by maintaining a climate of personal insecurity: the politicians, the media, and the police.

The Arsenal of Demagoguery

Black and white politicians over the last century have consistently played on—and often intentionally exaggerated for political gain—their constituencies' fears and mistrust of the "other." Greater Detroit blacks and whites can agree on few things. But one thing brings consensus for sure: when a local politician is in trouble, the most effective, time-tested response is playing the race card.

Whites had more time to perfect this technique since they held power first in Detroit. Racial demagoguery got off to a raucous start during the 1925 mayoral campaign, when incumbent John Smith took on avowed Ku Klux

Klan sympathizer Charles Bowles. With Bowles's resounding victory in the August primary, Mayor Smith was not about to let himself be outflanked on the lunatic right. Thus, after the Ossian Sweet incident in September, he blamed Dr. Sweet for his reckless, selfish ambitions. Nevertheless, the Klan rallies continued to mobilize Bowles's supporters, and he outpolled Mayor Smith in the general election that November. But Bowles did not become mayor in 1925. In a disturbing foreshadowing of the "hanging chad" recount circus in Florida during the 2000 presidential election, 17,000 Bowles votes were thrown out for spurious irregularities by the Smith-dominated elections board, just enough to give the election to Smith. In 1929, Charles Bowles finally won the mayorship. His vindication proved short-lived; he was recalled from office for corruption eight months after his inauguration.

Race-baiting again took center stage in the 1940s Detroit mayoral races. This period saw once-liberal Edward Jeffries morph into a segregationist in the desperate search for white votes, most infamously by praising the work of the Detroit police during the 1943 riot. Even UAW vice president Richard Frankenstein, a working-class hero who was among the union organizers beaten at the "Battle of the Overpass" outside the Ford Rouge complex in 1937, was trounced by Jeffries in 1945. The mayor played to whites' racial fears by condemning "neighborhood invasions" and vowing to preserve the sanctity of all-white havens. In the 1949 race, another liberal integrationist, George Edwards, lost to Republican Albert Cobo, despite strong backing of the UAW. Cobo artfully manipulated the worst nightmares of socially conservative, white working-class voters, the same group who became known as "George Wallace Democrats" in 1968 and 1972 and "Ronald Regan Democrats" in 1980. The election set turnout records: 62 percent of those registered voted. Cobo won all the city's white-dominated wards and Edwards all (seven) of the black-dominated wards. Cobo got 76 percent of the votes, as the racial conservatism of the UAW rank-and-file clearly revealed in the voting patterns. As one unionist wrote the disheartened Edwards in the wake of his defeat, "We don't want you or any part of your stuff . . . .In the shop we may be CIO but when we vote we vote *American*." As recounted by Mary Stolberg, such sentiments led Edwards to pen a poignant letter to his father after the crushing defeat, lamenting the prospects for "when a big overgrown industrial village will act like a modern city with a soul." Cobo was handily reelected 1953 using the same tactics. Detroiters honor Jeffries and Cobo—quintessential race-baiters—in perpetuity with the names of a major freeway and the convention center.

Most Detroit mayors were rank amateurs in the fear-mongering department, however, compared to Dearborn mayor Orville Hubbard—the demigod of racist scare tactics and the nationally infamous symbol of suburban Jim Crow-style segregation, as David Good documents. This is a man who did not hide behind politically correct code words. "I am not a racist," he once said to his assembled Dearborn City Department heads. "I just hate those black b_____!" In a 1956 interview with a delighted Alabama newspaper reporter, he proclaimed himself "for segregation 100 percent." And he knew how to achieve this goal politically. In 1948, Mayor Hubbard wanted to drum up opposition to a large apartment complex proposed by the John Hancock Insurance Company, so he issued a flyer subtly proclaiming:

KEEP NEGROES OUT OF DEARBORN
X VOTE NO ON (ADVISORY VOTE)
(the John Hancock Rental Housing Project)

PROTECT YOUR HOME AND MINE!

Mayor Hubbard proved that such fear tactics were political gold in Greater Detroit. He was elected in 1941 and 14 more consecutive terms spanning thirty-six years, still a U.S. record for mayors.

Numerous local and national white politicians panned for this mother lode of racial fear in Greater Detroit over the years. Gerald L. K. Smith, a white supremacist preacher from Louisiana who merged his demagogic prowess with Father Charles Coughlin's in a campaign to elect a "populist" president in 1936, found such fertile ground for his message in Detroit that he moved his church headquarters here at the start of World War II. Despite his extremism, Rev. Smith won a third of the votes in the 1942 Michigan Republican primary for U.S. senator. In 1972, Alabama governor and infamous segregationist George Wallace won the Democratic presidential primary in Michigan, garnering the bulk of his votes from Greater Detroit's white-dominated districts. Currently, suburban politicians like Oakland County executive L. Brooks Patterson play the race card by derisively joking about the incompetence and corruption of elected officials in Detroit. When in 2006 the Detroit City Council rejected a plan for transferring ownership of Cobo Convention Center to a regional authority, Patterson responded, "By and large, they're an embarrassing group, and they are continuing to embarrass the city nationally with their behavior." He then took a swipe at the city councilor who led the opposition: "I'd rather own a 1947 Buick than own Barbara-Rose Collins."

Detroit's black leaders also gained traction by playing racial politics for several generations. Often these politics took on a radical, separatist flavor, beginning with the founding of the Nation of Islam ("Black Muslims") in Detroit by Wallace D. Fard in 1930. The Shrine of the Black Madonna church was founded in 1967 by the Rev. Albert Cleage. He espoused the philosophy that Jesus was a black revolutionary and that the Promised Land could be reached only through grassroots struggles. Conflict was inevitable, Rev. Cleage preached, unless whites transferred power. During a dramatic and controversial 1967 Easter Sunday service, Rev. Cleage's invited guest, famed black radical H. Rap Brown, ominously warned that blacks "would burn Detroit down" if whites did not accomplish this power transfer quickly. Rev. Cleage then unveiled an 18-foot painting of Mary and baby Jesus depicted as blacks, the symbolic namesake of his church. The following year, the New Republic of Africa was founded in Detroit as a reaction to white racism. This organization advocated the U.S. ceding five southern states to create the territory for a new black nation.

Mainstream black politicians did not shy away from racial fear mongering when they sensed electoral trouble, as Wilbur Rich showed. In the midst of the city's fiscal crisis of 1981, Mayor Coleman Young mounted a desperate campaign for a referendum instituting a city income tax that would include a tax on commuters. Mayor Young asked during a revealing speech before Baptist ministers, "Are we going to do what we have to do to guarantee the city continues to move forward and our destiny remains in or own hands? Or will we do what thousands of bigots hope we'll do: vote 'no' and the state takes over?" Later, in attacking unnamed suburban organizations opposed to the new tax, Young said, "Some people in this state are playing a dangerous, divisive game. What they want is to take over Detroit . . . .They are after us."

The trump card played time and time again by Detroit's black politicians is inciting fear that white suburbanites want to control "*our* city's resources." Mayor Young hurled the epithets "Uncle Tom" and "Great White Hope" at black challenger Tom Barrow in the 1989 campaign, to drive home his assertion that Barrow's proposals served hidden suburban interests. Sharon McPhail used similar labels (ultimately, unsuccessfully) to smear fellow black mayoral aspirant Dennis Archer during the 1993 campaign. Incumbent Mayor Kwame Kilpatrick could not resist watering the seedling of fear at a get-out-the-vote rally before the 2005 election. "This is *our* town, and *our* town is coming back," he asserted. "The question is: Will Detroiters be involved in the comeback?" Race-baiting is now institutionalized in Detroit in the form of the Call 'Em Out Coalition. This organization annually sponsors the "Sambo" awards for local politicians who reputedly sell out to white interests. The winner for 2005: Mayor Kilpatrick.

In Greater Detroit, there is one topic that both white and black politicians agree can be the focus of an effective campaign of racial fear mongering: property values. Ironically, each race uses the property value gambit in the opposite way. As illustrated by the Orville Hubbard flyer above, white politicians scored points for generations by "protecting" their constituents against the loss of property values that would inevitably follow if blacks were to move into their neighborhood. Now some Detroit politicians whip up their black constituents' fears over possible *increases* in property values (and corresponding losses of "affordable" housing) that might follow from proposed downtown real estate developments. Their racially loaded dirty words: "white gentrification." During the mini-boom in speculative housing construction in Detroit in 2003, real estate developers brought a half-billion dollars' worth of desperately needed proposals to City Council for approval. During the hearings, a key promulgator of the white gentrification fear campaign, councilwoman JoAnn Watson, was only interested in learning where the developers lived.

Demonizing Detroit

Greater Detroit's local news media embrace a perpetual campaign of fear because it helps them get readers and viewers. Their message is simple: "What's goin' on" in the region is usually "bad," and if it's bad, it's usually in Detroit. The local media select and mold the "news" to remind their predominantly white, suburban customers that they voted wisely with their feet. Fear has a face, and that face is black and male.

The *Detroit News* infamously fomented fear in the wake of Mayor Coleman Young's inaugural speech in 1974, during which he urged criminals to "hit the Eight Mile Road," an obvious euphemism for "get out of town." But the *News* found and quoted on its front page an obscure suburban public official who was convinced that Mayor Young was urging black criminals to victimize white suburbanites instead of Detroiters.

"If it bleeds it leads" still seems to be the editorial talisman for choosing stories that will begin the nightly TV news broadcasts in Greater Detroit.

Nina Butler, then a Wayne State University Urban Planning Master's student, conducted a content analysis of the three nightly local news broadcasts for a three-month period during 2007. She found that 85 percent of all lead stories showing faces of black people emphasized negative content and that 89 percent of lead stories about Detroit had negative content.

The national and international news media also have a field day demonizing Detroit. The fearsome stereotypical image of Detroit is widely promoted. The rest of the world seems to take comfort—even perhaps some voyeuristic pleasure—in the myth that "Detroit could never happen here" and that, however bad things are, "at least it's not Detroit." Ever attuned to selling comfort and voyeuristic pleasure, the media have generously obliged. The media act as the pimp doctors of Detroit, exposing the patient's tantalizing symptoms in graphic detail for their own profit, while offering no diagnoses, let alone prescriptions.

There is no lack of illustrations of the media pimping Detroit. The August 14, 1967, cover story on *Life Magazine* breathlessly described Detroit as "the city at the blazing heart of a nation in disorder." The national wires gleefully disseminated photos of drunken fans burning police cars after the October 1984 Tigers Baseball World Series victory. Israeli journalist Ze'ev Chafets labeled Detroit "America's first Third World city" in his 1990 *Devil's Night and Other True Tales of Detroit*. In October 2009 *Time Magazine* featured a cover story titled "The Tragedy of Detroit." This was the first of a series of articles by the *Time-New York Times* publishing consortium, which sent a cadre of reporters on "Assignment Detroit" for a year, as if it were some exotic foreign correspondent locale. Were they issued flak vests, one wonders, as if they were headed for Baghdad or Kabul? *NBC Dateline* featured a 45-minute special on Detroit in April 2010. Despite hours of interviews with Detroiters who emphasized the positive features of the city and why they lived there, only footage of the bizarre and depressing was aired.

This mercilessly myopic media mania is successful. Much of the world apparently *does* think Detroit is a place where the weak are killed and eaten. As an illustration, a student in the Wayne State University Master of Urban Planning Program had a penchant for exploring nearby cities on "road trips" organized with a group of her girlfriends. She once chose to visit "The Hill" in Pittsburgh, the neighborhood made famous in August Wilson's plays that carries its own reputation for toughness. As this clearly out-of-place gaggle of petite young blonds walked past a barber shop, they were playfully accosted by a group of patrons who helpfully offered to provide them with an unrepeatable variety of "personal tours." "No, thanks," the intrepid student leader replied, "We're from Detroit!" "Whoa!" the would-be tour guides exclaimed, eyebrows raised, as they hastily retreated into the barber shop, undoubtedly anticipating that these ladies "were packing" (or worse), and *mos def* not to messed with.

To Serve and Protect

It is no wonder that demand for police in Greater Detroit seems insatiable, given its history of competition via robbery, renewal, and riot and of politicians and the media continually fomenting fear. Unfortunately, security personnel have not typically been used evenhandedly to deter and apprehend lawbreakers. Throughout Detroit's history, security forces have been ruthlessly and selectively set by the more powerful against the less powerful, by the "ins" against the "outs." Thus, police both responded to and fomented fear, allaying the fears of those in power (capitalists, whites) but abetting more fear for the less powerful (unionists, blacks).

Greater Detroit's police repressed strikes from the 1920s through the 1970s. Their political role evolved over the last century into agents of racial repression. The Detroit Police Department's implicit mission became clear in the early 1920s, when it actively began recruiting southern-born whites, many of them avowed Ku Klux Klan members. These recruits performed their mission with great efficiency and brutality. Between January 1925 and June 1926 (exactly the period surrounding the Ossian Sweet incident), the police killed 25 black Detroiters. Though blacks represented only 8 percent of the city's population, they represented 51 percent of the victims of police violence. In contrast, in New York City, with three times the black population, police killed only three black citizens during this span.

Police racial biases grew even more transparent during the 1940s. The police arrested only two whites, but 102 blacks, during the 1942 Sojourner Truth Homes riots. A group of religious and union leaders accused the police of conspiring with the Klan to foment this disturbance. But these outrages paled in comparison to what would come the following year.

From the earliest stages of the 1943 riots, the police force showed its true racial colors. On that fateful June Sunday night on Belle Isle, police searched only cars driven by blacks. On Monday morning, instead of stationing police to protect stores on the Hastings Street retail district of Black Bottom, whose windows had been broken the night before, they cruised around, stopping only occasionally to take potshots at looters. Later Monday, as rampaging whites turned over and burned black-owned cars, assaulted black pedestrians, and beat black transit riders in the heart of downtown, police tried only to "reason" with the mobs, not arrest the perpetrators. The cops' cynical passivity was most tragically displayed when a black man on his way to work at a downtown bank was pulled from his streetcar, assaulted, and eventually shot while in the presence of four police who were escorting him through the mob "for his own protection." That night provided an eerie foreshadowing of police antiriot tactics perfected a quarter-century later. On June 21, 1943, a black man shot a policeman patrolling in a vacant lot on the 200 block of Vernor Avenue, then was immediately shot and killed by other police. The police vented their rage by firing machine guns, rifles, and tear gas canisters into the fully occupied Vernor Apartments next door. After their assault, police lined up shell-shocked tenants on the street and ransacked their apartments "searching for weapons," stealing any valuables uncovered. Police on the scene claimed that "they were going after snipers in the building," though a subsequent police report confirmed only the single shooter in the vacant lot.

As the blood dried and debris was cleared, two parallel narratives of blame emerged. Mayor Edward Jeffries articulated the opinion held by most Detroit whites that the blacks (or an equivalent but less polite appellation) were responsible for inciting violence. In this way, he could justify that 85 percent of those arrested were black and of the 25 blacks who died in the disturbances, 17 were shot by police "in the line of duty." Future Supreme Court Justice Thurgood Marshall articulated the other narrative in a NAACP report documenting police brutality during the 1943 riots: "The affidavits we have taken are more than sufficient to justify the calling of a special grand jury to investigate the nonfeasance and malfeasance of the police as a contributing factor in the Detroit riots. . . . The trouble reached riot proportions because the Detroit police once again enforced the law under an unequal hand." Yet another major event produced parallel narratives of blame, cementing another row of bricks on the wall separating Greater Detroit's racial histories.

*   *   *

"What a gorgeous Sunday afternoon," Bruno and Helen's eldest son Karl thought, "Though unseasonably hot and muggy for June." He was pleased he could spend the day with his family, drinking beer and playing with his young son in the backyard, as this was his scheduled weekend off from police duty. Dinner ended abruptly with a panicky phone call from Karl's precinct commander. "The n_ _ _ _ _ s are rioting on Belle Isle! Report now!"

Before leaving, Karl took time to phone his parents to determine the whereabouts of his younger sister. He knew of Helen's fondness for spending "quality time" at Belle Isle with her fiancé, George Milton, and was relieved to hear that they both were safely at the family home on Balfour Road. Within minutes, he was riding into action, siren screaming, astride his police Harley-Davidson.

Like virtually all white Detroiters, Karl did not know any black people well. Neighborhoods and schools where he grew up were rigidly segregated, so there was little chance for contact there. Only 1 percent of his fellow police were black, so there was little chance for collegial contact there. Karl's main interracial contacts came on the beat, and they were the sort of interchanges that were fraught with power imbalances, misunderstandings, tensions, and the latent potential (and often actual) use of violence. As with his fellow officers, the context of contact merely reinforced Karl's prejudices and legitimized use of repressive tactics.

It was thus not at all surprising that Karl's commander ordered him to arrest any young black males he saw who "might seem capable of making trouble." Those who were thereby "preventively detained" were brought before a sympathetic judge, who listened to the rote (and totally fabricated) testimony of a police officer stationed in his court, who would dictate from a template of minor offenses that the hapless arrestee had supposedly committed during the riots. A sentence of a few days in jail proved sufficient to intimidate (and infuriate) the Black Bottom community, as well as reify the existing power structure.

Karl heard that on Monday some of his police brethren intentionally rerouted unsuspecting black motorists from Black Bottom toward the white mob violence on lower Woodward Avenue. But this gratuitous police maliciousness had its limits, as Karl learned first hand. As the trouble was abating, he and the three other police in a cruiser patrolling Black Bottom spotted a group of black youth loitering outside a movie theater. The police pulled up, and the sergeant bellowed through his bullhorn that they all should clear the street and go inside the theater. After they obeyed, the sergeant guffawed to his colleagues, "Now watch this, boys!" as he tossed a tear gas canister into the theater. The cops' laughter was quickly squelched as the hissing canister came bouncing back out of the theater, coming to rest directly under their squad car before exploding in a cloud of choking smoke that effectively camouflaged the gasping, burning-tires exit of the chastened police pranksters.

*   *   *

As Detroit returned to a "peacetime" environment in 1945, the war between the white police and the black citizenry continued. The more violently the police exercised racial repression in response to whites' fear, the more blacks' fears grew. "Law enforcers and keepers of order" as perceived by whites were "law breakers and oppressors" as perceived by blacks. A 1951 public opinion poll starkly revealed these parallel realities. Five times more black than white respondents included "the Police Department as one of top three matters needing attention in city." In 1957 the Detroit NAACP issued a scathing report documenting that

> the most frequent type of police misconduct . . . is physical assault, followed by insulting epithets. . . . The central problem . . . seems to be the unprovoked attacks by the police while questioning [blacks]. This, followed by false charges of "resisting arrest" has created distrust and bitter resentment of the police department. . . . Our reports show a total disregard, on the part of the policemen, for the complainant's rights as a citizen.

Instead of spurring reform efforts, such reports seemed only to provoke the police into even more outrageous misconduct. After the murder of two white women in the fall of 1960, the unfounded suspicion of a black perpetrator spurred a rabid police crackdown during which police stopped, frisked, and jailed thousands of innocent blacks.

The first serious reform effort began in 1962 with the appointment of Police Commissioner George Edwards by newly elected Democratic mayor Jerome Cavanagh. When Edwards accepted the position, he said his first job was "to teach police that they didn't have a constitutional right to beat up

Negroes on arrest." The Police Department reciprocated the obvious lack of affection. They tried to discredit Commissioner Edwards by delaying reporting of crimes occurring in prior months to "show" that crimes spiked in the first month after his appointment. Despite entrenched resistance, Commissioner Edwards's reform efforts eventually bore fruit during the June 23, 1963, Civil Rights march on Woodward Avenue that culminated with Rev. Martin Luther King's prototype "I Have a Dream" speech delivered at Cobo Arena. The police assigned to the march's route were so protective and courteous that Dr. King himself was moved to pen a letter of thanks to Commissioner Edwards.

Unfortunately, old habits died hard in the department. When Commissioner Edwards went on a European vacation during July 1963, the "old police" tactics resurfaced in the case of Cynthia Scott, a well-known, statuesque sex worker who happened to be black. The Police Department claimed that Ms. Scott was plying her trade on the street when two police attempted to arrest her. Police charged that she brandished a knife, slashed at an officer, and then ran down an alley, whereupon officers shot and killed her while in pursuit. The would-be customer at the scene reported a different tale: that Ms. Scott had not flashed any weapon and was walking away after arguing that there was no reason to arrest her when she was shot. The final shot entered her stomach from the front after she had been felled by a bullet in her back.

It is easy to appreciate how many black Detroiters saw the police as an occupying army. In 1967, over a third of the city's population but only 5 percent of the police officers were black. One among that 5 percent was Isaiah McKinnon, later named police commissioner by Mayor Dennis Archer in 1994. In July 1967, Officer McKinnon narrowly escaped being shot as a looter by his fellow officers, whose actions apparently were governed more by his complexion than his police uniform. Many other black citizens were not so lucky.

Vignettes of police brutality during the 1967 civil unrest are sufficiently copious to fill a book as Sidney Fine has done, but a sampling is instructive. Police dragged one black man into a hospital emergency room; he was handcuffed and bleeding profusely from the face. "Help me!" he moaned. An officer promptly kicked him in the groin, adding insult to injury, "You should have thought of that before you started this, n _ _ _ _ _!" In another case, a handcuffed black man was shouting familial curses at his captors from the back of a squad car. The object of ancestral derision shot back, "I won't kill you in front of these reporters, but I'll shut your mouth!" Whereupon the officer repeatedly pummeled the victim's mouth with the butt of his rifle until he collapsed on the squad car's bloody floor.

Yet one incident stands above the rest for the sheer arbitrariness of its violence and the baseness of the racial passions that motivated it: the Algiers Motel incident. As described by John Hersey, on the night of July 25, 1967, a National Guardsman and private security guard assigned to protect the Great Lakes Mutual Life Insurance Building on Woodward Avenue near New Center, claimed that snipers were firing from the nearby Algiers Motel. Other Guardsmen, federal troops, and Detroit and state police responded, surrounding and then crashing simultaneously into the motel through every door. Though the stories become murky at this point, no one uncovered evidence of weapons or shooting from inside the motel. What apparently was going on, however, was a shooting of a different kind: a sex party involving two white women and nine or ten black men. The partiers were questioned by the combined forces, found innocent of sniping, then allowed to return to their rooms. Three Detroit police officers stayed behind to "finish up the details." Soon thereafter the motel's night clerk found the bodies of three black men, ages 17, 18, and 19, killed by 12-gauge double-O buckshot at close range. Two were shot while kneeling. None could have been killed while engaging in a sniper duel with police outside the motel. Though three trials were held, no one was convicted of the killings.

> I . . . think of it [the 1967 disturbances] as an explosion—a chemical reaction to the prevailing conditions. The flammable element was police brutality. . . . The explosion of 1967 was not a race *riot* . . . there was a principal object of the rebels' vengeance, and . . . it was the white man in the blue uniform.
>
> —Coleman Young, Mayor of Detroit, 1994

> The DPOA believes . . . that charges of police brutality are part of a nefarious plot by those who would like our form of government overthrown. The blueprint for anarchy calls for the destruction of the effectiveness of the police.
>
> —Carl Parsell, president of the Detroit Police Officers Association, 1968

> We know that today we have the highly sophisticated Green Beret STRESS unit roaming our city at will and killing on whim . . . .It

promises to get better. [Police Chief] General John Nichols is in Germany tonight, studying police procedures in Munich, Frankfurt, and Berlin. Maybe he'll have ovens for the survivors and witnesses of STRESS murder.

—Sheila Murphy Cockrel, activist and future
Detroit city councilor, 1973

The Detroit police did have one notable accomplishment during the 1967 turmoil: they got blacks and whites to agree on *something*. Unfortunately, what they got them to agree on was that the police made both groups more afraid than ever. Blacks were convinced that the police represented a fearsome element of random violence in their lives. Whites were convinced that the police were unwilling or unable to keep blacks from breaking the law.

For their part, the police responded by cracking down even harder on anything black or leftist that moved, producing a string of ever more violent incidents. Police delighted in harassing patrons of the "Infernoburger," a teen club in northwest Detroit's Fitzgerald neighborhood dedicated to creating interracial solidarity. As Poor People's Movement activists gathered for a meeting at Cobo Hall in May 1968, mounted police charged into the crowd with no provocation. In October that year, police assailed a picket line protesting the presidential campaign appearance of Alabama Governor George Wallace at Cobo Hall. Then, in November, chance would play the provocateur by arranging two dances simultaneously at the Veterans Memorial building downtown: well-dressed black teens attending a major social event on one floor and off-duty policemen attending a Detroit Police Officers Association function on another. After the inevitable verbal confrontation between members of the two groups on an elevator, the police roughed up any black teens they could isolate in the building. In March 1969, two white police witnessed what they thought were several armed men leaving a meeting of the Republic of New Africa at New Bethel Baptist Church and were shot when they tried to challenge them. Responding police claimed they too were fired on and, forcing their way into the church, engaged in a brief gunfight. All told, 142 inside were arrested, and twelve guns were confiscated. At the urging of New Bethel pastor Charles L. Franklin, newly elected judge George Crockett set up a temporary Recorder's Court in the police station holding the crowd and quickly released most on their own recognizance. Those accused of shooting the white officers were acquitted, partly because defense attorney Kenneth Cockrel (father of Kenneth Cockrel, Jr., future Detroit City Council President and

Interim Mayor) secured a jury that actually represented Detroit by overturning the decades-long racist jury selection bureaucracy.

For their part, white Detroiters took security matters into their own hands by buying a record number of guns, electing Roman Gribbs mayor, moving from the city, or all the above. Wayne County Sheriff Roman Gribbs, the "law and order candidate," was elected mayor of Detroit in November 1969. He defeated Detroit's first black mayoral candidate, Richard Austin, by the narrowest of margins: 7,312 votes of 507,312 cast. Despite the cloven electorate, Mayor Gribbs knew what his constituents wanted: security. Thus STRESS was born in 1971: *Stop the Robberies, Ensure Safe Streets.* The acronym proved perversely appropriate, given its psychological impact on the black community. Here's how it worked. Specially selected police officers were trained to entrap "street criminals" by having one member of their team pose as a vulnerable target while his teammates hid nearby, ready to arrest the perpetrator. These "sting" operations mainly targeted black neighborhoods. They quickly proved that "apprehension of suspects" often involved firearms. Detroit's annual rate of civilian deaths at the hands of police (7.17 per thousand officers) jumped to the number one spot in the nation. Fully one-third of these deaths were caused by STRESS, even though the unit represented only 2 percent of the Detroit police force. Despite (or perhaps because of) these statistics, STRESS was politically invulnerable under Mayor Gribbs. Even the accidental entrapment and killing of a black Wayne County sheriff's deputy and the wounding of two other deputies by STRESS zealots on March 9, 1972, could not terminate it. It took a political sea change to "Stop the STRESS."

The sea change occurred with Coleman Young's mayoral win in November 1973. In an ideological replay of the 1969 election, Young ran against another "law and order" candidate, police commissioner John Nichols. This time the electorate's changing demographics and their outrage over STRESS were too much for the reactionary position to overcome. Mayor Young quickly instituted a controversial affirmative action hiring plan in the Police Department, which yielded dramatic results. Within three years, Detroit had its first black police commissioner and the share of blacks in the force had risen to 25 percent. By 1990, Detroit had the highest percentage of black officers—59—among all large cities, more than double the percentage of Philadelphia, the runner up.

Though the Detroit Police Department's racial composition changed, many of its fear-provoking proclivities did not. In June 2003, the U.S. Department of Justice signed two consent decrees with the department, forcing it to take specific steps to cease violating the civil rights of citizens. These violations included fatal shootings, abuse of suspects in lockups, and routine mass arrests of potential witnesses (not just suspects) in homicide cases. A week after the decrees were signed, seventeen Detroit police officers were indicted on federal charges including illegal search, false arrest, assault, theft, planting evidence, falsifying reports, and perjury. The acknowledged ringleader was a white officer living in Livonia who had been sued five times previously by Detroit citizens for unreasonable use of force. Four years earlier, he cost the city a $1 million legal settlement because he killed an unarmed black driver at a routine traffic stop. In 2002, this policeman—admiringly known as "Robocop" to fellow officers—was honored by the Detroit Police Department as "Precinct Officer of the Year."

The behavior of Detroit's police is so suspect that the Department of Justice consent decree mandated each squad car be equipped with a video camera system. The system proved a complete failure despite the city spending $2.5 million; one wonders if squad car occupants bore any responsibility for its malfunctions. Another new computerized Police Department record system designed to identify individual officers with patterns of problematic behaviors has yet to be fully operational at this writing. In June 2010, a federal judge began fining the Police Department $1,000 a day until it came up with an acceptable plan to undo a backlog of over 1,100 citizen complaints of police misconduct.

Of course, Detroit did not hold a patent on employing police as repressors. For years, Dearborn's police cars were emblazoned with the words "Keep Dearborn Clean." Everyone—white and black alike—knew what this meant. Blacks with the temerity to move into Dearborn were greeted with "intensive police protection," which took the form of hourly visits or phone calls to their homes (24 hours a day, 7 days a week) "to make sure they were safe."

Today suburban police harassment typically takes the form of arrests for "driving while black." Timothy Bates and David Fasenfest analyzed data on approximately two thousand traffic stops during 1996 and 1997 by police in Eastpointe, a city bordering Detroit on the north side of Eight Mile Road. Black motorists who ventured into the interior of Eastpointe along Nine Mile and Ten Mile Roads had a disproportionate chance of being arrested: they comprised a third of all arrests but only one twentieth of all drivers in Eastpointe. Moreover, when arrested they were more likely to be handcuffed than white motorists were. All these patterns appeared despite the fact that,

when motorists were stopped and their cars searched, whites disproportionately were found with contraband and arrested for more serious offenses.
Thus, the police were operating to intimidate black motorists and discour-
age their presence in a place where "they clearly did not belong."

> now that Jose cat on the southwestside
> talking trash to hook in the bar outside
> they screamed at him to put his hands up high
> now they in southwest Detroit
> how should they know he a Hispanic guy?
> and they was black police so you know it wasn't no racial brutality
> or nothing like that
> but Jose had no business not doing what he was told
> and that's just the fact
>
> i mean, what was he doing out that late at night
> and what was he doing not knowing how to speak English right
> he was lucky they only shot him five times
> i mean, what we pay our police for?
>
> a 16 year old running through a vacant lot
> Gary Glenn knew he was spose to be
> in the Youth Home the day he was shot
> now he hadn't caught a serious case
> it was just he was a habitual type runaway
> and thank God that the police have guns!
> and if he didn't do nothing then why did he run?
> police had to shoot him six times
> cause they thought he was strapped
> as his momma screamed "don't shoot my boy no more"
> what could they do but keep busting caps in his back
>
> but what was Gary Glenn doing out in the daylight?
> the daylight sun can blind just like it was midnight
> and though he was shot in the back and no guns was found
> by running away he could've still taken them policemen
> down
> i mean, what we pay our police for?

i was 9 years old in my Brewster project bed
71 was hot before Boyd and Bethune was shot dead
and we was under the Big 4 and under STRESS
hook shot first or put you under cardiac arrest

and a gun was put to my mother's head
and a gun was put to my brother's head
as i sat up in my bed
reading a Richie Rich comic book
i stared and waited to be dead

but what was I doing in my bed that night?

you know criminals often choose under bedspreads to hide
and who knows what kind of stories
my mother might've been reading me at bedtime
and what the hell we pay our police for?
                    —"Support Your Local Police: What We Pay
                        Our Police For?" by Errol A. Henderson

The Fruits of Fear-Mongering

Has fear-mongering been successful in Greater Detroit? The sad answer is clearly "Yes." A 2004 University of Michigan Detroit Area regional poll found that 84 percent of white respondents would not consider a redeveloped Detroit neighborhood as a place to live. Leading the list of reasons was "too much crime." A July 2005 *Free Press* survey revealed that 32 percent of suburbanites go into Detroit "once or just a few times a year," 10 percent "almost never," and 7 percent "never." When asked why they did not go more often, the leading response was "fear." A Kaiser Family Foundation poll of Greater Detroit residents in January 2010 revealed that 49 percent of suburbanites do not go to Detroit, mainly due to fear of crime. Of those living in or traveling weekly to the city, 35 percent feel "not too safe" or "not safe at all."

Powerful media and political interests in Greater Detroit benefit by promoting this fear. Police forces are another beneficiary. Unfortunately, one group's quest for security through police power creates a byproduct for other groups that leaves them feeling even less secure than before. Because this police power has traditionally been applied in a biased fashion, it undermines victims' respect for the legitimacy of the security forces. Lawlessness is, thus, abetted ultimately, not deterred. It is but one of many examples of the region's *collective irrationality*.

But one more powerful group feasting on fear has yet to be mentioned: Greater Detroit's residential developers. They play on whites' insecurities by offering seemingly safe havens far removed from the dangers of the city, thereby creating a housing "Disassembly Line" that produces an irrational, unsustainable urban form, as we will explore next.

Chapter 9

The Dynamics of Decay, Abandonment, and Bankruptcy

[On] Jefferson Avenue, roughly from Chene Street out to the Belle Isle Bridge . . . dwelt families . . . in quiet, unstudied magnificence hard to equal anywhere else on earth, then or now. Row upon rows of elms, maples, and oaks. Immense, dreamy lawns, stretching from the front gates clear down to the river; little boat houses on the shore; . . . mansions of brick, rather plain on the outside but luxurious inside . . . [Detroit of the late 1800s] had more old wealth and old culture by far than did any of the cities in the great line of march between the Atlantic and the Pacific. Beside it, Buffalo was a mere outhouse. . . . Beside it, Chicago was a dung heap. Bostonians declared it was more like Boston than any other place. Yet it was no more Boston than I am Lillian Russell. It was, in truth, Detroit and nothing else.

—Walter Pitkin, *On My Own*, his chronicles of growing up in turn-of-the-twentieth-century Detroit, published in 1944

Mercy, mercy me, things ain't what they used to be.

—"Mercy, Mercy Me," sung by Marvin Gaye in 1971

Playing Reverse Musical Chairs

Perhaps the Detroit car culture's fetish about the "latest model" and "planned obsolescence" carried over into its housing market. Perhaps the subliminal message drilled into the Detroit subconscious by the Big Three marketers that "you *are* what you drive" has extended to "you *are* where you live." Whatever its origins, Detroiters place huge psychic importance on their residence's status and security. This translates into a feverish desire to have one's domicile surrounded by other homes of comparable (if not superior) price and vintage (the newer the better), so that personal status can be reified by neighborhood prestige. For security reasons, the home should be as far away as possible from the dangerous ghetto. For whites, having a set of neighbors who are exclusively white offers an added status symbol. Even more perceived security of whites' person and status is achieved if through subtle or blatant means one's political jurisdiction discourages black households from moving in.

Detroit-area residential developers have been only too willing to accommodate these white household demands. The region's featureless but well-watered plain, fragmented political jurisdictional structure and impotent regional planning institutions have been permissive—if not downright encouraging—of unbridled development.

What results is a game that could be called "reverse musical chairs." Unlike the conventional game, where the number of chairs and contestants is steadily decreased until only one of each is left, in this game the number of contestants stays the same while the number of new chairs is steadily increased. Reverse musical chairs begins with a tight circle of outward-facing chairs of varying degrees of comfort and an equal number of contestants occupying them. The music plays and contestants walk about, as a brand-new, stylish, extremely comfortable chair is added outside the original circle. When the music stops, many contestants vie for the new chair, but only one succeeds in occupying it. Everyone else settles for the most comfortable chair he or she can get, though everyone gets to sit somewhere because there is an excess of chairs. The music plays again while another, even better chair is added to the outer circle; the music stops, contestants compete for the best chairs, and everyone settles back down into what he or she can occupy. As these rounds progress, an ever-larger set of chairs in the original, inner circle accumulates that no one has occupied for a long time because they are the room's least comfortable ones. Eventually, these superfluous chairs are removed from the room because they merely get in the way of playing the game.

The metaphorical game of reverse musical chairs has its real-world equivalent. "Chairs" are dwellings, and they are added to the game by developers; "contestants" are households; the "room" is southeastern Michigan. The rules of this game, to the extent that there are any, are set by suburban municipalities and townships on the developing metropolitan fringe. This game has been played in Greater Detroit since 1950. The result as of 2010: over 600,000 more dwellings were built in the region than there were households to fill them. The inescapable corollary is that almost an equal number of the least competitive dwellings were vacated, eventually abandoned by their owners, and ultimately demolished. The vast majority of these lost dwellings were older houses and apartments in the least secure neighborhoods occupied by the poorest (typically black) people, located in the jurisdiction with the least favorable fiscal conditions, public services, and schools: Detroit.

Census Bureau statistics in Figure 21 show this game of reverse musical chairs in action. The three-county region gained 210,000 households during the 1940s but, due to wartime constraints, was able to add a net of only 194,000 dwellings. But every decade since, regardless whether the number of households grew a little or a lot, the region's developers built many more additional dwellings—an average of *over ten thousand per year*—than the net growth in households required. Ironically, this proved true even through the recession of the last decade. Though construction rates declined, there was an even sharper contraction in the number of households, so the region's excess housing supply reached record levels by 2010. Developers built this perpetual excess supply since 1950 because they could make a profit; their new suburban subdivisions could win the competition for occupants against the older housing stock located in more dangerous, more deteriorated, lower-status neighborhoods. Almost an equivalent number of dwellings were rendered redundant by this excess supply, minus those relatively few lost due to highway construction or retail and industrial development. Some of these redundant dwellings were converted to nonresidential uses, but the bulk were vacated and eventually abandoned by their owners. Typically after years of increasing deterioration, many of these abandoned dwellings were demolished or left to arson or rot.

Where the resulting growth and decline of the region's housing stock took place is also obvious from Figure 21. Never-developed land within Detroit was not completely built out until the late 1950s; thus 112,000 dwellings were added to the city's stock between 1940 and 1960. Detroit's peak number of dwellings—553,000—occurred in 1960, and the number declined steadily thereafter. Since 1960 the vast majority of new construction has

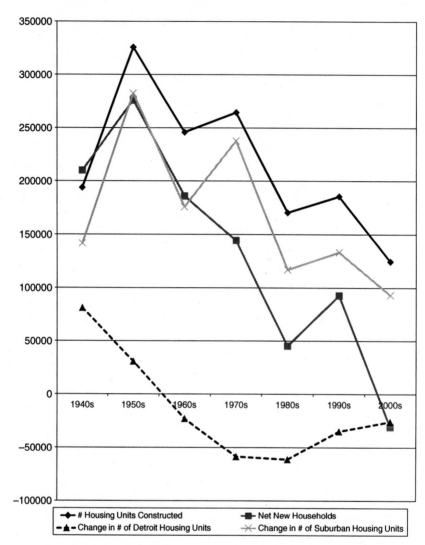

Figure 21. Housing and household changes in Detroit and its suburbs, 1940s–2000s.

Population Trends by Race in Metro Detroit Since 1900

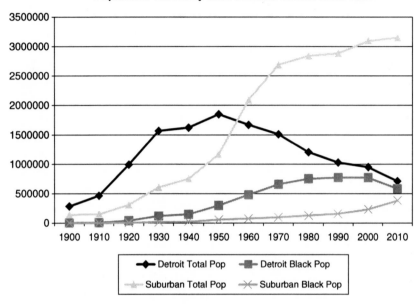

Figure 22. Population changes in Detroit and its suburbs, by race, 1900–2010.

occurred outside Detroit. As a result, the three-county suburban housing stock grew by 14,000 dwellings per year, on average, over the half century since 1960. During the same period, housing abandonment and demolition has continuously eroded the stock of dwellings in Detroit by an annual average of almost 4,000.

Not surprisingly, population trends tallied by the Census Bureau closely followed trends in dwellings, as seen in Figure 22. After rapid growth through the first half of the twentieth century, peaking at 1.85 million in about 1950, Detroit has been emptying out ever since; only 713,777 people remained in 2010. The three-county suburban ring's population rose from 1.17 million to 3.13 million during the same span. Sometime in the mid-1950s, the suburban population surpassed the city's and has not looked back since, literally and figuratively.

These population changes have been highly selective in terms of race. As Figure 22 shows, the black population of the region has always been disproportionately concentrated in Detroit. It surged during the Great Migrations from 1910 to 1930 and again from 1940 to 1980, almost exclusively within

Detroit. Only during the last three decades did blacks made any substantial population gains in the suburbs, rising to a 10 percent share of the suburbs by 2010. Yet the white shift to the suburbs was even more dramatic; only 8 percent of Detroit's population remains white in 2010.

Population shifts due to playing musical chairs in reverse have also been selective in terms of income, creating startling economic disparities between the core and the periphery. For example, David Crary, George Erickcek and Allen Goodman found that from 1995 to 2001—despite the period of relative prosperity in the region—almost 120,000 households moved out of Wayne County, the region's central county dominated by Detroit. Moreover, the out-movers' average income of $44,109 was 8 percent higher than the county average. This selective migration from the core county was associated with an annual loss of over $3.6 billion in household purchasing power. The consequences for local income, sales, and property tax revenues and the revenues for local retail enterprises were nothing short of devastating.

Playing musical chairs in reverse has systematically stripped value from homeowners in core neighborhoods. Allen Goodman found that, from 1970 to 2000, the median value of owner-occupied homes in Detroit, adjusted for inflation, fell 8 percent, from $67,000 to $62,000. During the same period, median home values in Detroit's suburbs rose 50 percent, from $94,000 to $142,000. Despite the fact that the region was at the peak of its last economic boom in 2000, almost 14 percent of owner-occupied housing stock (over 25,000) in Detroit was priced at or below that of a modest automobile: $25,000. At the other extreme of the Detroit market, less than 1 percent of the housing stock (a paltry 1,700 dwellings) was valued above $300,000.

The national mortgage market meltdown since 2007 hastened the downward slide of property values, not only in Detroit but in its suburbs as well. During 2009 the average price of a home sold in Detroit was less than $13,000. The local housing market is so depressed that some desperate owners are seeking divine intervention.

> With the real estate market stalled, some homeowners are looking for every possible advantage to help them find buyers. . . . This means there has been a rush for St. Joseph [patron saint of carpenters] statues. How is St. Joseph supposed to work? Bury the figurine upside down in the yard of the house you want to sell.
> —"St. Joseph Getting More Prayers," *Detroit Free Press*,
> February 26, 2010

Figure 23. Abandoned apartment building, Hamilton Avenue.

As property owners in Detroit find the value of their homes eroded by the lack of buyers and the rents collectible from their apartments atrophied as vacancies rise, they quite sensibly choose to invest less in maintaining and improving their properties. Eventually, no matter how much they lower the asking price or rent and how little they spend on upkeep, they lose money the longer they stay. The rational property owner will walk away from the property at this point. One such property is shown in Figure 23. Thousands of owners have been abandoning their properties each year in Detroit for decades. Allen Goodman estimates that 160,000 dwellings were abandoned in Detroit from 1970 to 2000. This process accelerated during the economic downturn since. In 2009, the city completed a survey of all 343,000 residential parcels within its borders. The results quantified what was obvious to the casual observer: 27 percent (over 90,000) of the residential parcels in the city are vacant land; another 3 percent (over 10,000 parcels) have houses vacant and open for trespass. Thus, nearly a third of Detroit's residential parcels have been wiped out by the game of reverse musical chairs; another 10 percent (33,000) have dwellings that are vacant and may soon be abandoned.

The staggering magnitude of the population loss and resultant vacant land in Detroit can be illuminated with a clever geographic juxtaposition devised by Dan Pitera. One could fit the City of Boston, the City of San Francisco, and the Borough of Manhattan (totaling 118 square miles) within the area of the City of Detroit (139 square miles), with room to spare. If you were to accomplish this geographic sleight of hand, the population of this hypothetical territory of three conjoined cities would be 2.87 million, over three times Detroit's actual population.

What would happen if you created a palette out of the household detritus left behind by former Detroiters, then brushed them onto an outdoor canvas of abandoned homes and vacant lots? The result would be the work of ever-evolving installation art known as the Heidelberg Project, located on Heidelberg Street and its environs in the decayed heart of the former Germantown community (see Figure 24). The Heidelberg Project is the brain child of resident homeowner-remnant artist Tyree Guyton. Here he has created a magical, bizarre landscape of lost communities turned inside out, the private turned embarrassingly public. Lonely stuffed animals stare from glassless window frames while others suffer crucifixion on peeling clapboards of the gaping homes their former child-masters once occupied. Countless shoes are piled in heaps, as if some Nazi concentration camp were operating nearby. Shopping carts dangle high above the sidewalk from amputated tree limbs, their trip to the long-departed grocery store indefinitely postponed. Ranks of vacuum cleaners stand at attention, eager for the command to clean up that will never come. Unplugged TVs sit blankly, mute, optimistically waiting for a picture—any picture—like so many local politicians.

In the 1980s, Guyton first gained notoriety by painting large, colored dots on abandoned homes all over Detroit, then covering his home on Heidelberg Street in similar dots. Perhaps the dots were designed to draw public officials' attention to the hazards of abandoned homes. Perhaps they invited the observer to "connect the dots" and discern the larger pattern of abandonment. Unfortunately, pinpointing the root cause of the abandonment would require Guyton to paint dots on thousands of new homes in Greater Detroit's suburban fringe, a prospect that would not amuse their developers or new owners.

> We're walkin' down to Jaybo's, see.
> Just walkin'
> And we turn down by where
> that boy got his nose sliced off
> and they put it up his you-know-what?
> That street there?

Figure 24. Heidelberg Project.

Well some guy gone and dumped
about ten dozen old shoes
right there on the street.
Right on the street,

It was on TV.
Not just the news.
Its been on "Oprah."

The guy, he says its art.
Them old shoes.
Dump on the street.
Don't give me that shit.

They closed all the art.
Shut it down to save money.
If it was art, sister,
it would be locked up inside,
where couldn't nobody see it.

—"The Heidelberg Project" by Ellen Hildreth

Liquor, Lotto, and the Lord

Playing musical chairs in reverse not only causes a loss of population in the core, a selective out-migration of better-off households, and a loss of residential property values culminating in abandonment, it also wreaks havoc on other aspects of the urban fabric. One of the first collateral casualties is the local retail and commercial sector. Statistics from the Economic Censuses indicate that from 1972 to 2002, the number of businesses in Detroit fell almost two-thirds, from 23,500 to 8,300. There are few more dramatic and depressing aspects of Detroit's landscape than the seemingly interminable miles of abandoned retail stores and vacant lots lining the main commercial corridors—Woodward, Gratiot, Jefferson, Grand River, and Michigan—from the downtown almost to the city limits. In certain pockets there are clusters of down-market merchandisers like dollar stores, check-cashers, rent-to-own outfits, fast food franchises, and drug stores. But most of the new retail structures are concrete block fortresses that dispense a limited palette of stale groceries, state lottery tickets, and strong booze. Many of the former stores have been converted into store-front churches, with hand-painted signs optimistically asserting that "Reverend ____" promises salvation from whatever plague is happening now. It is a landscape that can be encapsulated as the "Three Ls": Lotto, Liquor, and the Lord.

The saga of Hudson's Department Store epitomizes the retail sector's flight. Joseph L. Hudson began his retail business in downtown Detroit in 1881 on the location now occupied by Compuware headquarters on Campus Martius. He moved a block away on Woodward Avenue to a larger location in 1911. Soon his success required further expansion, so he bought up the entire block and, in 1923, erected his mammoth department store adjacent to his existing one. But Hudson's was only one of three major department stores—Kern's and Crowley's were the others—that dominated Detroit's downtown shopping scene through the 1960s. At its peak in the middle of the twentieth century, Hudson's had more than 12,000 employees making 100,000 daily sales. The continued loss of population and disposable income from the city, escalation of interracial tensions and fear of crime, and growing competition from retailers located in suburban shopping centers (including several Hudson's branches) eventually overwhelmed the behemoth flagship store. It closed its doors to customers in January 1983, but its numerous records still stood. At 33 stories, it was the tallest department store in the world; at 2.2 million square feet, it was the nation's largest store next to the New York Macy's. The largest U.S. flag in the world (3,700 square feet) was hung along Hudson's Woodward flank, beginning with Armistice Day in 1923. On October 24, 1998, Hudson's flagship set yet another record: the largest building ever imploded by controlled demolition. As the storm of toxic dust from the fallen skyscraper billowed through the downtown streets, scattering in panic the 20,000 onlookers, no one guessed that this was but a mild preview of what would occur within three years to two taller, more famous skyscrapers just south of Macy's in New York. Whites were saddened by this event because the repository of their childhood Christmas fantasies, Hudson's famous seventh-floor toy wonderland, would be forever gone. Blacks cheered the destruction of this bastion of discrimination. Well into the 1960s it was impossible for a black person to be hired as a sales clerk; perhaps a light-skinned black might be allowed to operate one of the elevators. Mayor Dennis Archer pronounced the demolition a watershed moment that would spur the revival of downtown retail. His idea was to build a city-owned parking garage in the basement of the former store, rendering the ready-to-build prime site irresistible for major new development at street level and above. Fourteen years later, this underutilized parking garage lurks underground next to Woodward, stubs of steel girders protruding from its ground-level roof, suggesting a cemetery of long-gone shoppers. Or perhaps the girders are better thought of as fingertips of outstretched, supplicant hands, begging for a building—any new building—to grasp.

> alone, breathing deeply
> looking about continuingly
> slow stepping hesitantly
> Ghosts watching ghosts,
> abounded in the silence
> imposing their illusory will.
> Unseen hands
> tending unseen mills,
> raised short neck hairs.
> Three generations of ghost autoworkers
> whispered, with hushed, groaning voices,
> from dusty corners,
> revealing billions of sweaty days
> birthing millions of Tin Lizzys.
>
> Highland park, mighty Highland Park,
> bombproof Highland Park,
> likewise, into history.
>
> —"Highland Park" by Leon Chamberlain

If Detroit were a football game the referee would be forced to call a penalty for "unnecessary roughness." As if widespread residential and retail abandonment were not enough, the prone Detroit was socked with other forms of land use abandonment "piling on." We've seen how capitalists' thirst for land-extensive plants in nonunion environments led to systematic abandonment of production facilities in Detroit. This obituary of hallowed and now hollowed monster factories includes Dodge Main, Continental Motors, Cadillac, Hudson, and Ford Highland Park. But the title "Most Spectacular Industrial Ruin" undoubtedly belongs to the Packard Motor Company complex at Concord and Grand Boulevard in central Detroit. (see Figure 25) The first building in the complex was finished in 1903, but the most historically significant

Figure 25. Abandoned Packard factory complex. Photo courtesy of Lina Hedman.

structure was 1905's Building 10, made of reinforced concrete with over-sized steel sash windows. It was designed by Albert Kahn, later of Ford's Highland Park and Rouge factories and Fisher Building fame. The Packard complex eventually grew to 47 buildings on 38 acres, 3.5 million interior square feet. Despite its strategic wartime significance, the plant was the site of the city's most virulent racial hate strike in 1943. When it closed in 1956, 11,000 were idled. In the inimitable style of Detroiters, the ruins were adaptively reused as a venue for raves that served as incubator for Techno music in the 1980s. Paint ball games, waste tire dumping, and incalculable added undocumented (and most likely illegal) activities also took place there. The shadowy Bioresources Inc. bought the complex in 1987 and has not made a property tax payment since. Detroit has repeatedly threatened the firm with fines for code violations and even foreclosure for failure to pay taxes. But Bioresources Inc., like so many other owners of derelict properties in Detroit, understands this is a hollow threat. Why would the city want to take title to this site? It is toxic. It would take $10 million to demolish the structures. And even if this were accomplished, who would want the land? The Packard complex, like dozens of Detroit's abandoned plants, are like fossilized bones of industrial dinosaurs. But unlike dinosaur bones, these plants cannot be easily moved into a museum where the public will pay to see them.

If industrial abandonment were not enough, Detroit's downtown office market adds yet another dimension. Ever since the Renaissance Center dropped its unwanted millions of square feet of office space into the mix, downtown has suffered from an excess supply. At least four 1920s-era skyscrapers now sit vacant, despite their prime locations in the Woodward corridor: the David Stott Building, Book Tower, David Broderick Building, and David Whitney Building. This amazing clutch of empty monoliths once prompted New York sociologist-photojournalist Camilo Vergara to propose with a straight face that Detroit create a tourist-oriented theme park of ruined high-rises, an "American Acropolis." The proposal produced quite a different, unhappy facial expression on city officials.

Places of worship are the last component adding gratuitously to Detroit's structural abandonment. Despite shifting denominations multiple times through a process of constant property depreciation, large, expensive-to-maintain edifices built to worship some deity or another are vulnerable. Most poignant are the remnants of the Roman Catholic Diocese in Detroit. The late nineteenth-century schisms that led to the sequential creation of the Polish congregations of St. Albertus, Sweetest Heart of Mary, and St. Josaphat now seem the heights of indulgent folly. These giant churches still stand—decaying, swaying on the precipice of oblivion over the bowed heads of their praying vestigial congregations of fading memories—lined up along Canfield Street like a trio of ornate, oversized tombstones marking the graves of the dead neighborhoods over which their scarred steeples cast uninterrupted shadows.

*   *   *

In 1923 George Jacob II, Emma, and their children Marvin, Ruth, and George Milton left the increasingly gritty, dense, heterogeneous neighborhood where the original German immigrant community settled in Detroit. They moved three miles east to Yorkshire Road in the leafy, tranquil, upper-class-only enclave of Grosse Pointe Park. There they built a fine brick home set far back from the street, a far cry from the modest wooden home hard by the sidewalk on Moran across from the Acme Wire and Iron Works in Germantown. It took over a decade for Bruno, Helen, and their children to follow suit and leave Hurlbut Street to move northeast about the same distance, to Balfour Road in the just-built East English Village neighborhood of Detroit. Though oldest son Karl by this time had married and moved out, Robert, Louise, Helen, and Betty had reached the age where they needed more space and privacy. Bruno and Helen shuttered the little delicatessen in the Broadway Market downtown and set up their own freestanding chicken pie and deli shop on Harper Avenue near Outer Drive.

Both families left their old communities long before the first black families arrived, so it was not classic racial "tipping" of neighborhoods that scared them out. Undoubtedly, their exits had something to do with growing dissatisfaction with their cramped quarters and tiny yards. They likely were tired of close proximity to industries large and small. By contrast, the substantial land plots on the far east side of Detroit and the Grosse Pointes were laid out in strict adherence to the new-fangled idea of "land-use zoning," which specified strict separation of residential and industrial uses. But their moves also represented an oft-repeated pattern of spatial assimilation: as German Americans rose in social status they successively moved into more prestigious neighborhoods farther and farther from the city center and the original Germantown.

For many years, both families maintained ties with the "old neighborhood." After all, the main German social clubs were still located at Harmonie Park downtown and on Mack near Mt. Elliott on the near east side. And, their First English Lutheran Church was still on the corner of Mack and Mt. Elliott. This location brought these two old-line German families together, in more ways than one. It was in this church in 1944 that George Jacob's and Emma's son, George Milton, married Bruno and Helen's daughter, Helen Mary.

But as decades passed there were fewer and fewer reasons for these now-united families to visit the old Detroit German haunts. War hysteria had closed the beer gardens once and for all, major factories had closed, neighborhoods had deteriorated, and black households had come to dominate the area. By 1948 both Emma and Bruno were widowed, so their incentive to engage with places associated with the past eroded further. The final straw that broke the pull of geographic gravity came in 1957, when First English Lutheran Church relocated to Vernier Road, the extension of Eight Mile Road in Grosse Pointe Woods. The old church building was sold to the St. James Missionary Baptist Church, and the parish hall was sold to the City of Detroit for use as a recreation center.

Soon, the locus of activity for Bruno, Emma, and their respective off-spring became the far east side of Detroit and the Grosse Pointes. No longer would regular shopping be done downtown at Kern's, Crowley's, or Hudson's. Rather, it would be done at Eastland Shopping Center, built in 1956 on Eight Mile Road in Harper Woods, anchored by a branch of Hudson's. They were but a few of the hundreds of thousands of white families who progressively shifted their locus of daily activities away from the core, based on their perceived personal interests. When all these individual geographic shifts get aggregated, the collective result is far different from what any of these families would have wished.

Though residentially separated only by a mile and joined by their children's marriage, these two families experienced distinct economic fates. Bruno's clan bought homes in Detroit neighborhoods. This meant that, sooner or later, they would experience the dislocations wrought by rapid neighborhood and school racial change, city fiscal stresses, and loss of their property's value and status. By contrast, Emma's clan bought homes in the Grosse Pointes, where the color line never moved, tax revenues never declined, and status never wavered. The Grosse Pointes are the only inner-ring suburbs of Greater Detroit that seem to have—so far—successfully opted out of playing musical chairs in reverse. One is left to ponder the degree to which this success was driven by their tawdry history of racially exclusionary actions.

I look west, down Merrick—
the sun fallen away
beneath layers of reds, oranges, purples, greys,
the vision through a smog-lensed sky,
the factorial West—
how those colors call back
another vanishing point—
how as a child I'd haunt
museum versions of older Detroits
where time falls back
down a single street
from the cinema to the druggist,
the five and dime and the firehouse,
the cobbler, the blacksmith,
the stable, the press—

falls back past the Fort and Cadillac
to the silhouette peaks of a picket fence
broken and weathered
like the soft ends of driftwood,
surges and echoes
into those hand-painted, back lit
tears of color
and how it felt precious and flirted
and promised something past it
and the song of my failed allegiance,
my false apology—
falls back on nothing that cares,
nothing that needs,
no one who waits.
How my street, Merrick,
empties into the West,
echoes the memory
of a museum.

—"Historical" by Kevin Rashid

Land Sharks

In 1975, as the *Jaws* movie phenomenon was sweeping the nation, Chevy Chase performed a *Saturday Night Live* skit where he pretended to be a "land shark" that solicited at apartment doors in an attempt to devour unsuspecting tenants. Though the skit was fictional, real land sharks have been prowling Detroit's murky housing market abyss for decades. Detroit's land sharks have evolved into bizarre species that can only survive in perpetually depressed property markets: speculators, skippers, strippers, rippers and burners. In concert, the actions of these housing market bottom feeders rapidly erode the quality of life for nearby residents and the prospect of profit for property owners.

Speculation on land and derelict buildings is rife in Detroit because vast amounts of both can be acquired and held over the years at virtually no cost. Many of the empty high-rise office buildings in downtown remain in private hands. As the head of a major commercial real-estate brokerage commented in 2010, these buildings are "owned by old money, waiting for Disney World to move to Detroit." The current alpha male of the land shark speculators is Manuel (Matty) Moroun, who in 2010 owned at least 625 properties in the city, including the infamous Michigan Central Station. Moroun's speculative holdings are clustered near City Airport, I-94 adjacent to the GM Poletown plant, and southwest Detroit near the Ambassador Bridge (which he also owns). These holdings place him in an enviable strategic position were the city's tiny airport or industrial district to expand or a proposed second bridge to Canada come to fruition. Speculators like Moroun have often avoided rehabilitating or even maintaining their buildings. All it takes is a promise to sell or redevelop the building, and the desperate city's bluff is called.

"Skippers" perpetrate mortgage scams, then skip town with the cash. The first member of the skipper team, posing as a *bona fide* buyer, approaches the desperate seller of a large, older home in Detroit and offers the deflated asking price. On acquiring title to the property, this skipper secures a ridiculously inflated appraisal from a coconspirator appraiser. This inflated appraisal is used to support a second sale to yet another skipper teammate. But this sale involves only a minimum down payment and a maximum amount of mortgage from some out-of-town lender. The unwitting mortgagor, unaware of the depths to which values in Detroit have plummeted, suspects nothing because such an appraisal seems "reasonable" given the size and features of the home. Having secured the mortgage, the first skipper "sells" the home to his teammate. Then both walk away without ever making a mortgage payment. Their ill-gotten gain is the large difference between the fraudulently obtained mortgage and the original seller's asking price, since the "down payment" was merely a transfer between teammates.

Strippers loot homes for profit from salvage. As you can imagine with the hundreds of thousands of homes that have been abandoned over the last decades in Detroit, stripping is a well-developed (if entirely underground) industry. Scouts for the strippers prowl neighborhoods looking for tell-tale signs of recent vacancy: no interior lighting for several nights, fresh plywood on the windows, newly posted foreclosure notices. They also look for rarer homes that have recently been renovated but are not yet occupied. Having identified their dwelling victims, the strippers pounce during the night, focusing on the home's most precious and easiest-to-fence assets: copper piping, chandeliers and light sconces, decorative wood or metal fixtures. They will come back in successive waves, ripping out toilets and sinks, air conditioners, kitchen cabinets and appliances, doors, and even furnaces.

Then they switch to the exterior, where bricks and aluminum siding disappear. The feeding frenzy of the omnivorous land shark strippers continues until the bones of the home are picked clean.

Rippers pose as legitimate owners of vacant properties and rent them to unsuspecting tenants. As soon as their rip-off of the legitimate owners is exposed they disappear, leaving hapless tenants with worthless leases, facing eviction notices or trespassing complaints. The stock of vacant properties in Detroit is so vast and dynamic that it is impossible for city officials to know which properties have been abandoned by their owners, which are in the process of being foreclosed on for failure to pay property taxes or mortgages, and which have titles that are clearly held by the city. This gives rippers plenty of room to run their scam. In a particularly disturbing variant of ripping, several city housing department employees were recently convicted of renting out city-owned houses for personal gain.

Burners set fires to properties for fun and profit. The most infamous example is "Devil's Night," a Detroit Halloween tradition from the early 1980s to mid-1990s. Each Devil's Night, hundreds of vacant homes across the city were set ablaze by arsonists, so overwhelming the fire department's capacity that many would burn to the ground before any response was forthcoming. Today the number of fires on Halloween is not much higher than the normal rate of structure fires, calculated in 2007 as an average of 33 daily. On average, 18 fires a day are of suspicious origin. So "Little Devils' Night" is every night. Presumably, the values of these intentionally torched structures less their unpaid property taxes are far less than the insurance value, rendering them prime targets for arson-for-profit. With Greater Detroit's property market depressed even farther from the mortgage market meltdown, more and more desperate homeowners are resorting to the arson option. It is not unusual for firefighters to arrive on the scene of a home fire in the middle of the night only to find all the occupants—including the children—"visiting" a neighbor's home down the street. There is clear reward and little risk in this strategy; though firefighters can often smell gasoline fumes at the scene of a fire, they know that the arson squad is so underfunded and backlogged that there is little sense in gathering evidence. Since insurance companies often do not find it cost effective to conduct their own arson investigation for such a comparatively small claim, they simply pay and then adjust upward yet again the premiums of all other local policyholders.

We got pride, we got anger, little else. Houses gone, stores gone;
   double nothin' . . .

—"Uprising," by Dennis Teichman

Losers and Winners of the Game

As long as the game of musical chairs is really a game played in an actual room with actual chairs, there are probably no losers of importance. When the real-world equivalent "game" of reverse musical chairs is played with houses embedded in neighborhoods and political jurisdictions, the big losers are legion. They can be identified clearly: Detroit residents and property owners, who are disproportionately poor and black. The losses manifest themselves in more ways than declining real estate asset values. They also show up as a deteriorating municipal fiscal situation and eroded quality of life, as blight, inferior public services, incivilities, and danger squeeze the community ever tighter.

As documented by the Citizens Research Council of Michigan, losing residential and nonresidential property values and residents with sizable disposable incomes imposes an ever-tightening financial constraint on Detroit, which relies on property tax, income tax, and other fee revenues for 31 percent of its budget. Perversely, the city's property and income tax bases are eroded at the same time as its operating costs are increased: more firefighters are needed to deal with arson, more health and social services are needed for an ever-poorer population, more abandoned buildings need to be demolished, and more clouded titles need to be cleared so the land can eventually be transferred to the city. The extent of this capacity-needs mismatch was made clear in a 2007 HUD-commissioned study, which found that Detroit had the lowest fiscal capacity—ability to raise revenues for city services—but the greatest community needs, among the nation's fifty largest cities.

In attempting to meet its growing needs with a shrinking base of properties and people for raising revenue, Detroit has made the agonizing and ultimately self-defeating choice to increase the rate at which property is taxed and institute the region's only income tax for residents and city workers. The results are twofold. First, Detroit puts itself at a competitive disadvantage, as households must pay three times more in taxes to live in Detroit than in the average Michigan city; the comparative figure for businesses is twice as much tax in Detroit. Second, Detroit has created an exceptionally burdensome and unfair tax regime. A Detroiter earning $50,000 can expect to pay 11 percent of that income in city and state taxes each year, eighth among fifty major cities nationwide. Tragically, the burden is disproportionately heavier for Detroiters earning just above the poverty line, $25,000. They pay almost 14 percent of their income for city and state taxes, the second highest in the nation, primarily due to the regressive nature of the city's steep property taxes.

Despite raising tax rates, Detroit's total revenues fell, forcing it to trim the quality and quantity of services it provides. Parks, clinics, recreation centers, and fire stations closed, departmental staffs shrunk, and modern technology installations were postponed. Ironically, some cutbacks in building code enforcement and property tax collection proved financially short-sighted. A 1998 study revealed that the city failed to collect around a tenth of the property taxes due, a rate five to ten times higher than peer cities.

The city's strategy to trim services while simultaneously raising tax rates has not been enough to avoid imminent bankruptcy, however. A Citizens Research Council report estimated that, in Detroit's $1.6 billion general fund, there is a $346 million (22 percent) accumulated deficit and a $100 million (6 percent) current operating deficit.

Detroit's fiscal stress stands in marked contrast to most of its suburbs. The Metropolitan Area Research Corporation estimated that the 2000 property tax base—the assessed value of all residential and nonresidential properties—was only $21,546 per resident in Detroit, less than a third of the regional average of $68,286 per resident. Yet Detroit tries to squeeze much more out of that base. Its property tax rate of $68 per thousand dollars of assessed property value was $28 higher than the metro-wide median, meaning that a Detroit property owner pays $2,800 more in property taxes annually for each $100,000 in assessed value compared to the regional median.

The Detroit public schools face increasingly dire fiscal problems akin to those of the city, while attempting to serve a more disadvantaged population than the city as a whole. In 2006, 94 percent of the students in Detroit Public Schools (DPS) were black and 80 percent received free or reduced-price lunches because their families had extremely low incomes. This mix of a weak, underfunded (and often corrupt) institutional infrastructure and an overwhelmingly impoverished student body presenting massive pedagogic challenges produced an educational disaster. Only 22 percent of ninth-graders graduate in four years, according to a respected 2006 national report; this placed DPS dead last among the fifty large school districts surveyed. Detroit's figure was only a quarter of the top rate (83 percent); even more discouraging, it was 17 percentage points below the 49th ranked district. In 2009, DPS fourth-graders and eighth-graders scored the lowest among the nation's large-city school districts on standardized National Assessment of Educational Progress reading and math tests. An appalling 73 percent of fourth-graders and 60 percent of eighth-graders performed below the "basic" level in reading, compared to national averages of 34 percent and 26 percent. Michael Casserly, president of the Council on Great City Schools, observed that Detroit's NAEP scores were "barely above what one would expect by chance, as if the kids had never been to school at all and simply had guessed at the answers."

At the same time as Detroit's municipal fiscal situation and public school performance become ever more desperate, its residents are pummeled with multipronged assaults on their residential quality of life. As homes and commercial properties are progressively undermaintained, abandoned, and torched in the reverse musical chair game, the landscape assumes a depressing dusting of desolation and danger. Despite the punishing tax rates, Detroiters are provided a third-rate portfolio of public services. Petty incivilities and vandalism become epidemic as residents adopt the attitude "Why not litter, spray paint graffiti, or dump truckloads of refuse on empty lots? The place is already a mess!" "Why not steal metal plates covering the wiring connections on street light poles? No one will care. And if it makes the street lights short out every time it rains, so what? The neighborhood is a wreck anyway!" Perceived and actual insecurities intensify as the proliferation of broken windows, inoperative street lights, and paucity of police officers signals the evaporation of informal and formal social control. The surplus abandoned structures provide havens for drug dealers and addicts, becoming the focus of systematic turf wars between rival drug gangs, as well as random acts of senseless mayhem. It is no accident that the ultraviolent Barksdale cocaine gang in the hit HBO series *The Wire* was modeled on Detroit's YBI (Young Boys Incorporated), based in the Dexter-Davison neighborhood on the near west side.

Unlike the conventional game of musical chairs, reverse musical chairs yields many winners. Those who produce the new "chairs" win because they seemingly have an inexhaustible market for their new suburban homes. Households with higher incomes seem to win because they get to occupy newer, more comfortable homes in seemingly more secure neighborhoods as the game progresses. Suburban politicians win because they gain the power and prestige that comes with expanding tax bases and the *cachet* of "a growing community." As long-time Oakland County Chief Executive L. Brooks Patterson succinctly expressed it, "I love sprawl. I need it. I promote it. Oakland County can't get enough of it." Not surprisingly, a coalition of developers, upper-income households, and powerful suburban politicians will have no interest in changing the rules of Greater Detroit's development game called reverse musical chairs.

> Nowhere to run to, baby; nowhere to hide
> Got nowhere to run to, baby; nowhere to hide . . .
> > —"Nowhere to Run," sung by Martha (Reeves) and the
> > Vandellas in 1965

The Disassembly Line

Henry Ford has been quoted as famously asserting, "History . . . is bunk!" He probably did not have in mind that his home region would perpetually support his dictum by creating and operating a housing development machine that annually erases thousands of historical artifacts from the landscape. Greater Detroit has indeed perfected the Fordist-style mass production of something besides automobiles: abandoned housing. The region's combined easily buildable topography, unfettered development rules, fragmented local government, and frightened populace have constructed a continuous Disassembly Line stretching from urban core to suburban fringe. Like some giant conveyor belt, each time a new house is added to the suburban fringe all older houses built on the line drop in value a little more, and one more house—the least valuable one located in the core—falls off the line and crashes to earth because it is no longer worth owning.

As a result of this newly abandoned house, the social, fiscal, and physical condition of its surrounding neighborhood—indeed, the entire core urban community—decays a little farther. The drug trade and ancillary crime proliferate in abandoned structures. The visage and actions of this place increasingly feed a voracious climate of fear. Home insurance rates go up as the danger from arson and other crimes intensifies. Weakened municipal fiscal capacity erodes the quality of public services provided to households and businesses, and the jurisdiction loses its ability to enforce laws or collect property taxes, while simultaneously requiring that tax rates be raised to uncompetitive, unfair levels. An ever more vacant, dilapidated, dangerous wasteland, served by a high-insurance/high-tax/low-service municipality, becomes a progressively less-attractive location for current and potential households and businesses. Those with options, thus, move ever farther from the core. The demand for yet another new house on the suburban fringe is created, and the conveyor belt keeps moving. Each house already on the line and the community in which it is located inch a little closer to the precipice. Ultimately, there is nowhere to run, nowhere to hide from the Disassembly Line. It violates the laws of thermodynamics: it powers itself.

The massive impact of the regional Disassembly Line on Detroit over the last half century can be summarized in four cold statistics. From 1950 to 2005, Detroit lost 29 percent of its homes, 52 percent of its people, 55 percent of its jobs, and 60 percent of its property tax revenue. Today, the detritus left by the Disassembly Line is painfully visible over vast swaths of Detroit, yet the city is in no position to do anything fundamental about it. The city did not build the Disassembly Line. It does not operate it. It does not have the political power to stop it. All it can feebly try to do is clean up the never-ending mess it produces with progressively fewer resources at its disposal.

The regional Disassembly Line makes a discordant duet of sucking sounds as it operates. From the suburban fringe of northern Oakland and Macomb Counties and western Wayne County emanates the sound of Detroit's people, businesses, and financial resources being sucked away. From the core emanates the sound of a once great but now impotent city going down the drain.

Back to the Future?

Back to the Future is not just a movie title; now it is a mantra for public policy proposals in Detroit. How far back should we go to see the future? German immigrant Johann Georg's farm should be sufficient, because much of his former lands have returned to their prairie state, just as he found them in 1851. The crucial difference is that in 1851 this vacant land was at the fringe of the metropolitan area two miles from downtown Detroit; today, it is thirty-six miles from the fringe of the metropolitan area. Nevertheless, some think that, if farming this land was appropriate a century and a half ago, it must be appropriate now. The now-*chic* notion of agriculture as the savior of Detroit is an old one. During the terrible depression of 1893, Mayor Hazen Pingree proposed (unsuccessfully, it turned out) hiring 25,000 unemployed to plant community gardens in the city.

Despite this dubious precedent, the painfully oxymoronic notion of "urban farming" has hijacked the judgment of many otherwise sensible people. In May 2009, an American Institute of Architects Sustainable Design Assessment Team suggested with a straight face that Detroit could re-create itself as a twenty-first- (i.e., seventeenth)- century English countryside, replete with "villages" separated by agricultural tracts and parklands. That same year, wealthy Detroit stockbroker John Hantz proposed investing $30 million of his own money in a high-tech urban agricultural scheme involving hundreds of acres of vacant Detroit land. The irrationality of trying to recreate nontoxic farmland in the metropolitan core at huge expense, while verdant farmland is being ravaged every day by developers at the fringe, instead of forcing development back to the core by changing rules of the reverse musical chairs game, is exceeded only by its irony.

Few have considered another downside of urban farming: prime pheasant habitat would be lost. Just as apparently it was in the days of Monsieur Cadillac, pheasants now are plentiful. It is common to drive through Detroit and have pheasants fly in front of the car as they are flushed from the brush. Perhaps it, therefore, would be simpler to propose "urban hunting" as the savior of the city. In this fashion, we could go *all the way* back to the future to the very origins of French Fort Detroit in 1701. Moreover, think of how the prices of *pheasant à l'orange* would plummet in the local French restaurants were we to pursue this strategy!

Though now pheasants dominate, Detroit once was home to splendid peacocks. Charles Freer made a boxcar of money by making railroad cars in late nineteenth-century Detroit as the founder of the Peninsular Car Company. He spent a goodly chunk of that cash in 1892 building a sprawling, cedar-shingled mansion on Ferry Street just east of Woodward Avenue. Nor did he skimp on the vast collection of Winslow Homer, John Singer Sargent, and James McNeill Whistler paintings for its interior. But the undeniable showpiece of the mansion was a custom-built addition in the carriage house for Whistler's *Peacock Room*, a floor-to-ceiling, four-walled fantasy of avian-motif filigree in gold and green, which Freer acquired in London in 1904.

Like so many of Detroit's wealthy over the years, Freer abandoned Detroit for a higher-status venue. Though his mansion remains (housing a famous children's research institute founded by the wife of Senator Thomas Palmer), all his art treasures are gone, including the magical *Peacock Room*. His legacy now reposes in splendor in the Freer Gallery of the Smithsonian Institution on the National Mall in Washington, D.C. The only birds in the vicinity of the old Freer Mansion are the pheasants in the weedy vacant lots of the neighborhood.

A group of University of Chicago scholars made a lasting contribution to urban sociology in the 1920s by extending the biological ecology notion of "invasion and succession" into the realm of human settlements. According to this view, a few members of one group would "invade" the territory dominated by members of a different group. If the dominant group "retreated" in light of this invasion, the new group would gain dominance in the area and eventually succeed the original group entirely. Just so for Detroit. Blacks have succeeded whites. Poor have succeeded rich. Pheasants have succeeded peacocks.

> [Detroit is] America's last limits of civilization.
> —Alexis de Tocqueville, French visitor and social
> commentator, 1831

> *Speramus meliora; resurget cineribus*—"We hope for better things; it shall rise from the ashes."
> —Official motto of the City of Detroit

Chapter 10

What Drives Detroiters?

What you need, you know I got it . . . What I need is just a little bit
of respect, just a little bit . . . just a little bit . . .
            —"Respect," sung by Aretha Franklin in 1967

Resources of Respect

People are people, and psychologists have observed some common behavioral and psychic characteristics that unite our species. What humans
everywhere need are three basic sorts of resources: *physical* (like food,
clothing, shelter, time, energy), *social* (like love, status, affirmation, community), and *psychological* (like identity, esteem, efficacy, and purpose). We
all strive to obtain, retain, and expand resources of all three types, though
the physical is more basic in terms of biological survival. When people have
attained a sufficient amount of all three sorts of resources, they will have
gained what I call in shorthand "respect." Given the crucial importance of
the resources comprising respect, it is no wonder that their potential or actual loss creates psychological stress for humans. How people respond to
such stress offers a provocative lens through which to perceive and better
understand Greater Detroiters.

Psychologists have suggested that these motivations can extend beyond individuals to groups and organizations as well. They have advanced
two principles. The first states that resource gains and losses are not symmetric; losses are much more damaging than similarly sized gains. This
explains why so many organizations and cultures have frequent rituals and

commemorative events attempting to restore resources lost in significant disasters.

The second principle states that people must invest resources if they want to expand their stockpiles or protect them against potential losses. For example, individuals must continually invest resources in interpersonal relationships if they want love to be maintained or grow. Organizations must invest in developing the skills and behaviors of their employees if they wish to become more productive.

These two principles lead to a corollary with crucial implications for Greater Detroit. Those with only meager resources and those suffering repeated events where resources were lost will adopt a defensive posture to conserve remnants. Confronted with the terrifying prospect that their resources may fall below the minimum threshold of acceptability, people and groups behave conservatively. They practice cognitive denial and hoard resources in the short-term, while avoiding investing resources to create a more secure or expansive future. Thus, ironically, such folks often respond in the short term to stressful situations in ways that produce self-defeating long-term consequences.

Greater Detroiters are no different from other Americans in their motivations to secure respect: adequate physical, social, and psychological resources. What distinguishes them are the uniquely daunting obstacles they have faced in their search for respect. Greater Detroit creates these obstacles with its economic base and housing market, abetted by external media and federal government forces. Its economic base and housing market are "engines of anxiety": fundamentally corrosive of the physical, social, and psychological resources that people expect to reap from their places of work and residence. How Detroiters have tried individually to cope with and collectively adapt to these corrosive forces at the heart of their metropolis has taken extreme—and extremely dysfunctional—forms.

A good many men break down mentally and physically . . . [under the strain of] continuous application to one line of work.
—Samuel Marquis, Ford Motor Company executive, 1918

A city which is built around a productive process . . . is really a kind of hell . . . Thousands in this town are really living in torment while the rest of us eat, drink and make merry.

—Reinhold Niebuhr, Detroit minister before moving to Union
Theological Seminary in New York, 1929

It has been asserted that machine production kills the creative ability
of the craftsman. This is not true.

—Henry Ford, 1929

Life in Detroit . . . is empty as a dried gourd for the creatures of the
assembly line. Empty and insecure. . . . It is a city of strangers.

—Forrest Davis, first director of the Detroit Urban League, 1936

The Economic Engine of Anxiety

Greater Detroit's economy has been dominated by the automobile industry
for over a century. Throughout these decades, it has tantalizingly offered a
Faustian bargain to its people: you will gain immense physical resources
relative to your skills, but you will need to sacrifice psychological resources
to get them. Generations of Detroiters have willingly sealed the deal, with
predictable and some unpredictable consequences for themselves and their
metropolitan area. Like Faust, auto workers found that the devilish font of
their physical resources extracted considerably more sacrifices of psychological resources than anticipated. Four core characteristics of the Detroit
auto industry—assembly line production, draconian management, cyclical
instability, and long-term employment declines—ally to forge an economic
engine of anxiety. It is an engine that drives away fundamental psychological resources that workers might expect to gain from the workplace: self-
esteem, personal efficacy, security, pride of accomplishment, a modicum of
appreciation and understanding from management.

The nature of production in the auto industry is especially degrading
to its workers. Assembly line work is uncomfortable, monotonous, and
completely beyond the control of the worker on the line. Not only what
you do but how fast you do it is controlled by someone else. Karl Marx
had it right—this kind of work makes the employee nothing more than
a machine-like appendage to a machine, an appendage that, the more
machine-like the tasks it performed, the more likely it would be amputated
and replaced by an actual machine. Thus, the cruel, ironic capitalist maxim

is true in Motown: as workplace dehumanization rises, so does job insecurity from automation.

Auto plant work is also notoriously dangerous, especially in the foundry, stamping, welding, and painting divisions. Cuts, bruises, burns, and punctures are normal; noxious inhalations, broken bones, and dismemberments are frequent; deaths are not uncommon. In 1916, Ford's Highland Park Model T plant alone recorded 192 severed fingers, 68,000 lacerations, 5,400 burns, and 2,600 puncture wounds. Though conditions improved with unionization, UAW records indicated over 15,000 serious industrial accidents in the notorious year of 1970.

As if the ambient conditions of the auto workplace's physical environment were not sufficiently challenging, a long tradition of demeaning management styles has infected the industry. As a Depression-era federal government report uncovered by Mary Stolberg put it, worker dissatisfaction in the first-generation auto plants arose from industry practices generating "insecurity, inequitable hiring methods, espionage, speedup and the displacement of workers at an extremely early age."

In the front line of management, foremen acted as petty tyrants, daily fomenting insecurity and stress for the hapless workers. In pre-UAW days, foreman were the workplace cops, judge, and jury, bullying and threatening workers and dispensing "justice" as they saw fit. Their powers even extended to rehiring workers (or not) after the weeks-long annual retooling process to accommodate the latest-model vehicle. Foremen corruption was rampant because no jobs were guaranteed through the retooling cycle. The UAW scored a major victory in 1936 when the Kelsey-Hayes strike was settled with a guarantee that foremen could not arbitrarily fire workers. Yet problems persisted even in unionized plants. Bigoted foremen remained catalysts for racial angst through the mid-1970s, generating an epidemic of workplace absenteeism, grievances, violence, wildcat strikes, and antiestablishment organizations like the Dodge Radical Union Movement.

Petty tyrants were the norm higher up the management food chain as well. Detroiter Philip Levine, 2011 poet laureate of the United States, has written poignantly about job applicants standing for hours in the cold rain outside an auto plant, only to be told eventually by some company official that "we're not hiring today" for any arbitrary reason he wanted.

In the top line of management, bosses' attitudes and policies showed a similar disrespect for working people. Ford Motor Company was exceptional is this regard. Ford's fabled 1914 announcement of the $5 a day wage immediately had its intended effect of reducing labor turnover and aiding recruitment. It was so spectacularly successful that a week later, on January 12, 10,000 men gathered on Manchester Avenue outside the Highland Park plant seeking work, despite the nine-degree temperature and howling winds. The company made no provision for an orderly application process. Instead, officials inside the plant repeatedly bellowed through a megaphone that Ford was not hiring today. The frustrated, freezing crowd refused to disperse unless they could apply. The company responded by calling out the Highland Park police and dousing the crowd with two of the plant's fire hoses. The outraged, ice-covered crowd responded by throwing stones at the plant, the public by fuming indignantly over Ford's callous behavior.

When it came to stripping workers' psychological resources of identity and self-esteem, the ultimate insult, however, was Ford's "Americanization Project." The "$5 a day plan" came with conditions: it was only available to workers who met certain standards. The first was to speak English. So Ford set up its own English School and required all non-English-speaking employees to enroll in its 72-session course. Between 1914 and 1917 over 14,000 did so. In this English course workers also learned "American-style" table manners, personal hygiene, punctuality, and prejudice. Other "American" behavioral standards were enforced by Ford's Sociological Department, a corps of investigators who visited workers' homes in off-hours to inspect, interrogate, and, if needed, educate. Grounds for disqualification from the $5 a day plan included gambling, drinking, taking in boarders, poor hygiene, buying on credit, or having a wife in the labor force. Because Ford thought that a woman's place was in the home, no women were ever eligible for the $5 a day plan unless they were the family's sole breadwinner.

James Johnson's case epitomizes the intense stress the auto plants created through inhumane working conditions and intolerable management practices. The twelve months preceding July 15, 1970, were particularly deadly for workers at Chrysler Corporation plants. Mamie Williams was forced back to work from her doctor-ordered sick leave under threat of dismissal, to die on the job soon thereafter. Rose Logan was struck by a motorized jitney in a factory and later died. Gary Thompson was ordered to load a five-ton pallet of steel into a railcar using a defective forklift he was not trained to operate; he was crushed to death in the attempt. These and other run-of-the-mill workplace atrocities spawned a series of wildcat strikes called by the Eldon Radical Union Movement (ELDRUM) at Chrysler's Eldon Avenue Gear and Axle plant. Yet, the capitalist cancer of disrespect could not be so easily excised; on July 15, James Johnson could not stand it any more.

Hampered by a weak education and a racially oppressive childhood in the South, Johnson had cycled from one bad job to another since moving to Detroit. Finally, he had found steady, decent-paying work at Eldon Avenue and was preparing to buy his family's first house. But there had been disputes with management over lost vacation days and arbitrary pay reductions where he was treated unfairly. So, on July 15, 1970, Johnson refused to participate in an assembly line speed up. When he was suspended from work, the accumulated disrespect crossed Johnson's tolerance threshold. He returned to the plant later that day, an M-1 rifle camouflaged under his clothing, and shot to death two foremen and a machine-setter before quietly surrendering.

A few days later, ELDRUM published at leaflet entitled "Hail James Johnson." It recounted the events leading up to Johnson's outburst, blaming it on the plant's working conditions. It argued that Chrysler Corporation in effect pulled the trigger and that the indifferent UAW was an accessory after the fact. Kenneth Cockrel, Sr., fresh from his victory defending those charged in the New Bethel Church incident, used a similar strategy to defend Johnson. After the jury visited the Eldon Avenue assembly line and saw how alienating it was, their verdict—"not guilty by reason of insanity"—was a foregone conclusion.

Visibly outraged trial judge Robert Colombo, the Detroit Police Officers Association's former attorney, urged Ionia State Hospital to confine Johnson for life. It was not to be, because in 1974 the Michigan Supreme Court ruled that those acquitted for reasons of insanity could not be detained indefinitely unless their mental illness persisted. Johnson was released in 1975 since the Ionia psychiatrists never thought him clinically insane in the first place.

This proved a bittersweet victory for James Johnson, however. In May 1973, the Workman's Compensation Board had ordered Chrysler Corporation to pay him $75 per week for the rest of his life, retroactive to the day of the shootings, based on the putatively permanent psychological harm its workplace had caused. With these harms now apparently mitigated with his release from Ionia, the Workman's Compensation Appeals Board ruled in 1975 that compensation need only be paid for sixteen months.

Please Mr. Foreman, slow down your assembly line.
No, I don't mind workin', but I do mind dyin'.
> —"Please Mr. Foreman," written and sung by Joe L. Carter,
> a worker at the Rouge complex during the 1930s

The Roller Coaster of Angst

Even with the most humane work processes governed by the most enlightened management practices imaginable, the auto industry would still be an engine of anxiety because of its cyclical instability, and its long-term trend of falling employment. Motor vehicles occupy a special niche in the world of goods: mass consumer, big-ticket durables. An inevitable (if uncertain duration) period of slumping sales and idle capacity, followed eventually by a sharp recovery, is the auto industry norm. From the auto workers' perspective, the result is cyclical layoffs, followed by potential callbacks after an indefinite period, followed by a potential period of overtime work with extra hourly pay. The livelihoods of nine times as many other Detroit region workers who directly or indirectly earn a living from the auto workers by selling *them* goods and services also become cyclically unstable. Thus, Greater Detroit's hyper boom-bust local economy has created a stressful way of life due to persistent economic insecurity. Just because insecurity is expected, however, does not make it psychologically easy. In the region's Second Great Depression from 1979 to 1983, for example, the suicide rate rose 20 percent and deaths from drug overdoses doubled.

Like a roller coaster, Greater Detroit's auto-based economy not only goes up and down, but it trends downward. Compared to forty years ago, there are relatively few auto industry jobs—white- and blue-collar alike—left in Greater Detroit due to the Big Three's constant cost-cutting pressures to automate and outsource overseas and to intensifying competition from foreign-based companies. This steady hemorrhaging of its economic base has affected the economic security of everyone in the region, not just those directly employed by the auto companies. This is reflected in a November 2009 Kaiser Family Foundation poll in Greater Detroit: a whopping 65 percent said that the current economic situation was a cause of stress.

The desperate stench of evaporating economic, social, and psychological resources fills the Greater Detroit air, even among the population segments for whom insecurity was previously unknown. Between 2006 and 2008, each of the Big Three firms announced that tens of thousands of their Detroit-area white-collar, salaried retirees would no longer get company-provided group health care benefits. As one Chevy white-collar retiree said in July 2008 after GM's surprise announcement, "We just feel betrayed." In May 2009 a Grosse Pointe career counselor described a palpable fear among her executive friends: "A few years ago, an executive from GM would never have asked me for advice [about reentering the job market]. People came to equate the company with stability. You had a job for life. It had 100 years of prosperity and suddenly that's all gone."

> Why do they always say: Don't look back. . . . Don't hold on to the
>   past?
> Well, that's too much to ask.
>   —"This Used to Be My Playground," sung by Madonna in 1995

*   *   *

It was all gone. Everywhere George Milton and Helen looked around the city where they were born and raised they saw empty spaces where memories used to reside. Helen's childhood home on Hurlbut near Ossian Sweet's house and George's childhood home on Moran near Acme Wire and Iron Company were weedy vacant lots. The social clubs where they had partied with their friends had vanished. Their original First English Lutheran Church on Mt. Elliot, where they met, married, and baptized their son, was boarded up awaiting the wrecking ball. Drug addicts camped under the main entrance portico. So, it was time for them to disappear too, never to set foot in Detroit again.

*   *   *

> When they bring
> a building down,
> when they make

history absent,
when they implode
a cistern of memories
into a basement grave,
where do
the ghosts go?

another landmark gone—
another space left behind,
another hole in a story,
another burial
to collect bones,
another place
from where
ghosts
are gone.

—"The Burial of a Building" by Melba Joyce Boyd

The Housing Engine of Anxiety

In normal places, workers can put workplace stresses behind them when they reach their homes' front doors. But Greater Detroit is not a normal place. For over a century, its housing market stressed out residents who feared loss of physical, social, and psychological resources.

First, the stress on whites associated with threats of neighborhood racial invasion and transition began with the Great Migration during World War I. Whites were in constant fear of the next Ossian Sweet moving into their neighborhood. Not only would their property values plummet, but their local networks and social status would be compromised. The threat to their physical, social, and psychological resources was thus palpable. Hence, the origins of the "white protection racket" can be easily understood.

Second, the regional Housing Disassembly Line began in the 1960s to produce stress on all households living in older neighborhoods associated with threats of neighborhood decay and abandonment. Owners of homes, apartments, and stores in these areas faced stress over potential property devaluation. Residents faced distressing prospects of deteriorating quality of life or, if they could afford to, moving somewhere else until the decay caught up with them again. But the Housing Disassembly Line produced a loss of more than physical resources.

Neighborhood decay and abandonment also levied a heavy psychological tax on Greater Detroit residents, for both those who lived amid it and those who managed to escape. Those who must live with proximate decay suffer erosion of their self-respect. If all around one sees dilapidated homes, burned-out hulks, and vacant lots of dumped tires, what does that do to one's self-image? As Kenneth Clark summarizes the psychological impact, who of worth would live in an environment like this? Those who escape before the decay arrived suffer from erosion of their histories. They witness their sacred ground—homes and stores built, owned, and occupied by their forebears—deteriorate, become abandoned, and eventually demolished. The places of their past are erased, replaced by feelings of never being able to go home again, a peculiar rootlessness. Thus, the Housing Disassembly Line strips a sense of humanity both from those who have (temporarily) escaped the decay and those who have not.

The Housing Disassembly Line creates a space for *imagined memory*. Because so much of the built environment has disappeared or is present only in ruins or vestiges of former grandeur, Greater Detroiters have few tangible, legible mementos of their past. Like the film *Memento*'s protagonist, they are condemned to live in a state of partial amnesia, informed only by faded photographs with mysterious captions. With amnesia, one has no context to make sense of a current event or assess the reality of someone else's historical assertion. Instead, the past must be perpetually reinvented by the amnesiac, and here is where imagination necessarily comes into play.

When imagination invents the past, a romantic nostalgia—filled with sanctified (if nonsensical) myths, heroes, and villains—has free rein. All these aspects of imagined memory are dysfunctional. Hypernostalgia leads Greater Detroiters to live in an invented past, which proves a huge barrier to investing bravely and creatively in the future. The future can never be as great as the glorious, albeit imagined, past. Besides, we now have so little that we cannot risk it on an uncertain future. So, like Madonna and her playground, Greater Detroiters cling to the past and leave the future to fate or divine intervention. Or, like George and Helen, stripped of much of their historic home, they see no reason not to leave the metropolitan area and start a home afresh.

"You came all the way from London to Detroit on holiday?" the U.S. Customs official at the Big Mac airport terminal asks the two female U.K. visitors with first incredulity and then suspicion. "Was that a bad idea?" they enquire. "Well," he grunts, "I'd have gone to Chicago . . . I mean, why would you want to come to Detroit?"

—As told by reporters Laura Barton and Amy Fleming
of the *Guardian*, July 2004

Greater Detroit has long been overlooked as a site for major military installations. The one exception is Selfridge Air Force Base, opened in 1917 near the northeastern suburb of Mt. Clemens. Congress named the base after army lieutenant Thomas Selfridge, the first air passenger fatality in history. He died in a crash of a Wright Flyer aircraft piloted by Orville Wright at Fort Meyer, Virginia, on September 17, 1908. Isn't it just like Washington to give the region a memorial to a passive victim!

Dissing the D

The region has been perpetually disrespected by the national media, as if its economy and housing market did not already provide enough barriers to its population's quest for psychological resources. It now seems as if the federal government has joined in gratuitously heaping on insults.

At no time did this become clearer than in fall 2008. Top executives from GM and Chrysler, supported by UAW officials, testified before Congress about the auto industry's dire conditions and their needs for short-term federal financing. By the harshness of the congressional inquisitors' tones and their patronizing, accusatory lectures, observers might have thought they had magically time-traveled into a 1951 House Un-American Activities Committee hearing with Senator Joe McCarthy at the microphone. The contrast could not have been starker to Congress's deferential, kid-glove treatment of major financial institution representatives at similar hearings a few months earlier. Leo Gerard, president of United Steelworkers union, had this take on the hearings, "Washington will bail out those who shower before work, but not those who shower afterwards." In the end, Congress gave nearly $1 trillion with no strings attached to the perpetrators whose risky and often illegal financial machinations brought the world economy down. GM and Chrysler, clearly victims of the credit crunch and resultant economic meltdown, got $14 billion conditional on subsequent hearings, draft plans to review and approve, and close federal oversight.

This and the other not-so-subtle messages have not been lost on Detroit's collective psyche. No wonder that eventually Greater Detroiters internalize this disrespect and are prone to display an inferiority complex. This seems to be true across the socioeconomic spectrum.

The inner-city crowds filling the pews on Sundays and weekday services, in grand cathedrals and storefront churches alike, testify to the aching need for the psychological resources of efficacy, dignity, and self-respect:

> Within the church the Negro porter or maid can assume responsibilities and authority not available to him elsewhere. Only there can he participate . . . in decisions open to whites in many other aspects of their lives. Here the Negro domestic exchanges her uniform for a "high-fashion" dress and enjoys the admiration and envy of other friends . . . .The Negro has managed to salvage some self-esteem from his church, and until he achieves such self-esteem elsewhere he will not give up this, the last and only sanctuary.

Although originally written by Kenneth Clark about Harlem in 1965, this quotation equally applies to Detroit today. It is not coincidental that, if you are a good customer in a black-owned store in Detroit, you will be blessed farewell with the ultimate compliment: "With respect!"

Even the most successful Detroit capitalists have not been immune to an inferiority complex about their hometown. A legion of wealthy Detroiters have invested their philanthropic legacies in ways that met their drive for self-esteem but did not redound to the benefit of their home town. Railroad car magnate Charles Freer built a permanent gallery for his impressionist masterpieces, including James McNeill Whistler's *Peacock Room*, on the mall in Washington, D.C. Henry Ford established his foundation in New York, only a few blocks away from where Walter Chrysler built his iconic skyscraper. GM's Alfred P. Sloan endowed the business school at MIT and a foundation in New York. And, of course, Berry Gordy moved Motown Records to Los Angeles. All these captains of industry must have felt that the grandeur of their legacies would be tarnished if they were left to languish in a third-rate place like Detroit. The implicit message conveyed to the troops commanded by these captains is unmistakable.

And what about the average, white suburbanite? Unfortunately, there are no good psychological surveys to tap on this point, but we can draw some inferences from their observed driving behaviors. Their penchant for large, American-nameplate vehicles, and their fascination with speed in excess of legal limits, is well documented. Oakland and Macomb County commuters also led the nation for the last quarter-century in the percentage driving single-occupancy vehicles. Put these facts together and you have the portrait of someone who desperately seeks personal efficacy.

> We curse
> congestion, honk
> and gesture, punch
> up all-news,
> all-sports, all-
> oldies all-the time, cut
> each other off,
> whatever we can do
> to simulate control.
>
> —"Motor City Trilogy III," by Kristin Palm

Detroit is a new city. Here is the utmost in technology . . . a city where nothing in sight existed yesterday; the last word among twentieth century communities, in which, one might suppose, the scientific spirit had swept aside such anachronisms as night riders. Detroit is bounded on the west by Fordissimus—by Ford's Rouge plant . . . . By Ford's company town . . . by Ford's presence as a disguised feudal monarch. On the north, Detroit is bounded by the Reverend Charles E. Coughlin's pulpit—a triumph of that other modern engine, the microphone. In between these points of interest, Detroit's million and a half souls go through the gestures of moderns. Yet this brittle new town harbored the Black Legion [responsible for several gun and bombing murders of labor leaders from 1933 to 1935]. . . . The truth, it would appear, is that there are at least two Detroits—Fordissimus and night riders, side by side. The marvels of industrial production on the one hand; on the other, reactionary night skulkers. . . . Two Detroits apparently far apart but not total strangers.

    —Forrest Davis, first director of the Detroit Urban League, 1936

Coping with Stress, Motown Style

Systemic forces of disrespect attack from many fronts in Greater Detroit, stripping physical, social, and psychological resources from its population and institutions. Disrespect attacks internally through its regional labor and housing markets and externally through the media and the federal government. These attacks motivate individual psychological coping mechanisms attempting to cushion the intense stresses that most face. These coping mechanisms have four distinctive qualities: fealty to hierarchy, forming oppositional identities, sanctifying intolerance, and creating scapegoats.

Greater Detroiters seemingly need a hierarchical social order. With a hierarchy, one can be reasonably sure of one's place in life and can take satisfaction in knowing there is almost always someone below one in the rankings. One's personal resource stock is evaluated relative to individuals in another group considered the *inferior other*. It is the opposite of *relative deprivation*: Greater Detroiters more often look down to feel satisfied than look up to feel dissatisfied.

Who Greater Detroiters *are* is typically defined by who they are *not*. Their identity is formed in opposition to the inferior other: "I am not poor, not black, not union, not *whatever*." The 2004 Detroit Area study of the University of Michigan revealed that many whites hold deep-seated feelings of superiority over blacks. High percentages thought that, compared to blacks, whites tend to be more intelligent (50 percent), prefer being self-supporting instead of living off welfare (47 percent), tend not to be involved with street crimes and gangs (58 percent), and do a good job supervising their children (53 percent).

Intolerance is the necessary consequence of oppositional identity formation. To "live and let live" is anathema to intergroup competition and establishing one's own superiority. The 2004 Detroit Area Survey also revealed that both whites and blacks think much more warmly of members of their own group than the other, but both think more warmly of the other than of Arab Americans. A 2006 Detroit Renaissance/*Crain's Detroit Business* survey of more than 350 executives, entrepreneurs, venture capitalists, real estate developers, and institutional board members found that 43 percent believed the region was unwelcoming for people of diverse backgrounds. Greater Detroiters of certain religious and ideological persuasions have turned this coping response of intolerance into a virtue: "the savior of society's true values." Most such absolutists would opt for Henry Ford's brand of "education" or Rev. Pat Buchanan's brand of "conversion." It is only a short intellectual walk, however, to the costume shops that so many intolerant Greater Detroiters have patronized over the years, where they purchase white robes of the Ku Klux Klan, black skull-and-bones hats of the Black Legion, and camouflage fatigues of the Michigan Militia. Given these individual coping mechanisms, the dualities of Greater Detroit are not as mystifying as Forrest Davis's observations imply.

Herding the Scapegoats

Any real or prospective loss to an individual's resources cannot be perceived as the responsibility of that individual, given these coping reactions of hierarchy, opposition, and intolerance. Instead, the fault must lie in what some *other* person or group did or did not do. Given the region's chronic labor and housing market-generated insecurities, Greater Detroiters have had a lot of practice blaming someone besides themselves. Usually, the scapegoating followed the fundamental dichotomies: blacks and whites blame each other; unionists and management blame each other.

The career of the Catholic "radio priest of Royal Oak," Father Charles Coughlin, iconically represents the region's gift for scapegoating. He blamed all the troubles of the 1930s world on the "twin secular manifestations of Satan": Wall Street and Communism. Conveniently, he saw Jewish conspirators at the heart of both evils. At the height of his popularity in the early 1930s, Father Coughlin's radio broadcast drew tens of millions of listeners, and his office received 80,000 letters of support weekly. These letters often contained coins and dollar bills, enough eventually to build the opulent Shrine of the Little Flower Church, which cannot be overlooked while driving by on Woodward Avenue.

White and black politicians alike over the years scored easy points with racial scapegoating based on imagined memory. Politicians added a pinch of historical fact and a generous helping of imagined memory in a recipe to convince their constituents that their turf was violated by the other: "It used to be wonderful, but *they* ruined it." Essentially, they tried to build a case of "space rape." This charge stuck readily because it constituted for both races a deeply felt and profoundly insulting loss of identity and spatial roots, for which the perpetrator must "pay."

White politicians make their space rape recipe by fingering black scapegoats for the decay, abandonment, and eventual demolition of their constituents' ancestral homes, the "loss" of their religious institutions to new users, and the pitiful decline of the once-magnificent city they loved. Black homeowners are blamed for "not keeping up their homes" and "letting the city go to hell." The City of Detroit's near bankruptcy is offered as proof of the incompetence and corruption of black public officials. Similarly, the 1967 riot showed that blacks are thieves and only want to tear up the place. The upsurge in gang violence associated with distributing the "new" 1970s drug—crack cocaine—made it clear that Mayor Young could not control the city. So, the space rape recipe white suburbanites are fed is essentially summarized, "Everything was fine for us in our wonderful city until *they* came in hordes, *they* rioted, and *they* took power."

Here's how black politicians make their equivalent recipe for space rape. Black Detroiters are encouraged to blame white suburbanites for "abandoning the city." By moving their residences, businesses, and patronage of retail and commercial establishments, whites have caused systematic deterioration of the building stock and erosion of the tax base. Even worse, whites are portrayed as aggressively destroying hallowed black turf, a now-idealized place with a vibrant black business-professional-entertainment district embedded in the heart of a thriving community. Here is how Councilwoman JoAnn Watson framed this imagined memory in September 2004:

> The famed "Black Bottom" and Paradise Valley were replete with black-owned hospitals, hotels, restaurants, grocery stores, pharmacies and entertainment clubs that provided an important network of commerce, social and family resources for Detroit's black community. Urban renewal programs supported by federal, state and local governments effectively dismantled the black businesses and disenfranchised the black owners and their customer base.

Though Watson never used the word "white," the scapegoating recipe of space rape worked fine without it.

We want the river dragged
for distraught souls.
We want our homes rebuilt.
We want the guilty
to pay a greed tax
for the living they stole.
We want our city back.

We want our streetlights on.
We want our garbage gone.
We want to be rid of smack and crack.
We want to retire
by the river.
We want our ancestors
to rest in peace.
We are claiming our history,
seizing the hour.
Cause, we mean to take
our city back.

—"We Want Our City Back" by Melba Joyce Boyd

The scapegoating space rape game is not just a black-white thing. In 2004, Detroit City Council commissioned an economic development analysis by former Detroiter Claud Anderson at a cost of $112,000. The resulting report, "A Powernomics Economic Development Plan for Detroit's Under-Served Majority Population," concluded that immigrants from Mexico, Asia, and the Middle East were stealing the city's resources and a black-owned "Africantown" must be developed in response. In line with the report's recommendations, the Council passed two resolutions by 7-2 majorities in July that year. The first established an economic development agency supported by casino revenues that would authorize business loans and grants only to the "major underserved minority" in Detroit. The second resolution designated blacks as that "major underserved minority." One opponent, Councilwoman Kay Everett, said with considerable psychological insight, "The rationale for this ill-conceived plan is rooted in victimhood justifications that scapegoat those of other ethnicities." On the bright side, it is perhaps a sign of growing multiculturalism that now the finger of blame is pointed in more than one direction.

The key correlate of scapegoating is *passivity*. Other than perhaps exacting retribution from the culprits, failure to take responsibility for one's own loss of resources fundamentally means that one does not need to change behavior or devise resource-strengthening strategies for the future.

Some for One and One for Some

Like all humans, Greater Detroiters have responded to environmental stress not only through individual coping mechanisms but also through collective adaptations. All these adaptations can be characterized as "some for one and one for some": limited collectivities of perceived similar people whose actions try to thwart the aims of dissimilar others.

These adaptations took four primary forms: unionization, segregation, fragmentation, and identity politics. The first three need no further elaboration. Working-class Greater Detroiters relied on unionization as a collective vehicle for offsetting management power and thereby extracting their rightful share of physical and psychological resources from the workplace. Whites and economic elites used segregation of neighborhoods and schools by race and class to preserve their physical, social, and psychological resources. Political jurisdiction fragmentation offered new tools for furthering race and class segregation (like exclusionary zoning) and gave residents an enhanced sense of power over local decision making.

The fourth collective adaptation meshes neatly with the others. Identity politics means voting primarily on the basis of a candidate's "being like me," rather than policy proposals or competence. Greater Detroit has been the longtime playground of identity politics, for understandable reasons. What could be better for those desperately seeking self-esteem and a sense of efficacy than to have perceived alter-egos in power?

The power of identity politics was not lost on former Detroit Mayor Kwame Kilpatrick during his 2005 reelection campaign against H. Freman Hendrix. After running far behind Hendrix in the primary because of his numerous first-term scandals, Mayor Kilpatrick stooped to a bizarre, albeit effective, form of racial identity politics. Noting disapprovingly that Hendrix was the offspring of a union between a German woman and a black U.S. soldier, the mayor implied that his opponent was not a "real black man." To remind campaign crowds that Hendrix's identity was suspect, the mayor only referred to him by his heretofore-never-used first name, "Helmut." Kilpatrick won the general election handily but was later convicted of perjury, bribery, and obstructing justice; forced to resign; and imprisoned halfway into his second term. Apparently, there are some charges that identity politics cannot deflect, even in Detroit.

Denial in the D

Despite Greater Detroiters' individual coping mechanisms and collective adaptations, the regional economic and housing market engines of anxiety often extracted too many of their resources. More and more individuals and organizations fell below the lower threshold of respect—that modicum of economic, social, and psychological resources considered bare minimum. As a consequence, these individuals and organizations frequently adopted the two defensive responses psychologists would predict: denial and myopia. Both came at the expense of conceiving and investing in longer-term strategies for resource conservation and expansion.

Denial is rampant in Greater Detroit. In a 2003 televised public hearing, Detroit Councilman Alonzo Bates criticized a white developer who wanted to buy some vacant, city-owned parcels to build market-rate housing: "Now that the city is *worth something*, you want to take it back!" Bates bellowed. In 2006 Bates upstaged this remark by muttering "Ku Klux Klan" when a federal jury convicted him of corruption. In 2007, a year of record-high gasoline prices and record-low auto sales, a large billboard next to I-94 coming into Detroit from Metropolitan Airport showed a powerful, gas-guzzling car with caption "There's No Muscle like Detroit Muscle." In 2007, Deputy Police Chief Gary Brown and two other black police officers sued the City of Detroit for wrongful termination, claiming that, in the course of an investigation, they were about to expose a sexual affair between Mayor Kilpatrick and his chief of staff. In September, the Wayne County-based jury, eleven white and one black, found in favor of the three officers. After the city settled out of court for $8.4 million plus legal fees, Mayor Kilpatrick shrugged off the verdict, commenting, "I can't help it if 12 people—11 who don't live in Detroit and one who did—decided to decide this way." In February 2008, the *Detroit Free Press* revealed text messages showing that the two indeed were having an affair, proving that the mayor had lied under oath at the

September trial when he denied this allegation. Nevertheless, the mayor re-fused to step down because, as he said in a radio interview, "I believe I'm on an assignment from God in this position." It took the subsequent felony convictions for perjury, obstruction of justice, and corruption to make him face reality.

Statistical evidence shows that denial is more widespread in the region than these vignettes imply. A November 2005 *Detroit News* poll found shock-ingly low percentages of respondents from Greater Detroit who agreed with the statement "People who have a college education are usually better off than people who don't." Only 47 percent of black, 57 percent of Hispanic, and 68 percent of white respondents agreed. Despite the decade-long drubbing the region has taken, only a third of the Greater Detroit respondents in the Kaiser Family Foundation poll taken in November 2009 said that they were pessimistic about the future of the Detroit area, and only 22 percent ex-pected that their standard of living would be lower in ten years. In the same poll, 22 percent said they would recommend a career in manufacturing to their children.

Greater Detroit once was a place of dynamic ingenuity and entrepreneur-ship. It was a place where multiple paths to opportunity beckoned, though the difficulty of the path depended on the current state of play in the power struggles between labor and capital, blacks and whites. It was once a place where many people with modest talent but oversized dreams could make decent lives for themselves, whether it be from baking chicken pies like Bruno and Helen, rolling cigars like Emma, or twisting wrought iron like George Jacob.

Today the old Germantown neighborhood where those opportuni-ties were realized and lives lived—their former homes, social clubs, and church—has been swept away. The exception is Acme Wire and Iron Works—one of a handful of hundred-year-old companies still in opera-tion in Detroit (see Figure 26). It is owned by a fourth-generation descen-dent of the founder. The factory would easily be recognized by George Jacob, for remarkably little has changed. The company still uses the origi-nal building to produce the identical wire mesh product with the origi-nal, leather belt-driven machinery installed in 1899. To walk inside Acme is to travel through time, or at least through Greenfield Village. It is a vestige of nineteenth-century technology improbably hanging on against all odds—as is its city. And like its host city, it is stubbornly unchanging,

Figure 26. Acme Wire and Iron Company factory amid the fields of the east side of Detroit.

locked in the past as everything crumbles to dust around it, denying that tomorrow will come.

Myopia up Close and Personal

It is also easy to find instances in Greater Detroit where individuals behaved myopically, desperately grasping in the moment for some morsel of power or self-esteem, while ignoring negative longer-run implications. A few involved famous protagonists. In 1923 a few Klansmen thought that preserving their place in the social hierarchy warranted burning out a Catholic priest from his recently occupied northwest side home. The priest in question, Father McNichols, was then undertaking the nefarious task of building a new campus of the Jesuit-run University of Detroit on Six Mile Road. Fortunately, the priest was neither injured nor deterred, and new higher educational opportunities for both Catholics and Protestants (like George Milton) were created on the now-renamed McNichols Road.

Generic myopic acts are more frequent. For example, to "diss" someone in Detroit is to ask for a fight. Only in a world bereft of resources of all kinds would people be so willing to risk injury, death, or prison time for the immediate gratification of preserving shreds of self-respect through violence. One day in May 2010, a skinny, seventeen-year-old named Je'Rean Blake gave a dirty look to Chauncey Owens, age thirty-four, in a party store on Mack Avenue near St. Jean Street. A short while later, Owens returned to the store, shot Blake to death, and drove off in his SUV.

> Soft Side of Hasting, Oakland Avenue,
> Wilfred's Billiard Parlor jammed between
> The Pig Bar-B-Q and the Echo Theatre.
> Slick Herman chalks his cue with resolution,
> blue powder whispers to the floor.
> he misses an easy bank shot in the corner.
>
> Safe Eddie would always leave you on the rail
> or hidin' behind balls you didn't want to shoot.
> And steady Jerome looks for nonbelievers.
> Hasn't missed a bank shot in four days.

Silent Ambrose shoots 9 ball
with Ralph, the Merchant.
Ralph accuses Silent of moving his balls
for a better angle, calls Silent a name.

Silent flashes quicker-than-light
2 inches of switchblade to Merchant's jugular.
In the stop-stillness of the moment,
you could hear a rat piss on cotton,
Don't you ever call me that . . . ever.

Silent wins the 9 ball game by forfeit.
Merchant can't find a cue
that will sit still in is hand.

—"8 Ball in Side Pocket" by Murray Jackson

Myopia in the face of organizational resource scarcity abounds in the City
of Detroit. First, take the Detroit Public School Board. Frustrated by the lack
of progress in improving student outcomes and financial accountability, in
1999 the Michigan State Legislature imposed a new governance structure on
the DPS. Instead of being elected directly, now the Board would be appointed
by the mayor of Detroit, except for one member appointed by the governor.
Despite notable successes under the new appointed Board structure, it was
met with fierce opposition when it came up for renewal in the Proposition E
vote on the November 2004 ballot. Characterizing the new structure as "a
takeover," opponents cynically capitalized on the populace's thirst for efficacy:
"We believe that this extension of the takeover is being driven by people like
the owner of [construction company] Barton Malow, who are current benefi-
ciaries of contracts at DPS," contended Heaster Wheeler, executive director of
the Detroit NAACP. Victor Marsh, coordinator of the Just Say No to Proposition E group, laid the core issue bare: "It's all about controlling the dollars. . . .
[If Proposal E is passed] the [DPS] Chief Executive Officer would be nothing
more than a puppet for the Detroit Regional Chamber of Commerce." Proposition E was soundly defeated. Detroiters needed control and the respect that
came with it, and they needed it right away. To get it, they would willingly
sacrifice a structure that insulated the DPS chief executive from the vagaries
of a patronage-elected, micro-managing, preening, and often-corrupt School

Board. Predictably, the resulting fiscal chaos led the State of Michigan to take over complete control of the finances of DPS in December 2008.

Robert Thompson made a fortune in the private sector and generously wanted to pay it forward. So, in 2003, he proposed donating $200 million to build charter schools in Detroit. Thompson had two big problems, however, that rendered his philanthropy suspect in resource-starved Detroit: he was white, and he lived in the suburb of Plymouth. The Rev. Wendell Anthony, former head of the Detroit NAACP, publicly decried this initiative at a 2004 school summit by appealing to the need for self-respect. He rhetorically asked, "What would Grosse Pointers think if Oprah Winfrey approached them about building a school for *them*?" Thompson's largesse was refused. Short-run gains in psychological resources for adults again trumped potential long-term economic gains for children.

The DPS Board lags far behind Detroit City Council, however, in demonstrating resource-hoarding myopia. In the aforementioned 2004 controversy over the "Africantown" proposal, Council overrode a mayoral veto, defiantly reiterating their belief that blacks indeed were the city's "major underserved minority" and that immigrant groups had unfairly acquired economic resources at their expense. This represents a textbook example of short-run resource hoarding with negative long-run consequences. This resolution discouraged desperately needed immigration that might provide a huge financial boost to primarily black owners of homes and businesses in this rapidly depopulating city. One Africantown opponent, Councilwoman Sheila Cockrel, saw this short-sightedness clearly: "[The proposal] advocates exclusionary classifications and illegal set asides [for blacks] that only serve to divide and polarize within the city and the region. And we have plenty of that already."

The Detroit City Council repeatedly demonstrated unwillingness to consider long-term benefits if it risked losing control in the short term. In 2003 the Michigan Legislature passed a bill facilitating the establishment of land banks: independent, nonprofit organizations whose job would be to assemble derelict properties and vacant land owned by local governments through the tax foreclosure process and speed their redevelopment. Despite its surplus of city-owned land, Detroit did not create a land bank, because it would only have the power to appoint a minority of seats on the land bank board. Council refused to cede control of city-owned land—worthless in all but symbolic terms—to a body that was not controlled exclusively by Detroit. Only in 2008, after the unique advantages of a land bank in acquiring foreclosed properties became irresistible, did the council relent and agree to establish one.

In another bizarre case, the City Council voted in March 2008 to withhold federal funds from Detroit-based charities, unless 51 percent of their board members were Detroit residents. One councilwoman defended her vote by caustically suggesting that non-Detroiters have a "slave-master mentality." Never mind that these suburban board members typically have the deepest pockets and the wealthiest networks that ultimately funnel more economic resources into Detroit. No, city control is more important; short-term psychological resources are more important than long-term physical resources.

Consider the Cobo Convention Center expansion controversy of February 2009. A $288 million deal to expand and upgrade the city-owned home of the internationally renowned North American Auto Show was painstakingly negotiated by representatives of Wayne, Oakland, and Macomb Counties, state legislators, and Detroit Interim Mayor Kenneth Cockrel, Jr. The proposal would give Detroit $20 million to retire debt incurred in building the Cobo parking garage and would relieve it of both an annual operating deficit of $15 million and deferred maintenance charges of $200 million. In return, Cobo would be put in the hands of a regional authority directed by a five-person board. Although only one board member would be appointed by the City of Detroit, each member would have veto power. The City Council turned this sweet deal down on a 5-3 vote. As if to underline the myopic response that psychologists would have predicted, Councilwoman JoAnn Watson said, "Detroiters have spoken loud and clear in opposition to giving away or transferring another Detroit asset."

Finally, the city fights changes in its water system as if it were a matter of life and death. Now, the city provides water for the entire region. Though paid for providing this service, Detroit must bear the financial burden of maintaining and updating the ancient system of pipes and complying with strict new federal water quality mandates. Many proposals have arisen over the years to create a regional water administration, sharing the responsibilities for delivering this vital service; all have been defeated by Detroit. The latest proposal was greeted with predictable public outcries as in March 2011: "Detroit is facing a hostile takeover from greedy suburban lawmakers for control of our water system!"

Detroit is a poster child for how threats to already meager resources are met with a defensive posture, a crouched position that inhibits seeing the future. Potential resource gains of all kinds are sacrificed on the blood-stained altar of fragile civic ego. The city fairly shouts, "It's *OUR* land, it's *OUR* water, it's *OUR* schools, it's *OUR* convention center, and we are going to keep control of them whether it makes long-term sense or not! They all may be like an albatross around our neck, but at least it's *OUR* albatross!"

Detroit's suburbs are not, however, immune to myopia. Their myopic strain is different from the city's in that it focuses on conserving economic resources and social status in the short term, instead of ceding either to an "undeserving" city occupied by "the others.". The behavior of the suburbs fairly shouts, "It's *OUR* money; why should we share it with *them*?"

In 2005, Wayne and Oakland Counties voted on a proposed property tax assessment to be used for ongoing support of cultural institutions and recreation programs in the two counties. Though the proposal would raise the typical homeowner's taxes only $100 annually, it would provide a critical revenue stream for a myriad important institutions, mostly based in Detroit, such as the Institute of Arts, Symphony, Opera Theater, Historical Museum, and Museum of African American History. The Detroit Regional Chamber of Commerce provided a comprehensive rationale for how the added funding would redound to the benefit of everyone in the region and led an aggressive publicity campaign in support. The referendum passed in Wayne County but lost so heavily in Oakland County that the measure was defeated.

Suburban Detroiters must put up with an inefficient, fragmented bus system because they have steadfastly refused to vote taxes on themselves. As of 2005, fifty suburban communities had opted out of the Suburban Mobility Authority for Regional Transportation (SMART)—costing it a quarter of its budget. More perversely, this frugal shortsightedness imposes costs on the suburbs that do participate in SMART, by forcing convoluted bus routing that delays and discourages riders. Suburbanites have also been unwilling to fund the requisite local match for building a regional mass transit system, thereby failing to secure generous federal matching monies. Their first opportunity was in 1976; Detroit came up with its share of the local match but the suburbs did not. The result was that the city ended up building its downtown loop "People Mover," but the light rail transit lines designed to feed suburban commuters into it never materialized.

Why would suburbanites respond in such a myopic way? Could it have anything to do with the fact that Coleman Young had become Detroit's mayor in 1974? Or perhaps because today over 80 percent of the region's bus ridership consists of black people? Why indeed should they support a decent transit system for *them*?

Rosa Parks died in Detroit on October 24, 2005, five weeks shy of the fiftieth anniversary of her famous act of civil disobedience on that Montgomery,

Alabama, bus. To mark her passing, all Detroit Department of Transportation buses (which serve only the city) had one *front* seat cordoned off with a black ribbon until the day of her funeral. After lying in state in the Capitol Rotunda in Washington, Parks' remains returned to Detroit for a seven-hour funeral at the Greater Grace Temple. A horse-drawn cortege proceeded majestically from the church down Seven Mile Road to Woodward Avenue and interment in Woodlawn Cemetery. Thousands of mourners lined the miles-long route. Parks' coffin had been interred less than a week when Livonia, an inner-ring suburban municipality of 89,000 white and 3,000 black residents, voted to withdraw from the SMART bus system.

The Last Chicken

How markets in an American metropolitan area operate holds profound implications for the abilities of its populace to gain respect: fundamental physical, social, and psychological resources. In the case of Greater Detroit, century-long reliance on assembly-line manufacturing of a durable consumer good meant that economic opportunities were cyclically unstable and increasingly scarce over time. The workplace itself, potentially a core vehicle for human actualization, proved corrosive to self-esteem, efficacy, pride, and fulfillment in the auto industry context. It proved the Engine of Anxiety. Instead of a sanctuary from the workplace, the home was yet another source of stress over threatened resource losses. This was guaranteed by rampant racial tipping and the inexorable degradation and devaluation of neighborhoods produced by the Housing Disassembly Line. The resulting abandonment and demolition of the city's physical history created a vast prairie of the imagined past where the weeds of rootlessness, mutual blame, and hypernostalgia sprout.

As abrasive as it has been to the human psyche and soma, Greater Detroit might more aptly be named Grater Detroit. It is a place that fundamentally and perpetually *disrespects* its citizens. Perhaps the deepest meaning symbolized by the Joe Louis *Fist* statue in downtown (see Figure 5) is the devastating punch in the gut this region gives its citizens as they quest for respect.

Greater Detroiters coped with and adapted to their disrespectful metropolis as best they could in an attempt to gain and preserve resources. Individually, they coped by glorifying hierarchy, emphasizing oppositional identity formation, and raising intolerance to a virtue. This led to epidemic-level scapegoating whenever resources were threatened or lost. Collectively, they adapted by forming unions, segregating themselves according to income and ethnic status, and creating tiny, homogeneous political jurisdictions that they could control and in which they could elect those "like themselves." These adaptations may seem rational and functional in the short term, the best choices in a bad situation. Denial and myopic hoarding, instead of investing resources in the future, are understandable responses of people who have suffered repeated and increasingly severe losses at the hands of the disrespectful metropolis called Motown. But, as psychology has shown, these are also desperate, conservative, ultimately self-defeating responses. And when aggregated to the metropolitan scale, these responses indeed have produced pernicious, unintended consequences in the long run.

Greater Detroiters fear they have only one chicken left in their coop after the seemingly endless raids by the foxes, so they hold on to it for dear life, strangling it in the process.

The Detroit Public Library stands regally on Woodward Avenue in the Cultural Center. Its second floor Grand Hall proudly displays the city's other great mural, *Man's Mobility*, painted by John S. Coppin. Though less famous than Diego Rivera's *Detroit Industry* in the Detroit Institute of Arts only 300 yards across the street, *Man's Mobility* offers a powerful lens through which to examine the ultimate concerns, aspirations, and myths of Greater Detroit. The mural is a triptych portraying the transportation technologies of three eras to which Detroit's industries have contributed mightily. The 1855 panel shows a steam locomotive and steamship figuratively passing a Conestoga wagon, ox cart, and sail-powered ship. The 1905 panel portrays a horse rider, bicyclist, and mother with baby pram frightened by a prototype horseless carriage as it careens past, belching smoke from its tailpipe. The 1965 panel has a group of white males gazing admiringly skyward as jets roar overhead and a rocket blasts off to outer space.

The caption next to *Man's Mobility* reads, "Man's will and his creative imagination have impelled him ever onward; thus has come new knowledge, understanding, peace, dignity, and fulfillment." Ah, if only this were true for Greater Detroit today.

Though Pilgrim Church is located near the MotorCity Casino in west-central Detroit, it caters to a distinctly different clientele. Every evening at Pilgrim Church, I Am My Brother's Keeper Ministries opens for business.

The group provides a place where some of Detroit's homeless people can get the most basic physical, social, and psychological resources: a warm meal, shelter, and some sympathetic human attention. These people are the ultimate victims of the region's degrading job and housing markets. Before eating, they are asked to repeat over and over, following the leader's chant: "I Am Somebody!"

Chapter 11

From Motown to Mortropolis

This place is cruel; nowhere could be much colder.
If we don't change, the world will soon be over.
—"Living for the City," sung by Stevie Wonder in 1973

What happens when you drop a giant, oligopolistic, land-hungry auto industry on a featureless plain in a state that gives tiny local governments the power to control their own development patterns and to decide who lives in their communities? What happens when that industry's degrading nature of work and exploitative excesses are countered by a union movement that eventually becomes equally gigantic, conservative and bureaucratized? What happens when that industry's strongest labor demands must be met by importing hundreds of thousands of blacks and whites from the Deep South who brought along their cultural attributes but not the de jure structures of segregation to codify them? What happens when permissive geography and local governments decisively tilt the developmental playing field in favor of excessive new housing construction at the suburban fringe, leaving in its wake abandoned neighborhoods in the central city?

What happens is that you get a metropolis that is deeply cleft by competitive tensions between capital and labor, blacks and whites, city and suburb. You get a metropolis that, at its heart, renders peoples' livelihoods, neighborhoods, housing assets, social status, personal safety, and self-esteem insecure. You get a metropolis that fundamentally *disrespects* its residents by systematically frustrating their quest for respect.

This book applies brushstrokes portraying these distinct aspects of Greater Detroit. Each adds a different hue, a richer texture of pigments, to the metropolitan portrait in process. Now it is time to step away from the canvas, for no portrait can be fully assessed without examining the impression it gives as a whole. Be forewarned that the holistic view is more akin to one of Francis Bacon's paintings, not one of John Singer Sargent's.

The Metropolis of Disrespect and Dysfunction

Throughout the twentieth century, Greater Detroit's music morphed to correspond to the evolving opportunities and quality of life it offered its residents. The optimism and faith embodied in James Weldon Johnson's "Lift Every Voice and Sing" in the 1900s and Wes Montgomery's "Goin' on to Detroit" in the 1960s succumbed to the confusion, depression, and desperation of Stevie Wonder's "Living for the City." The tenor got even grimmer in the decades following the 1960s; surreal Techno and angry rap music made 1960s Motown music seem as quaintly irrelevant as the Model T. This musical transformation reflected the on-the-ground realities: Greater Detroit had become the metropolis of disrespect.

The region's auto manufacturing economy and housing market development rules conspired to create tremendous personal and organizational insecurities associated with threatened or actual losses of physical, social, and psychological resources. This systematic and prolonged process of disrespect triggered a predictable series of individual coping mechanisms and collective adaptations. These were seen by each person and organization as functional in the short term. Ironically and perversely, these responses proved dysfunctional because they frustrated the efforts of *other* people and organizations to gain and protect *their* resources. Detroit is fundamentally a metropolis whose labor and housing markets disrespect people; then, people and organizations adapt to their frustrated quest for respect in ways that ultimately intensify the disrespect for everyone.

First, take Detroiters' fealty to hierarchy and oppositional nature, summarized by this dictum, *I am not [union/management; white/black]. I am better than they are. I must have more power than they do. I must consume more than they do and be safe from them. If I have all this, I will have self-respect and their respect.* This sort of mindset inevitably leads to a "zero-sum" way of thinking. I win if you lose, even if I gain nothing in absolute terms. I lose if you win anything because it threatens the rankings; the gap between "us" and the "them" below us may narrow relatively or (even worse) absolutely. From this perspective, seeking out opportunities for win-win collaborations is unthinkable. Greater Detroit's virulent and often violent dual competitions between labor and capital and between blacks and whites are especially pernicious in this regard. This dysfunctional, zero-sum mindset was flaunted in 2009 by two suburban elected officials who tried to convince major Detroit institutions to relocate. Warren mayor Jim Fouts proposed tax breaks worth tens of millions of dollars to General Motors if it would move its headquarters from the Renaissance Center to his suburb. County executive L. Brooks Patterson darkly threatened, "I'm going to call around to see if there's any interest in attempting to move the venue of the North American International Auto Show to a site in the suburbs, including Oakland County."

Second, consider Greater Detroiters' intolerance. Defining one's own "group" in a narrow, ethnocentric way retards regional economic growth that could potentially benefit everyone. Intolerance creates shriveled interpersonal networks and bonds of trust, discourages immigration from elsewhere in the nation and abroad, and is corrosive to the entrepreneurial spirit. Sam Logan, a black executive with the *Michigan Chronicle*, blasted Detroit officials on this point in a front page column of *Crain's Detroit Business* on June 17, 2005:

> White-owned businesses [in Detroit] are routinely subjected to every form of shakedown imaginable. Unjustly castigated gas station and store owners are forced to pay hush money to loudmouth malcontents for urban peace. Developers and investors aren't allowed to set up shop [in Detroit] unless a majority of the construction and other jobs go to their black friends, whether they qualify for them or not.... Hostility and intolerance toward private-sector voices deprives Detroiters of the opportunity to explore and expand business formation.... This mindless, ill-informed approach—which is somehow being confused with the concept of black pride—is not in our collective interest and will ultimately be to our undoing.... Detroit will remain black, proud—and broke.

Third, the scapegoating coping mechanism hurts everyone by undermining synergistic regional cooperation among jurisdictions. The rhetoric of race-baiting politicians—both black and white—as they whip up "space rape" grievances shows how this happens. Detroit politicians "exercise their independence and demonstrate their power" without investing in building alliances with white suburbs, both because they have few resources to invest and because they fear constituent backlash if they were to play nice with representatives of the folks who fled Detroit as it got blacker. Suburban politicians want to hold on to their resources and avoid cooperation for symmetric reasons. They ask, "How could we ally with those who ruined our city, overran generations of our neighborhoods, and threaten us today?" In the wake of the 2005 racist outbursts at the Livonia Planning Commission and in the midst of his own hotly contested reelection campaign, Detroit Mayor Kwame Kilpatrick ranted, "In Birmingham, Bloomfield Hills and all these places they do more meth . . . ecstasy . . . and acid than all the schools in the City of Detroit together." L. Brooks Patterson rejoined, "We've been waiting for this race card to be played for months now, and the unfortunate comments made in Livonia played right into Kwame's hand. . . . They're spoiling for a fight, a racial fight." City and suburbs are implicitly saying the same thing: "How could you respect yourself if you bonded with those who so badly disrespected you?"

As if these individual coping mechanisms were not sufficiently dysfunctional, add the consequences of the collective adaptations. The first is unionization. For all their obvious benefits as a counterweight to capitalist exploitation, unions implicitly taught their members some unfortunate lessons. Unions countered workplace exploitation by instituting rigid work rules and an ethos of gain through extortionist redistribution from employers, not through increasing productivity, teamwork, or regular work habits. Unions assured laborers in Greater Detroit that union membership and seniority—not education, creativity, entrepreneurship, or productivity—were keys to their success.

The second collective adaptation, the segregation of neighborhoods and schools based on race and class, has disastrous consequences for individual opportunities. Minority and lower-income families are typically segregated in Greater Detroit municipalities that have the weakest fiscal capacity, the lowest quality of public services and schools, and the highest tax rates. Their neighborhoods have the most environmental dangers—from highways, incinerators, former industrial sites, and lead-painted homes. These places usually are far removed from where most jobs in the region are now located, and they are poorly served by public transportation. Their neighborhoods are at the wrong end of the Housing Disassembly Line, so they are plagued with homes that are badly devalued if they can be sold at all. Finally, such geographic isolation abets the development of distinct subcultural traits regarding patterns of speech, dress, and social intercourse that differ from the mainstream and, thus, are more easily stigmatized.

The third adaptation, political jurisdictional fragmentation, makes it easier for higher-income groups to separate themselves from lower-income groups and avoid any financial responsibility for them. This yields a desperate duo in Detroit—spatially concentrated poverty coupled with a dysfunctional public school system—that tamps down potential workforce productivity. Detroit is woefully undereducated compared with its competitors. Basil Whiting and Tony Proscio document that in 2004, only 11 percent of Detroit's population had a college degree, much lower than in Philadelphia (20 percent), Baltimore (24 percent), Pittsburgh (34 percent), Boston (41 percent), or Atlanta (43 percent). The nonprofit Pro-Literacy Detroit estimated that over half the city's adults were functionally illiterate in 2009. Not surprisingly, a 2010 ranking by America's Most Literate Cities of the seventy-five cities with more than a quarter-million population placed Detroit dead last in library usage, even though it ranked near the top in library books available to residents. This lack of basic—let alone advanced—education does not bode well for the prospects of developing homegrown entrepreneurs, keeping existing companies prosperous, or attracting new capital from outside the region. The benefits of realizing any of these prospects would extend, of course, far beyond the boundaries of Detroit.

Identity politics, the last collective adaptation, creates the perverse consequence of tolerance for underperforming local public officials. Citizens are reluctant to criticize incompetent or corrupt local officials when they previously bought into the notion that "they are like us." Besides, they rationalize, "Who among us is perfect? We all deserve a second chance, even politicians who do wrong, especially when some outsiders are out to get them." Citizens and institutions with connections outside the jurisdiction in question are reluctant to demand accountability and efficiency for fear of being labeled "disrespectful." As for the underperforming local public officials themselves, victimhood absolves all personal responsibility. Incentives for public accountability, thus, evaporate. In the wake of his son's charging personal luxury items on the city's credit card and having the Police Department buy a red Lincoln Navigator for his wife's personal use, Mayor Kilpatrick's father rose to his defense. At the May 2005 kickoff of the mayor's reelection campaign, dad explained that criticisms in the "white" press were unfair; his son, the embodiment of "strong, young black manhood," had followed all society's rules yet was being persecuted anyway. "If *they* can do it to him, *they* can do it to any of us," Kilpatrick the elder warned. The shadowy "other" again was blamed in March 2008 at the height of the mayor's text message scandal. "Perhaps it is because Mayor Kwame Kilpatrick has brought such unprecedented change and reform to our city that some feel threatened by his leadership and will go to any lengths to remove him from office," his Web site darkly insinuated. Given that the former mayor and his father were subsequently convicted on federal indictments of conspiracy corruption, perhaps the Kilpatricks' paranoia was justified.

Collective Irrationality

Collective irrationality means that doing certain things achieves its purpose only when one person does it and everyone else refrains from doing it; when everyone does it, the opposite is achieved. For example, if only one person takes more than the legal limit of fish from a lake it would serve the purpose of fulfilling the greed of that single fisher. However, if everyone were to do likewise, there would be no fish left to spawn, and all would go hungry next season.

Greater Detroit is a blinding example of collective irrationality at a metropolitan scale when we view its individual and collective responses to disrespect in a holistic way. In response to the disrespecting labor and housing markets, individuals have chosen to cope as best they can by emphasizing hierarchy, oppositional identity formation, intolerance, and scapegoating. Often they have joined with others also trying to protect their resources and formed unions, segregated themselves into their own neighborhoods and political jurisdictions, and supported identity politics. The crowning irony is that these individual responses have not only failed to attain the individual's goal but, because everyone has tried to do the similar thing, they have increasingly—if unwittingly—frustrated goal attainment by *all* parties. Greater Detroiters' seemingly rational actions as individuals aimed at gaining respect have produced irrational collective outcomes when the actions are aggregated.

Greater Detroit's whites and upper-income families take the lead in responding to anxieties produced by the region's labor and housing markets by segregating their neighborhoods and schools and, whenever possible, escaping to separate political jurisdictions. This hypersegregation and jurisdictional fragmentation erect barriers that make it more difficult for minority and low-income individuals to be well-educated, healthy, employed, wealthy, and able to act "middle-class white." These barriers objectively perpetuate intergroup disparities and, thus, legitimize the dominant group's prejudiced stereotypes. They thus, can smugly say with some justification, "See, I *told you* that they were stupid, lazy, sloppy, incomprehensible, and dangerous! *They* are not like us!" The dominant group is thereby *further* motivated to segregate and jurisdictionally fragment themselves, enlisting the aid of local police, municipal land use zoning boards, and real estate industry operatives to hold these lines of race and class ever-more vigilantly. They intolerantly point fingers at the "other," define themselves in opposition to them, and see the world in zero-sum terms. They avoid vast swaths of the metropolis, re-elect race-baiting and underperforming local officials, and resolutely reject efforts at regional mass transit, service coordination, or resource sharing. Their unions taught them the superiority of seniority over creativity, security over risk-taking, so they invest too little in education and entrepreneurship. They remain "better than *they are*," but their collectively irrational actions make them fall ever-farther behind world-class standards and undermine their families' future prospects for respect.

From the perspective of Greater Detroit's minority and low-income individuals, their senses of victimhood, resentment, and anger are legitimized as well. They can glimpse the structure that is out to make them fail from childhood through adulthood. It is thus understandable that they often reject trappings of success laid down by the rulers of that structure, such as educational credentials and mainstream dialect. They can also say, "*They* are not like us!" Instead, they follow incentives to seek physical, social, and psychological resources where quite different sorts of opportunities present themselves: having children as teens and participating in the underground economy. Over time, these second-best choices further limit their ability to participate lucratively in the legitimate labor market, as their child-rearing obligations, exposures to violence, and criminal convictions multiply. They, too, take comfort in pointing intolerant fingers at the "other," defining themselves in opposition to them, seeing the world in zero-sum terms, reelecting race-baiting and underperforming local officials, and opposing regionalism as a further loss of their already meager power. They also increasingly become less secure due to these collectively irrational adaptations.

The distinctly drawn boundaries of race, class, physical decay, crime, and violence collude with subcultural differences to create miniworlds within Greater Detroit. And with stark differences and implied threat comes fear. Fear is the Petri dish medium in which the race-baiting politicians and media purveyors of hysteria grow their self-serving spores of paranoia with which to infect a vulnerable population. With fear comes ever more emphasis on police and self-armament. But when the gun-toting citizenry and police try to secure their constituencies, they exacerbate the insecurity of others, in yet another illustration of collective irrationality. The only thing we can be secure in is the knowledge that fear is fatal to cooperation and creative, long-term thinking.

Greater Detroiters' individual quests for respect, perpetrated over generations, proved collectively irrational because they created a perverse metropolitan structure. This structure creates a distorted landscape of incentives and constraints where all Greater Detroit residents ultimately become less educated, entrepreneurial, cooperative, tolerant, and civil. Instead, they become more myopic, suspicious, irresponsible, passive, and violent. Over time, this situation erodes the region's productivity, quality of life, and economic competitiveness on a global stage. It also frustrates the attempts of labor, capital, blacks, and whites alike to achieve their goals of respect.

Double Bipolar Disorder

Not one but two intersecting tension lines—between black and white and between capital and labor—tug at the soul of Greater Detroit, magnifying the forces of disrespect. These lines of tension arose primarily from the century-long auto production dominance of the region's economy. Competition along these lines has been as perpetual as it has been violent. Yet the relative powers of capital and labor, black and white, have not remained constant historically.

On the contrary, Greater Detroit's history reveals a dual dialectic. In one dialectic, excessively powerful capitalists' labor abuses during the late nineteenth and early twentieth centuries engendered massive labor organizing in reaction. This, in turn, generated a counter-reaction by the capitalists: automation, relocating factories, and outsourcing internationally. In the other dialectic, excessively powerful whites' racist abuses from the late nineteenth to the mid-twentieth centuries engendered virulent identity politics emphasizing black power and pride above everything in reaction. Whites, in turn, responded by willfully boycotting the central city, moving ever-farther away from it, and frustrating attempts to coordinate infrastructure, improve education, or share resources regionally.

These dual dialectics were mutually dysfunctional. They led to the ruination of both the domestic auto industry and its dominant union. They led to the pauperization of both blacks and whites, as the region failed to invest in its people and its infrastructure to make it globally competitive. This dual dialectic, thus, represents another key force in Greater Detroit that deeply frustrates it citizens' quest for respect by producing collectively irrational outcomes. One, therefore, can diagnose Greater Detroit as a fatal case of "double bipolar disorder:" capital polarized from labor, black polarized from white.

> Don't find fault—find a remedy. Anybody can complain.
>
> —Henry Ford

> This is an insular industry in an insular town.
> —William Clay Ford, Jr., Chief Executive Officer of Ford Motor
> Company and great-grandson of Henry Ford, 2006

The Auto Mortropolis

Auto production's historical dominance bequeathed Greater Detroit four powerful legacies related to the nature of capital, technology, labor, and race relations: the high-octane hangover. The super-sized, oligopolistic nature of the corporations led to bureaucratization, complacency, conservatism, and stifling of entrepreneurial spirit both inside and outside the Big Three. The gigantism of the auto companies required an equally gigantic counterweight if workers were to get some relief from inhumane working conditions and wrest their fair slice of the economic pie from the companies. As the UAW grew it, too, bureaucratized, got complacent, and lost its creative, organizing fervor. Its efforts to smooth the inherently rough edges of auto work saddled the industry with unsustainable labor costs. The UAW and other unions taught rank-and-file Detroit the lesson of zero-sum outcomes and the primacy of seniority over creativity.

The nature of auto production technology pushed both factory size and the land demand under them ever higher. Plants did not value proximity to the city's historical core along the Detroit River because auto production did not require access to navigable water. This triggered their inexorable relocation to ever larger, more peripheral sites, forcing the region to become decentralized and auto-dependent for commuting. On the flip side, this relocation meant leaving behind industrial relics whose very mass inhibited their subsequent reuse and discouraged the city's preservation and redevelopment, setting it up for fiscal failure.

The nature of auto industry labor was fundamentally characterized by the insecurity of basic physical and psychological resources. From its inception, the industry tried to deskill, disempower, and eliminate workers through a division of labor, repressive shop-floor management practices, and automation. It attempted to counter workers' collective union efforts through race-baiting, outsourcing, and factory relocation. It is an industry that fundamentally disrespects workers by frustrating in multiple ways any efforts to secure and conserve a modicum of physical and psychological resources.

The nature of race relations encouraged by the auto industry was both intentionally and unintentionally divisive. Intentional efforts by the industry to foment racial tensions as a way to thwart union organizing efforts exacted their own "legacy costs." Ironically, the unions' postwar success in wresting economic gains for their primarily white members indirectly contributed to racial tensions. As more and more white unionized workers bought their own homes, they simultaneously bought into the White Protection Racket and thereby became more vested in maintaining residential segregation and suburban jurisdictional fragmentation.

Greater Detroit's workers tried to cope with the ongoing stress barrage caused by this disrespectful economic base by emphasizing hierarchy, defining themselves in opposition to others, scapegoating, and intolerance. Their quest for respect led them to create a peculiar set of institutions (like police forces, unions), political entities (like fragmented suburban municipalities, identity politics), spatial structures (like race and class segregation), and physical-psychic boundaries (like Eight Mile Road, the Dearborn city limits). In consort with a permissive geographic and jurisdictional setting, the quest for separation, security, and efficacy helped empower a regional Housing Disassembly Line that perversely intensified the threat to physical, social, and psychological resources of workers living in older neighborhoods. These collective adaptations produced dialectical responses and counter-responses yielding a double bipolar disorder and a pantheon of prismatic symbols that inhibited interracial and interclass communication.

This panoply of individual and collective respect-seeking actions produced the extreme socioeconomic and physical dualities that characterize Greater Detroit today: racial polarization of opportunities, places, and politics; concentrations of poverty and affluence; city-suburban fiscal disparities; massive disinvestment and abandonment in the core, coupled with unbridled fringe development. These actions ultimately created a place structured to encourage its people to become less productive, entrepreneurial, and cooperative and instead become more polarized, violent, and vengeful. So it is a place that could not constructively respond to progressive deindustrialization and cannot compete effectively in the new global economy. Ultimately, it is a place where the quest for respect is continually frustrated by the collectively irrational actions of its people in their individually rational responses to its industrial legacy.

The auto industry and those dependent on it have unwittingly built a suicidal metropolis, a place where bodies, psyches, and opportunities die all too often, a mortuary where the dreams of respect are embalmed. It is the "Auto Mortropolis."

Is Detroit Unique?

Many of the phenomena visible in Greater Detroit are present in other American metropolitan areas, especially in the Midwest. Deindustrialization, decay, central city population loss, sprawl, segregation by race and class, and jurisdictional fragmentation certainly exist elsewhere. Greater Detroit is distinguished by the intense degrees of all these phenomena and their special origins.

The dominant reasons for these extreme circumstances are a result of the Auto Mortropolis. No other major American metropolitan area has been so dominated for so long by one industry, one with all the pernicious idiosyncrasies associated with the High Octane Hangover. If this were not enough, Greater Detroit also had the misfortune of being in a locale where topography, weather, and rainfall erected no developmental barriers of consequence and the state's "home rule" structure abetted a fragmented, pro-development jurisdictional context ripe for the creation of the Housing Disassembly Line. In addition, Greater Detroit suffered from bad timing. In its two strongest labor demand periods, it was forced by war and immigration restrictions to import vast numbers of black and white southerners whose volatile relations contributed to the already-tense racial climate. This mix produced spasmodic outbreaks of violence unparalleled in any other American metropolitan area. The postwar combination of a rapidly decentralizing auto industry and housing construction that could only be purchased by whites (due to federal mortgage policies), juxtaposed against perpetual racial tensions, led to the wholesale abandonment of Detroit by whites. No other major American metropolis has such a black-dominated central city surrounded by such white-dominated suburbs, unleavened by substantial representations of other minority or immigrant groups. This stark geography of black-white inequality, in turn, catalyzed the incomparable degrees of race-baiting politics, fear, and distrust that distinguish Detroit's unusually toxic city-suburb relations.

What Can Be Said in the End?

Our exploration of the marvelous, horrible, dysfunctional place called Motown is over. We excavated its history, analyzed its economy, dissected its society, and probed its collective psyche. We traversed its highways, sifted through its ruins, and heard its voices, whether they be lifted in song or in anguish. In the end, what can we say of this place?

Greater Detroit is *driven*. Though an accidental metropolis, the automobile eventually became its vehicle, driving urbanization, industrialization, sprawl, and unprecedented (if transitory) blue-collar prosperity. Motown drove it and drove it and drove it some more until the gas is now about run out. But the industry driving Detroit proved as sclerotic in its response to the changing global competitive environment as it was deeply wounding to the population's psyche. Thus, the region drove a Faustian bargain, and the devil now awaits payment. That's OK, because Motown knows how to deal with the devil.

JSTPRAY
—Michigan license plate spotted on a car in Detroit, May 2010

In December 2008, at the same time the Big Three went to Congress requesting a financial bailout, a bizarre photo appeared on the front page of the *New York Times* national edition. It showed a choir lifting their voices, a dancer gyrating her hips, and a preacher raising his hands toward the sky in supplication. The caption read "Praying for a miracle: SUV's sat on the altar of Greater Grace Temple, a Pentecostal church in Detroit, as congregants prayed to save the auto industry." Yes, this was the same venue as the Rosa Parks funeral three years earlier, but this scene was entirely different.

The photo brought to mind a movie still from the 1956 Hollywood epic *The Ten Commandments*. The original screenplay was written several thousand years ago, of course, with Moses taking the part of Charlton Heston. The scene being played out was when the Israelites were getting tired of their exodus wanderings in the Sinai desert. Hungry, thirsty, bored, and in need of a miracle, they melted down their precious metals and forged a golden calf. They sang, danced, and prayed to this graven image representing the god Baal.

Suddenly, it all made perfect sense. Back to the future: a *Baal-out*! That's what Detroit needed, and the good folk of Greater Grace Temple knew exactly that. Pray not only to demigods in Washington, but to the graven SUVs on the altar. They have the horsepower to deliver the exorcism we need!

The only thing that would have made this idolatrous spectacle even more surreal is if some tall, old man with a long beard and raggedy cloak came charging down the aisle toward the altar, a carved-stone Prius under each arm, bellowing vengeance from Yahweh Toyota.

> Baal, we cry to thee! Hear and answer! Heed the sacrifice we offer!
> Baal, O hear us and answer us!
> —*Elijah*, oratorio written by Felix Mendelssohn, 1846

Detroit is indeed driven. It worshiped devoutly the auto and the companies that built it. But the auto industry proved a false god, infecting Motown's workplaces, culture, social structures, politics, urban form, and collective psyche with the deadly and apparently incurable mortropolis virus. If ever a headstone is erected over the grave of Greater Detroit, the inscription must read

> WE LOVED THE AUTOMOBILE
> WE LOVED IT TO DEATH.

> We're goin' riding on the freeway . . . in a pink Cadillac;
> We're goin' riding on the freeway . . . and we ain't coming back.
> —"The Freeway of Love," sung by Aretha Franklin

Two Daughters of Detroit Revisited

Greater Detroit's struggles for respect between labor and capital, blacks and whites created a landscape of radically different opportunities. This landscape's topography is shaped not only by things that people partly can control, such as their educational credentials and their work efforts, but even more by things beyond their control, such as their race. This is epitomized in the fates of our two emblematic daughters of Detroit, Marguerite and Helen.

Marguerite never had a chance to prove herself by amassing educational credentials and working hard, despite the good fortune of being born into an extremely well-educated family headed by a prosperous, highly respected medical doctor. For Marguerite was the only daughter of Ossian and Gladys Sweet, whose attempts to move their family out of the ghetto and into Helen's neighborhood were met with such fierce resistance. Marguerite was unable to share the same opportunity space as Helen because the Sweets never occupied the house on Garland Avenue, even after they ultimately were acquitted of murder and released from prison. Marguerite had little chance to occupy *anyone*'s opportunity space, as a matter of fact. Ossian and Gladys Sweet were exposed to tuberculosis during their long incarceration awaiting the outcome of their trial. When they finally were reunited with their daughter, they exposed her as well. She died from it soon after her second birthday.

Helen, on the other hand, was able to attend Howe Elementary School, located diagonally across the street from Sweet's house. She later graduated from Southeastern High School and attended Wayne University (before it became a state school), thus outstripping the educational credentials of her chicken-pie-baking parents, Bruno and Helen. Her networks built around the First English Lutheran Church in the old Germantown neighborhood led her to meet and fall in love with George Milton, the son of fellow parishioners George Jacob and Emma, and grandson of the founder of Acme Wire and Iron Works. They married soon after George, parlaying his excellent training at Grosse Pointe High School, graduated with honors from the University of Detroit with a degree in engineering. Helen and George led a happy, prosperous, fulfilled life during their fifty-three years together, while George rose steadily up the corporate ranks, finishing his career as vice president of a Fortune 500 company supplying auto parts. Helen's and George's ashes are scattered on Belle Isle near the place where they once parked to make out. Helen and George had two children; their son has now finished writing this book.

Selected References

Baba, Marietta and Malvina Abonyi. *Mexicans of Detroit*. Detroit: Wayne State University, Center for Urban Studies, 1979.

Babson, Steve. *Working Detroit: The Making of a Union Town*. Detroit: Wayne State University Press, 1986.

Bates, Timothy. Race, *Self-Employment and Upward Mobility*. Washington, D.C.: Woodrow Wilson Center Press, 1997.

Bates, Timothy and David Fasenfest. "Enforcement Mechanisms Discouraging Black-American Presence in Suburban Detroit." *International Journal of Urban and Regional Research* 29, 4 (2005): 960–71.

Beasley, Norman. *Made in Detroit*. New York: Van Rees Press, 1957.

Bjorn, Lars and Jim Gallert. *Before Motown: A History Jazz in Detroit, 1920-1960*. Ann Arbor: University of Michigan Press, 2001.

Boyd, Melba Joyce and M. L. Leibler, eds. *Abandon Automobile: Detroit City Poetry 2001*. Detroit: Wayne State University Press, 2001.

Boyle, Kevin. *Arc of Justice: A Saga of Race, Civil Rights and Murder in the Jazz Age*. New York: Henry Holt, 2005.

Bunge, William. *Fitzgerald: Geography of a Revolution*. Cambridge, Mass.: Schenkman, 1971.

Carson, David A. *Grits, Noise and Revolution: The Birth of Detroit Rock and Roll*. Ann Arbor: University of Michigan Press, 2005.

Chafets, Ze'v. *Devil's Night and Other True Tales of Detroit*. New York: Random House, 1990.

Citizens Research Council of Michigan. *The Fiscal Condition of the City of Detroit*. Livonia, Mich.: Citizens Research Council, memorandum 1098 (April 2010).

Clark, Kenneth B. *Dark Ghetto: Dilemmas of Social Power*. 2nd ed. Hanover, N.H.: University Press of New England.

Clemens, Paul. *Made in Detroit: A South of 8 Mile Memoir*. New York: Doubleday, 2005.

Conot, Robert. *American Odyssey*. New York: Bantam, 1973.

Cosseboom, Kathy. *Grosse Pointe, Michigan: Race Against Race*. East Lansing: Michigan State University Press, 1972.

Crary, David, George A. Erickcek, and Allen C. Goodman. "The Economies of Michigan's Major Cities." In *Michigan at the Millennium: A Benchmark and Analysis of Its Physical and Economic Structure*, ed. Charles L. Ballard, Paul N. Courant, Elisabeth R. Gerber, Douglas C. Drake, and Ronald C. Fisher. East Lansing: Michigan State University Press, 2003. 215–33.

Eisinger, Peter. "The Politics of Bread and Circuses: Building the City for the Visitor Class." *Urban Affairs Review* 35, 3 (2000): 316–33.

Farley, Reynolds, Sheldon Danziger, and Harry J. Holzer. *Detroit Divided*. New York: Russell Sage, 2000.

Ferry, W. Hawkins. *The Buildings of Detroit: A History*. Detroit: Wayne State University Press, 1968.

Fine, Sidney. *Violence in the Model City: The Cavanaugh Administration, Race Relations, and the Detroit Riot of 1967*. Ann Arbor: University of Michigan Press, 1989.

Ford, Henry. "My Life and Work." *McClure's Magazine* 54, 5 (July 1922).

Freund, David. *Colored Property: State Policy and White Racial Politics in Suburban America*. Chicago: University of Chicago Press, 2007.

Gallagher, John. *Reimagining Detroit: Opportunities for Redefining an American City*. Detroit: Wayne State University Press, 2010.

Gavrilovich, Peter and Bill McGraw, eds. *The Detroit Almanac: 300 Years of Life in the Motor City*. Detroit: Free Press, 2000.

Georgakas, Dan and Marvin Surkin. *Detroit: I Do Mind Dying: A Study in Urban Revolution*. New York: South End Press, 1998.

Good, David L. *Orvie: The Dictator of Dearborn: The Rise and Reign of Orville L. Hubbard*. Detroit: Wayne State University Press, 1989.

Goodman, Allen. "Central Cities and Housing Supply: Growth and Decline in US cities." *Journal of Housing Economics* 14 (2005): 315–335.

Hartigan, John. *Racial Situations: Class Predicaments of Whiteness in Detroit*. Princeton, N.J.: Princeton University Press, 1998.

Hendrickson, Wilma Wood, ed. *Detroit Perspectives: Crossroads and Turning Points*. Detroit: Wayne State University Press, 1991.

Herron, Jerry. *AfterCulture: Detroit and the Humiliation of History*. Detroit: Wayne State University Press, 1993.

Hersey, John. *The Algiers Motel Incident*. New York: Knopf, 1968.

Hill, Eric J. and John Gallagher. *AIA Detroit: The American Institute of Architects Guide to Detroit Architecture*. Detroit: Wayne State University Press, 2003.

Hyde, Charles K. *Detroit: An Industrial History Guide*. Detroit: Detroit Historical Society, 1980.

Iceland, John and Daniel Weinberg. *Racial and Ethnic Residential Segregation in the United States: 1980–2000*. Washington, D.C.: U.S. Census Bureau, 2002.

Jackson, Murray. *Bobweaving Detroit: The Selected Poems of Murray Jackson*. Ed. Ted Pearson and Kathryne V. Lindberg. Detroit: Wayne State University Press, 2002.

Jacoby, Tamar. *Someone Else's House: America's Unfinished Struggle for Integration.* New York: Free Press, 1998.

Jargowsky, Paul. "Take the Money and Run: Economic Segregation in U.S. Metropolitan Areas." *American Sociological Review* 61, 6 (1996): 984–98.

Johnson, Arthur L. *Race and Remembrance: A Memoir.* Detroit: Wayne State University Press, 2008.

Jurkiewicz, Theodore. "Citadels in the Suburbs: White Resistance to Black Neighbors in Southeast Michigan from 1950 to 1970." Ph.D. dissertation, Department of Political Science, Wayne State University, 2006.

Katzman, David. *Before the Ghetto: Black Detroit in the Nineteenth Century.* Urbana: University of Illinois Press, 1973.

Klepper, Steven. "The Origin and Growth of Industry Clusters: The Making of Silicon Valley and Detroit." *Journal of Urban Economics* 67, 1 (2010): 15–32.

Kellogg, Paul. "Ford Motor Company's Changeover from the Model T." In *Detroit Perspectives: Crossroads and Turning Points,* ed. Wilma Wood Hendrickson. Detroit: Wayne State University Press, 1991. 351–61.

Levine, David A. *Internal Combustion: The Races in Detroit: 1915–1926.* Westport, Conn.: Greenwood, 1976.

Levine, Philip. *What Work Is.* New York: Knopf, 1996.

Meier, August, Elliott Rudwick, and Joe William Trotter. *Black Detroit and the Rise of the UAW.* Ann Arbor: University of Michigan Press, 1979.

Mirel, Jeffrey. *The Rise and Fall of an Urban School System: Detroit, 1907–1981.* Ann Arbor: University of Michigan Press, 1981.

Nawrocki, Dennis Alan and David Clemens. *Art in Detroit Public Places.* Rev. ed. Detroit: Wayne State University Press, 1999.

Palm, Kristin. *The Straits.* Long Beach, Calif.: Palm Press, 2008.

Poremba, David Lee, ed. *Detroit in Its World Setting: A Three-Hundred-Year Chronology, 1701–2001.* Detroit: Wayne State University Press, 2001.

Quaife, Milo M. *This Is Detroit: 1701–1951.* Detroit: Wayne State University Press, 1951.

Rich, Wilbur C. *Coleman Young and Detroit Politics: From Social Activist to Power Broker.* Detroit: Wayne State University Press, 1989.

Sauerzopf, Richard. "The Spatial Origins of National Politics: Place and Race in the Fragmented Metropolis." Ph.D. dissertation, Department of Political Science, State University of New York at Albany, 2002.

Shogan, Robert and Tom Craig. *The Detroit Race Riot: A Study in Violence.* Philadelphia: Chilton, 1964.

Sinclair, Robert and Bryan Thompson. *Metropolitan Detroit: An Anatomy of Social Change.* Cambridge, Mass.: Ballinger, 1977.

Smith, Suzanne. *Dancing in the Street: Motown and the Cultural Politics of Detroit.* Cambridge, Mass.: Harvard University Press, 1999.

Stolberg, Mary M. *Bridging the River of Hatred: The Pioneering Efforts of Detroit Police Commissioner George Edwards*. Detroit: Wayne State University Press, 1998.

Sugrue, Thomas J. *The Origins of the Urban Crisis: Race and Inequality in Postwar Detroit*. Princeton, N.J.: Princeton University Press, 1996.

Thomas, Heather Ann. *Whose Detroit? Politics, Labor, and Race in a Modern American City*. Ithaca, N.Y.: Cornell University Press, 2001.

Thomas, June Manning. *Redevelopment and Race: Planning a Finer City in Postwar Detroit*. Baltimore: Johns Hopkins University Press, 1997.

Thomas, Richard W. *Life for Us Is What We Make It: Building Black Community in Detroit, 1915–1945*. Bloomington: University of Indiana Press, 1992.

Warren, Donald. *Radio Priest: Charles Coughlin, the Father of Hate Radio*. New York: Free Press, 1996.

Watts, Steven. *The People's Tycoon: Henry Ford and the American Century*. New York: Knopf, 2005.

Widick, B. J. *Detroit: City of Race and Class Violence*. Detroit: Wayne State University Press, 1972.

Whiting, Basil and Tony Proscio. *Philadelphia 2007: Prospects and Challenges*. Philadelphia: Pew Charitable Trusts, 2007.

Wolf, Eleanor P. *Trial and Error: The Detroit School Segregation Case*. Detroit: Wayne State University Press, 1981.

Woodford, Frank B. and Aruthus M. Woodford. *All Our Yesterdays: A Brief History of Detroit*. Detroit: Wayne State University Press, 1969.

Wylie, Jeanie. *Poletown: Community Betrayed*. Urbana: University of Illinois Press, 1989.

Zunz, Olivier. *The Changing Face of Inequality: Urbanization, Industrial Development, and Immigrants in Detroit, 1880 to 1920*. Chicago: University of Chicago Press, 1983.

Index

Acknowledgments

I owe debts to many people who contributed to this book. But in the absence of one particular person, this book would never have been written: Professor Judith Martin of the University of Minnesota. Had it not been for her brilliant idea for a Metropolitan Portraits book series and her persuasive argument that I *needed* to write the volume on Detroit, I would not have attempted it. She demonstrated saintly patience as I assembled background materials at a glacial pace, fitfully revised already revised chapter outlines, and all-too-often let other, less important projects distract me. Her advice on drafts was unerringly on the mark. My thanks to Judith for this precious opportunity and not-to-be ignored challenge. It is a pity that she did not live to see the book in print.

I wish to thank many who generously granted me permission to quote their poetry and song lyrics, thereby making this a much more nuanced portrait of Greater Detroit: "Solidarity Forever," © Alpha Music Inc, All Rights Reserved; poetry selections from Murray Jackson, "Growing Up Colored" and "Eight Ball, Side Pocket" from *Bobweaving Detroit: The Selected Poems of Murray Jackson*, edited with a postscript by Ted Pearson and Kathryne V. Lindberg; Copyright © 2003 Wayne State University Press, quoted with the permission of Wayne State University Press. All other poetry is quoted with the permission of the authors holding copyright. Robert Lockhart, Alison Anderson, and the staff of the University of Pennsylvania Press provided excellent support and editorial guidance as the book was being produced.

Many faculty colleagues from several departments at Wayne State University generously shared their thoughts and research with me. I wish to thank Steve Babson, Tim Bates, Robin Boyle, Jorge Chinea, Mike Goldfield, Jerry Herron, Charles Hyde, Nate Israel, Rusty McIntyre, Gary Sands, Anna Santiago, Mike Smith, and Avis Vidal. Jason Booza of the Wayne

State University Department of Family and Community Medicine was extremely gracious with his copious supplies of demographic statistics and maps of Greater Detroit. Ann Slawnik helped shape my perspectives by involving me in her insightful Detroit Orientation Institute. Indeed, all the students, staff, and faculty in the Department of Urban Studies and Planning at Wayne State University implicitly assisted in the creation of this book by sharing their experiences and hopes, thereby helping me better understand this place called Motown and those who live here.

Several students at Wayne State University worked with me as Research Assistants for this book. Dan Beard, Nina Butler, Andy Linn, Lonnisha Thomas, and Noah Urban not only excavated the facts for which I asked, but contributed innumerable suggestions and insights for which I was not clever enough to ask but they were clever enough to provide gratuitously. I am indebted to the Clarence Hilberry Professorship for financially supporting these Research Assistants and for supporting my work in many other ways.

I was fortunate to be graced by innumerable insightful, vignette-laden conversations about Detroit from the "inside" by three long-time resident-activists. A special tip of the hat and wink to Sheila Cockrell, eternal institutional reformer and former City Councilor of Detroit, Eugene Kuthy, formerly the Michigan Banking Commissioner and perpetual community organization board member, and Peter Zeiler, formerly of the Detroit Economic Growth Corporation and now of the Charlotte (NC) Planning Department. Joseph Kassab and Mary Romaya of the Chaldean Cultural Center, Heidi Mucherie of Community Legal Resources, Erica Raleigh of Data Driven Detroit, and Sally Serrano of First English Lutheran Church graciously provided information that also proved invaluable.

Stefan van der Laan Bouma, Michael and Nell Darcy, Wenda Doff, Hartmut Häussermann, Lina Hedman, Ade Kearns, Sako Musterd, and Dirk Strijker provided keen questions, observations, and photographs of Detroit that only the fresh eyes of international visitors can perceive. I deeply appreciate their sharing of sights and insights.

Many neighbors, both in the immediate environs of my City of Detroit Palmer Woods neighborhood and in Greater Detroit, played a critical role in shaping this book, though unwittingly. Special thanks to Cleo and Jim Hamilton and Ann and (the late) Gerald Smith for their enlightening conversations and access to their vast interpersonal networks. Living among such people since 1996 has not only been a personal pleasure but a source of inspiration. They have taught me what it means to care deeply about a place and invest heavily in it financially and emotionally, often against all logic. They are the unsung heroes of Detroit and its hope for the future.

Finally, thanks and love are extended to my family, at least six generations of whom have been Detroiters and many of whom still live in the region. Their lives have epitomized the dreams both achieved and shattered on the hard ground of this strange, wonderful, awful, endlessly fascinating metropolis. It is parts of their lives that bring this text to life. But one member of the family is the recipient of by far the most gratitude: Nancy Galster, an inexhaustible font of energy, encouragement, and love.

CPSIA information can be obtained at www.ICGtesting.com
Printed in the USA
BVOW02*1810250813

329140BV00009B/10/P

9 780812 244298